W9-ASF-316

A Supreme Court Justice Is Appointed

STUDIES IN POLITICAL SCIENCE

KF
8745
.B8
D3

A SUPREME COURT JUSTICE IS APPOINTED

David J. Danelski

Yale University

Random House
New York

124205

FIRST PRINTING

© *Copyright, 1964, by Random House, Inc.*

All rights reserved under International and Pan-American Copyright Conventions. Published in New York by Random House, Inc., and simultaneously in Toronto, Canada, by Random House of Canada, Limited.

Library of Congress Catalog Card Number: 64-22706

Manufactured in the United States of America by The Colonial Press Inc.

DESIGN BY *Margaret F. Plympton*

IN MEMORY OF

James C. Rierdon

1930-1961

AND TO

His Wife and Children

10/26/65 ICS 3.22

"The process of living seems most satisfactorily conceptualized as a single, undivided, unitary, but extremely complex process which no single symbol is capable of expressing. Description is necessarily analytical and successive. As soon as one starts to speak or to write, something is left out. In short, one is already dealing with fictions, abstractions, or concepts at least one step removed from first-order data."

HADLEY CANTRIL *and* CHARLES H. BUMSTEAD
Reflections on the Human Venture

PREFACE

Every few years we read in the newspapers that the President has appointed a Supreme Court Justice. We know that the event is important, that the course and direction of constitutional interpretation may turn upon it, and that the new Justice's behavior in the Court may ultimately touch the lives of millions of persons in the nation. But in regard to the appointment itself, we know little. To most of us the inner aspects of the event are and remain a mystery. We do not know who was intimately involved in the selection of the Justice, how they proceeded, and why that Justice and no one else was appointed. Perhaps only a few persons possess even a part of that information and they carry it to their graves. Undoubtedly that is often the case. The appointment of Pierce Butler to the Supreme Court in 1922, however, is an exception. Those who possessed the central information did not carry it to their graves. Thousands of documents touching the event have survived in archives and manuscript collections in various places in the United States. With rare clarity and detail, they tell who selected Pierce Butler for the Supreme Court, how the selection occurred, and suggest why he and no one else was appointed.

The central portion of this study is a biography of that event. In writing it, I was struck by the richness of the data. It was as though I were looking through a microscope and seeing clearly the totality of a political event with all its minute activity relationships. With such an example of politics in action, I decided to do more than attempt to explain the Butler appointment. I felt that the data presented an unusual opportunity to consider some basic problems of political analysis and fashion analytical tools for future research. The final chapters are exploratory essays that tentatively consider the analytical utility of concepts like transaction, influence, and personality in terms of the activity comprising the event under inquiry. I hope the value of the study will go beyond the description and explanation of the appointment of a Supreme Court Justice.

I am indebted to many persons and institutions in making this study. I should especially like to thank Fola La Follette, Francis D. Butler, Pierce Butler III, and Rev. Richard Twohy, S.J., who gave generously of their time for interviews and helped in other ways; James Twohy and Nelson Phillips, Jr., who provided important information in response to written inquiries; John P. Frank, who made available prints of his microfilm of the Butler Confirmation Papers; Professor C. Herman Pritchett of the University of Chicago and Professor Walter F. Murphy of Princeton University, who read the entire manuscript and made helpful suggestions; Anne Dyer Murphy and Charles D. Lieber of Random House, who helped in countless ways; Diane Roseme, who commented on the style of an early draft of the manuscript; Robert Hallauer, Carl Hetrick, and George Roseme, who assisted in the content analyses in Chapters 1 and 11; Joyce Lamon, who typed the manuscript; Alan Thompson of the Library of Congress; Lucile M. Kane of the Minnesota Historical Society, Maxine B. Clapp of the University of Minnesota Library, Kenneth W. Duckett of the Ohio Historical Society, and Margaret Donlan of the Department of Justice, who assisted in the location of relevant data and made research a pleasant experience; the University of Minnesota for permitting me to examine its records; the University of Oklahoma for making available the William A. Schaper Papers; Carleton College for material concerning the student days of Pierce Butler; Yale University for use of the Charles D. Hilles Papers; and the University of Washington for financial assistance in the typing of the manuscript.

Finally, I am profoundly grateful to my wife, Jill Parmer Danelski, who, in addition to caring for our five youngsters, assisted in every phase of the book.

D. J. D.

August, 1964

CONTENTS

Part One: Who

Chapter 1

PIERCE BUTLER

At precisely noon on January 2, 1923 seven Supreme Court Justices took their places at the bench. The Marshal, in measured tones, thrice cried "Oyez," then asked God to "save the United States and this Honorable Court." The Supreme Court was now in session.

"Since the last meeting of the Court," the Chief Justice announced, "the President has nominated, and the Senate has confirmed, Mr. Pierce Butler to be an Associate Justice of this Court to succeed to the vacancy created by the retirement of Mr. Justice Day. Mr. Butler is in attendance and is ready to take the oath. The Clerk will read the commission." Butler—a tall, powerfully built man of middle age, with slightly stooped shoulders—looked at the bench. On the far left he saw an empty chair, then the men who would be his colleagues—Brandeis, Van Devanter, McKenna, Taft, Holmes, McReynolds, Sutherland—and finally another empty chair. When the Clerk finished, the Chief Justice administered the oath; then Mr. Justice Butler was escorted to the chair on Brandeis' right.[1]

Thus Pierce Butler became a Supreme Court Justice. In many ways the appointment was atypical. Unlike most of his predecessors, Butler was a man of humble origin, a

Roman Catholic, a self-taught lawyer, a member of a politically inactive family, a citizen of a state that had never before had a Supreme Court Justice, a Democrat appointed by a Republican.[2] And that was not all. So that he could be appointed, men like Benjamin N. Cardozo and Harlan F. Stone were passed over. To understand how all this came about, it is necessary to begin with Butler himself.

I

Butler's rise to the Supreme Court is the classic American success story.[3] His parents, Patrick and Mary Ann Butler, were immigrants who left Ireland soon after the famine of 1848. Although both were natives of County Wicklow, they met in the United States and were married in 1855 in the riverboat town of Galena, Illinois. There, for a time, Pat ran a tavern in one of the hotels, and it is said that Ulysses S. Grant was one of his better customers. But Patrick Butler—who had studied civil engineering at Trinity College in Dublin, who had participated in Sir Roderick Murchison's survey of Ireland, who had traveled the Continent, who had taught English in Germany—did not intend to spend the rest of his life as a tavernkeeper. The proud stern-wheelers that stopped at Galena, promising land and opportunity, beckoned the brave and the hardy to the frontier. In 1856 Pat Butler responded. He took his wife and baby Kate and journeyed up the Mississippi to begin life anew in the Minnesota Territory, where hostile bands of the Sioux and Ojibway Indians still roamed. At first Pat taught school; later he turned to farming. Acquiring a homestead in Dakota County in 1862, he built a log cabin, and in that structure, on St. Patrick's Day 1866, Pierce—the sixth of the nine Butler children—was born.[4]

The Butlers lived the rugged life of pioneers. The farm yielded the necessities of life, but only by dint of hard work. Diligently Pat and his boys plowed, planted, cultivated, garnered, and threshed each year, thankful that the locust, which had ravished Minnesota in the 1870's, missed Dakota

County. From an early age until he left the farm, Pierce did regular chores without complaint. But all was not work; in the evenings there was relaxation, a chance to read or engage in the usual family pastime—spirited conversation. By the light of homemade candles, and later the kerosene lamp, Pat would tell of the old days in Dublin, of his European travels, of his trip west, of Ulysses S. Grant at Galena. Sometimes he would sit at the supper table and hold school to supplement the three R's taught in the one-room common school. During these sessions young Butler was introduced to Latin, German, and mathematics. He proved to be an able student, for at fifteen he himself was teaching at the common school.[5]

That year, following in the footsteps of some of his older brothers and sisters, he enrolled in the preparatory department of Carleton College, located at Northfield, five miles from the Butler farm. Two years later, the course completed, he took an examination for appointment to the United States Military Academy. Though he did well on the examination, another candidate scored a tenth of one percent higher and received the appointment. Butler followed the career of his successful competitor until 1901, when he heard the officer was killed in the Philippines. He then wondered whether that would have been his fate had he scored a fraction of a percent higher on the examination. But in 1883 he had no such thoughts; the tenth of one percent difference meant only that he would remain at Carleton instead of going to West Point.[6]

The spirit of Carleton's Congregationalist founders still reigned at Northfield during Butler's student days. One of the school's avowed purposes was to develop "a symmetrical Christian character." Though Carleton maintained that it was neither sectarian nor denominational, it emphasized that it was "thoroughly Christian, and distinctly and earnestly evangelical." The curriculum, which was wholly prescribed, included such courses as Moral Philosophy and Evidences of Christianity. The former gave special attention "to the basis of our belief in God"; the latter considered the internal and historical evidences of Christianity. These courses, Butler later said, emphasized "things deemed essential to character building on the basis of Christianity." [7]

The secular gospel at Carleton was laissez faire. In his political economy text by Amasa Walker, Butler read:

> A just and efficient government of the state is important to realize the largest development of wealth, but only as a condition under which the laws of wealth, already complete and harmonious, may have their own proper sway.
>
> . . . .
>
> Labor is always irksome. This is law. Men do not voluntarily put forth their exertions, except for a reward.
>
> . . . .
>
> Whenever a population is sufficiently intelligent to understand its own interests, it should be left to direct its own labors. Its industry should never be interfered with by government.
>
> . . . .
>
> Economically, it will ever remain true, that the government is best which governs least.
>
> . . . .
>
> The law cannot say how much he [the laborer] shall accept for wages, how many hours shall constitute a day's work, nor how much the employer shall give him.
>
> . . . .
>
> Government should undertake nothing that can be accomplished by individual enterprise.
>
> . . . .
>
> To accept charity from a neighbor, under the pressure of extraordinary misfortune, could impeach the honor of no one; but to take bread from government carries with it a sort of taint of beggary through life.
>
> . . . .
>
> The truly helpless and suffering should be sheltered under the wings of charity; the indolent and wasteful, driven out into the storms of the world.[8]

The same year Butler studied Judge Cooley's text in constitutional law.[9] An abbreviated version of Cooley's *Constitutional Limitations,* which has been described as "the most fecund source of laissez-faire constitutional principles available during the period," [10] it neatly complemented Walker's work.

To young Butler, laissez faire seemed perfectly natural. He saw its principles operate on the frontier, where men rose from almost nothing because they were free and willing to work. He, too, worked for his education, and he saw his labors as an investment in the future. Surely, he felt, the rewards that might ensue should not be interfered with or taken away by government. Perhaps he had that in mind when, years later, he asked: "Should all the rewards which are due to the foresight, wisdom, and enterprise of the men who conceived and constructed wisely be transferred by legislative authority to others?" [11]

During his Carleton years Butler lived in Northfield with the family of his close friend, Frederick N. Dickson. Although Dickson was about a year ahead of Butler, the young men often studied history and literature together. According to Dickson, Butler liked Shakespeare and Bobby Burns and could recite many of the Scotsman's poems. "A Man's a Man For A' That" was Butler's favorite because of its fundamental democratic principle. The young men also used to read aloud to each other the speeches of great British and American orators. Butler loved debate and looked forward to argument, both in and out of the classroom. Later he said that his experience in debate and public speaking at Carleton was one of the most important aspects of his education.[12]

Butler's scholastic average at Carleton College was about a C+. He excelled in mathematics, and it was said that he was a favorite student of Carleton's professor of mathematics and astronomy, William W. Payne. Butler also did well in political economy; his lowest grades—those that fell below a C—were in chemistry, Latin, constitutional law, and logic.[13]

The year before Butler graduated from Carleton, Dickson went to St. Paul to read law in the offices of General John B. Sanborn and Walter H. Sanborn. Following the example of Dickson, who would later become a judge, Butler also came to St. Paul the month after his graduation in 1887. He arranged to study with two lawyers whose firm name—Pinch & Twohy—might have appeared in a Dickens novel. Although J. W. Pinch was the better lawyer, John Twohy proved more important in Butler's life. He took a fatherly interest in his clerk, often inviting him to Sunday dinner, where he would be paired with Annie M. Cronin, the half-sister of Twohy's wife. The Sunday dinners led to a courtship; and though Annie's friends were unable to see what she saw in the big, rawboned youth from the country, the young couple were married in 1891.[14]

Impressed by their clerk's sharp mind and ability to ask questions they could not answer, Pinch and Twohy marked him as a comer. So did other St. Paul lawyers. One of them was Dickson's preceptor, Walter H. Sanborn, who later became a federal circuit judge. Sanborn saw in young Butler intelligence, wit, common sense, and drive—in short, the potential of a first-rate lawyer. In 1888 he approved Butler's admission to the bar after quizzing him in open court, as was the custom in those days. Thereafter he followed the young man's career with fatherly interest, and a friendly relationship developed between the two that was to last until Sanborn's death more than thirty years later.[15]

In 1888 Butler cast his first vote for Grover Cleveland and henceforth was a Democrat. In 1890 he nominated Thomas D. O'Brien for county attorney in an eloquent speech at the Ramsey County Democratic Convention. Upon election, O'Brien (later a Minnesota Supreme Court justice) made Butler his assistant. Two years later, at the age of twenty-six, Butler himself was elected county attorney and chose as his assistant Stan J. Donnelly, son of the Populist leader, Ignatius Donnelly. Butler was known as a fearless and fair-minded prosecutor. When the Women's Christian Temperance Union asked him to prosecute Ed Murphy—king of the St. Paul saloonkeepers—Butler took immediate action, despite the fact that Murphy was a fellow Irishman, a Catholic, and a power in local Democratic politics. Butler went to Murphy's saloon as though he were a regular patron and personally gathered the evidence he later used in his successful prosecution of the saloonkeeper. The ladies of the W.C.T.U. were so pleased with the "manly" and "masterful" way Butler handled the case that they presented him with a resolution of appreciation.[16] In 1894, when Butler was seeking re-election, the *Minnesota Law Journal* appraised his record as prosecutor as "one of the best in the history of Ramsey County." "He has no equal for his age as criminal lawyer in the state," it added. "Personally he has a charming and agreeable manner, is an eloquent speaker, and his integrity, ability, and fearlessness has (*sic*) made him what he is today, viz.: one of the most popular young lawyers of the Ramsey County Bar." Although he was handily re-elected, he made it known at the end of his second term that he would not run again. Democrats, hearing this, tried to persuade him to run for Congress. He declined on the ground that if he were elected, he could not afford to go to Washington.[17]

Unlike many ex-prosecutors, Butler had no intention of making a career of defending persons accused of crime. In 1896 he entered into a partnership with Homer C. Eller and Jared How, older men with sterling reputations and a successful commercial practice. A year or so later Eller died and the firm continued as How & Butler until 1899, when Thomas Wilson, general counsel of the Chicago, St. Paul, Minneapolis & Omaha Railroad, asked Butler to join him as the railroad's general attorney. The offer was tempting, for Wilson, who had been chief justice of the Supreme Court of Minnesota, was one of the most respected lawyers in the state. Butler accepted and for five years worked as a railroad lawyer. Yet he knew there was something to the proverb "Whose bread I eat, his man I am," and yearned for private practice again. When he told this to Judge Wilson in 1905, Wilson replied that if he remained with the railroad he would shortly become general counsel. Butler thought the matter over but concluded he still wanted to leave. Judge Wilson said he understood and added that he thought it was the right thing to do.[18]

Butler returned to private practice, joining Jared How, his former partner, and William DeWitt Mitchell,* son of an eminent Minnesota Supreme Court justice. In a short time How, Butler & Mitchell was regarded as one of the leading firms in the state. Butler's personal reputation also rose. In the areas in which he specialized—litigation and railroad valuation—few lawyers were a match for him. Recognizing his stature in the bar, the Minnesota State Bar Association elected him president in 1908.[19]

Butler's six years as a prosecutor had made him an astute advocate. While still in his twenties, he had already tried hundreds of cases involving serious crimes, including murder, and had faced some of the best trial lawyers in the state, learning from them and often beating them at their own game, which, after all, was his game too. He loved the rough-and-tumble of fiercely contested cases. He appreciated the drama of the trial and intuitively understood the advocate's role in it. He knew the importance of careful preparation and often, in the middle of a trial, worked late into the night. And yet, as one of his partners put it, "the strain and tension of the hard-fought legal battle affected him less than any lawyer I have known." [20]

Butler's forte was cross-examination. Although he was familiar with Francis L. Wellman's book on the subject, he did not go along with its clever-courteous-conciliatory approach.[21] "The only way to treat a hostile witness," he used

---

* Mitchell was Solicitor General during the Coolidge administration and Attorney General during the Hoover administration. His life's ambition, however, was to become an appellate judge like his father. When Butler heard he was nominated to the Supreme Court, he exclaimed: "Billie Mitchell, not I, should have been named." In 1932 Mitchell was a leading candidate for the vacancy filled by Benjamin N. Cardozo. Chief Justice Hughes personally endorsed Mitchell and told President Hoover that most members of the Court thought he was especially qualified for the post. Holmes, Brandeis, and Stone, however, preferred Cardozo, though at one point even Stone thought Mitchell would receive the nomination. When Mitchell was passed over, Justice Van Devanter attributed Hoover's action to Mitchell's modesty in failing to press his own case and Hoover's great need of him as Attorney General. Van Devanter to Frank B. Kellogg, Jan. 14, March 10, 1932, Van Devanter Papers.

to say, "is to be hostile." [22] Wit, humor, and sarcasm were also his weapons—weapons that he used with skill and effectiveness. Referring to a case that Butler was trying in Kansas City in 1908, Mitchell wrote to his wife: "Butler & I make a good team for this kind of case. I feed out the 'dope' to him & keep him loaded with material, and he slams it in. The case has already attracted much attention, especially on account of the brilliancy & effectiveness of Butler's cross-examinations. Witness after witness of the plaintiff left the witness stand in about the condition of Tomlinson's soul, after it was 'shredded.' " [23] Butler's "shredding" cross-examinations led some to criticize his courtroom behavior. A respected historian and administrator at the University of Minnesota remembered Butler as "the most ruthless cross-examiner then practicing in the courts of that day." [24] Another critic called Butler "a veritable bully, aggressive to the point of being insulting," who treated "witnesses with a ruthlessness seldom seen in court." [25] Friends, on the other hand, saw Butler as "a hard fighter, but a fair and just one." [26]

Understandably, Butler was a dreaded antagonist in the courtroom. Yet he was generally well liked by fellow lawyers. There was little formality about him; he was simply "Pierce" to all who knew him. He was friendly, possessed a fine sense of humor, and delighted his brothers at the bar with his "inexhaustible fund of anecdote." [27] But he was not affable in the sense that he was condescending, nor did he seek popularity by pleasing. Lawyers detected "an indefinable reserve" about him—"the reserve which always accompanies strength." [28] A Minneapolis lawyer perceptively summed up Butler in a single sentence when he said: "He was a man easy to meet, but dangerous to oppose." [29]

By 1909 Butler's reputation as a trial lawyer extended beyond the borders of Minnesota. In that year, when the millers in the Midwest were prosecuted for selling flour bleached with nitrogen peroxide, Taft's Attorney General, George W. Wickersham, designated Butler a special Assistant Attorney General to present the government's case. Butler convinced a jury in Kansas City that the millers' practices were a violation of the Pure Food and Drugs Act, but on appeal before the Eighth Circuit—with Judge Sanborn sitting—the judgment was reversed.[30] While the *Bleached Flour Cases* were pending, Butler was one of the lawyers chosen by Wickersham to prosecute Louis F. Swift, J. Ogden Armour, and other midwestern meat packers for alleged violations of the Sherman Antitrust Act. Though the government won the early rounds of the litigation, the meat packers were acquitted after a lengthy trial in Chicago.[31]

Butler's other specialty, railroad valuation, grew out of his experience with the Omaha Railroad and his early interest in economics and mathematics. He successfully argued the valuation issue for the railroads in the *Minnesota Rate Cases* before Judge Sanborn,[32] and when the cases came to the Supreme Court in 1912, he and Charles W. Bunn were chosen by the railroads to argue them. Butler argued that cost of reproduction was the proper basis for railroad valuation, citing *Smyth* v. *Ames,* an 1898 case in which the Supreme Court decided that, for purposes of rate making, cost of reproduction might be considered in determining present value.[33] Ironically, that theory of valuation had been urged by William Jennings Bryan in the 1890's because it favored farmers and shippers. In the fourteen years separating *Smyth* v. *Ames* and the *Minnesota Rate Cases,* inflation had worked a curious change: the cost-of-reproduction theory of valuation had changed sides. What Bryan had wrought in his fight against the railroads, Butler now wielded in their defense. Although Butler's argument and brief, which was a 900-page effort, impressed the Justices,* the Court unanimously decided against most of the railroads' contentions.[34] It did not, however, strike down the cost-of-reproduction theory of valuation, and Butler's forcible argument of that position made him known throughout the nation as one of its leading exponents. Thus when Congress passed the Valuation Act of 1913, the presidents of the nation's

---

* Chief Justice Hughes later said Butler's brief was "one of the ablest, most comprehensive and most careful briefs ever submitted to this Court." 310 U.S. xvii (1940).

railroads selected Butler, former Congressman William G. Brantley of Georgia, and former Governor Herbert S. Hadley of Missouri to head a committee of lawyers who were to present the railroads' views on valuation before the Interstate Commerce Commission. The Presidents' Committee of Counsel functioned until 1918.[35]

In 1912 the Canadian Northern Railroad retained Butler to defend it in a personal injury case filed in St. Paul by one Walker, a trainman who had been seriously injured in Calgary. The railroad's case was so weak that Butler, after investigating the facts, offered to settle for $20,000. When Walker's lawyer refused the offer, the case went to trial, and Butler secured a verdict for the railroad. A lawyer who could produce such results was not forgotten. In 1918, when the Canadian government took over the Canadian Northern, the railroad's general counsel suggested that the shareholders retain Butler to represent them in the arbitration proceedings that would establish the value of their equity. Butler was retained and went to Toronto to present the shareholders' case before the Board of Arbitration. Though his opponent, Eugene Tilley, was one of the leading barristers of Canada, Butler scored one of the most notable victories of his career: the board not only awarded the shareholders the maximum statutory amount—$8,000,000—it also recommended that Parliament pay them an additional $900,000.

Three years later, when the Canadian government began proceedings to take over the Grand Trunk Railroad, Tilley asked Butler to act as co-counsel with him in behalf of the Dominion. One of the arbitrators in the Grand Trunk arbitration was former President William Howard Taft. For several weeks Taft watched Butler in action and was impressed by what he saw; the St. Paul lawyer more than held his own with the best barristers in Canada. The two Americans soon became friends. They stayed at the same hotel and dined together two or three times a week. When, near the end of the arbitration, Taft received word that he had been nominated Chief Justice of the United States, he and Butler celebrated the occasion. A little later Butler too had cause for celebration. Though the maximum statutory award to the Grand Trunk shareholders was $64,000,000, the Board of Arbitration voted, over Taft's dissent, to give them nothing. For Butler it was a victory as notable as the Canadian Northern arbitration.*

In 1922 Canadian shareholders again retained Butler—this time in the Toronto Street Railway arbitration. He was in Toronto summing up the case when he received word of his nomination to the Supreme Court. Again he was successful: the Toronto Street Railway shareholders were awarded approximately $12,000,000.[36]

II

Through the years Butler had maintained his early interest in politics. At one time he was close to James Manahan, staunch Bryan supporter and Nonpartisan League leader. In 1904 Butler referred to himself and Manahan as "lusty young Democrats" and pleaded for harmony in the party. "Now is the time," Butler told Manahan, "for men like you and me, all over the country, to consult together and put an end to the bickering within our party that will insure the success of the Republican party, which certainly no longer deserves the confidence of the people." [37] Two years later he ran for the state senate in a predominantly Republican constituency and came within twenty-three votes of victory. Thereafter his political activity was mostly behind the scenes. He was an adviser to Minnesota Governors John A. Johnson (1905–09) and Winfield S. Hammond (1915), both Democrats. Johnson appointed Butler to the Board of Regents of the

* The friendly relation between Taft and Butler continued. In June 1922 Butler wrote Taft recommending his friend, John F. McGee, for a federal judgeship in Minnesota. Though McGee was more than sixty at the time, Taft, on the strength of Butler's recommendation, wrote Attorney General Daugherty in McGee's behalf. Butler to Taft, June 3, 1922; Taft to Daugherty, June 25, 1922, Taft Papers. Writing to Senator Nelson on November 23 of the same year, McGee said that Butler's "intimacy with the Chief Justice is such that if you put the matter up to him, he will have the Chief Justice join with him in going to Mr. Daugherty and the President." Nelson Papers. McGee received the appointment.

University of Minnesota in 1907, and governors of both parties continuously reappointed him until he was named to the Supreme Court.

In 1912 Butler was chosen as an alternate delegate to the Democratic National Convention, and in 1920 he presided at a meeting of Minnesota Democrats that was addressed by the vice-presidential candidate, Franklin D. Roosevelt. Although he remained true to the Democratic party to the end of his voting days, at times Butler was sorely tempted to vote in Republican primaries to save "real" Republicans (especially friends like Governor J. A. O. Preus) from Nonpartisan League candidates (like Henrik Shipstead) running as Republicans. Nevertheless, he could confidently state in 1922: "As to my record as a Democrat—it is good." [38]

III

As one would expect of a lawyer, Butler highly valued law, order, justice, tradition, and freedom, but an analysis of some of his speeches before and immediately after his appointment to the Supreme Court reveals that he also highly valued patriotism, laissez faire, and morality. This trinity of values was prominent in his public statements.[39]

In 1915, for example, he said the strength of the state was limitless when erected by "loving patriotism." [40] Patriotism to Butler was not simply flag waving; he acknowledged such activity was easy and often pleasant, but "real patriotism" required the bearing of the burdens of taxation gladly as well as discharging the other duties of citizenship. The primary duty of citizenship, he said, was undivided allegiance to the nation. "Allegiance to government and protection by it are reciprocal obligations, and, stripped of all sentiment, the one is the consideration for the other; that is, allegiance for protection and protection for allegiance. Because the citizen is entitled to its protection, he owes allegiance in full measure to his country." [41] This idea, he thought, was implicit in the oaths taken by public officials and aliens, and, though most native citizens took no oaths, they owed the same loyalty. "Thus," he concluded, "it is that all, from the highest to the lowliest of our naturalized citizens, are, by legal obligation strong and binding, held to full and faithful loyalty." [42]

In the early 1920's Butler viewed the postwar restlessness with alarm. He felt that the agitation of the period was detrimental to the existing order and that, to some extent, college and university professors were to blame. "In some of our colleges and universities," he told the American Bar Association in 1923, "there is a good deal of false teaching in the field of politics and social sciences. Professors, sometimes, spread discontent among the students. The things that are good and essential to patriotism are neglected and existing ills in political and economic conditions are magnified, and the Constitution is sometimes condemned as archaic, and by some of them it is believed that religion is a hindrance to social progress." [43]

In making that statement Butler probably had in mind his experience as regent of the University of Minnesota. One of his fellow regents said that during the war Butler would not countenance even the suspicion of disloyalty on the part of any employee of the University.[44] The most sensational case of that period involved Professor William A. Schaper, chairman of the Department of Political Science, who was charged with being "a rabid pro-German" by the Minnesota Commission of Public Safety. He was called before the Board of Regents and rigorously cross-examined by Butler on his views concerning the war. Though Schaper maintained he was loyal and would obey all laws, he refused to say he would go out and "boost" for the war. Butler and the other regents were not satisfied with that kind of loyalty. They felt that during the crisis the faculty should not merely profess willingness to abide by the laws of the country, but should support its every act whole-heartedly and zealously.[45] Schaper's removal, said Butler, "is in harmony with the present tendency to silence disloyal communities, institutions, publications, officers and individuals. We must see that sincere, loyal Americans are made the instructors of our youths.

. . ." [46] By unanimous vote, the regents dismissed Schaper.* Though the action was led by Butler, he had some misgivings about it. "I didn't want to fire that man," he told one of his sons, "but he gave me no chance to save him." [47] A patriotic American, thought Butler, had no alternative but to dismiss Schaper.†

Butler felt as strongly about laissez faire as he did about patriotism. He remained true to the doctrine he had learned as a student from Amasa Walker's text. Indeed, some of Butler's statements might well have been made by Walker himself. "Contemporaneously with the ever increasing activities of government," said Butler in 1916, "there is a school of thought leading toward a kind of state socialism. Too much paternalism, too much wet-nursing by the state, is destructive of individual initiative and development. An athlete should not be fed on pre-digested food, nor should the citizens of tomorrow be so trained that they will expect sustenance from the public 'pap.' " [48] It was Butler's view that the state may not transgress "its true functions" and become a vast charitable machine, furnishing employment, doling out aid, and meeting the needs of the people. Such a program would ruin the nation, "weaken character and leave the individual man and woman without the motive or hope or inspiration necessary to freedom and morality." [49]

---

* The Schaper case must be understood in the context of the period. At about the same time in Lakeside, Minnesota, James Manahan was defending Joseph Gilbert, a socialist, who was charged with sedition for a speech he had made. At a recess during the trial, a mob threatened to lynch Manahan. "I heard myself say," Manahan recalled later, " 'Boys, I am only a lawyer, trying a case for a living,' and,—oh, the pity of it, I heard my lying tongue say, 'I have no use for those damn socialists.' Like Peter, I cursed. I denied my client and the truth. I cursed. . . . Thrice I lied that night. I said I didn't mean it." Abandoning Gilbert's defense, Manahan returned to St. Paul. Manahan, *Trials of a Lawyer,* pp. 232–38. Gilbert's case became a *cause célèbre.* See *Gilbert* v. *Minnesota,* 254 U.S. 325 (1920).

† On June 4, 1918 Butler wrote Justice Van Devanter: "Does not the present situation make us all feel what our boys are doing makes everything else unimportant?" Van Devanter Papers. Four of Butler's sons and his daughter Mary were in military service at the time. Mary died of influenza while on active duty at Fort Snelling the same year.

This, however, did not mean Butler opposed all social legislation. On the contrary, he led the fight for workmen's compensation in Minnesota. But compensating workers for their injuries on the job was not inconsistent with his conception of laissez faire. He felt that since every well-run business set aside funds to cover damage or destruction of machinery, there was no good reason for not doing the same for employee injuries; it was simply part of the cost of doing business that could be added to the price of the commodity. Furthermore, he believed the handling of workmen's claims by the courts was a waste of the taxpayer's money and the delay involved encouraged habits of idleness on the part of workers.[50]

Nor was his prosecution of the meat packers for alleged antitrust violations inconsistent with his conception of laissez faire. The purpose of the antitrust laws, he believed, was to insure competition by prohibiting only "unreasonable" restraints of trade. Thus at the state bar meeting in 1911 he staunchly defended the Supreme Court's use of the "rule of reason" in the *Standard Oil* and *Tobacco Trust* cases.[51] James Manahan debated the point with Butler, calling his defense of the Court sophistry. Manahan maintained the Court destroyed the Sherman Act by holding that it applied only to so-called "unreasonable" restraints of trade; he added that while Wall Street might be satisfied with this "rule of reason," the Court's decisions in the cases were "most damnably unsatisfactory" to the ordinary citizen whose respect and love of the Court were lower because of them. Butler totally disagreed.[52]

Patriotism and laissez faire were intimately connected with Butler's central value: morality. "The educated man," he told a Catholic audience in 1915, "whose character is not sound, whose conscience is not well-instructed and whose conduct is not guided by religion or morality, is a danger to the State and his fellowmen." [53] One of his favorite quotations was from Archbishop Spalding: "The end of all worthy struggles is to establish morality as the basis of individual and national life." [54]

Morality and religion to Butler were closely related. "The Catholic Church," he said with approval, "holds that religion cannot be separated from morality, that morals rest upon religion and that without it character will not be secure as against the attacks of selfishness and passion." [55] The teachings of the Church were undoubtedly an important source of Butler's conception of morality. He was born in the faith and had the example of parents who took it seriously.[56] Although he had no formal training in Catholic theology or moral philosophy, his reading included those subjects, and when he graduated from Carleton, the subject he chose for his oration was the greatness of the Roman Catholic Church and its good influence upon the world.[57] Among his friends were members of the Catholic hierarchy: Archbishop John Ireland of St. Paul and Bishops John P. Carroll of Helena and William Turner of Buffalo. He was also well known to other high Church officials, for in 1915, when the Catholic Educational Association met in St. Paul, he was the only layman to address a general meeting.[58]

Pierce Butler—moralist, patriot, laissez-faire champion—was the product of his age and environment. His was a world of either-or, of black or white, a world in which principle could never be sacrificed to expediency. He had a system of values for which he was willing to fight. And fight he did—in the courtroom, in the regents' room of the University of Minnesota, and finally in the conference room of the Supreme Court of the United States. One might disagree with him, but there was seldom any doubt as to where he stood or that his stand was based on deep conviction. "No one who dealt with him one day," said Mitchell, "was afterwards confounded or nonplussed by any subsequent act or declaration of his on the same subject." [59] Holmes characterized him with a single word—"a monolith," adding, "there are no seams the frost can get through. He is of one piece." [60]

Chapter 2

HARDING AND COMPANY

It is naive to suppose that because the President has constitutional power to nominate Supreme Court Justices, men come to the High Court solely as the result of his decision. President Harding sent Pierce Butler's name to the Senate, but the nomination was made by Harding and Company. Included in that group were not only Attorney General Daugherty but, surprisingly, Chief Justice Taft and Justice Van Devanter as well.

I

How Warren G. Harding was chosen for the Republican presidential nomination in 1920 by fifteen men in a smoke-filled room at 2:11 A.M. is now legend. That such a meeting occurred is fact; that Harding's nomination resulted from it is highly debatable.[1] The names of senators known to be present, however, are worth mentioning in connection with the appointment to the Supreme Court of Pierce Butler. They were William E. Borah, Frank B. Brandegee, William M. Calder, Charles W. Curtis, Joseph S. Frelinghuysen, Henry Cabot Lodge, Medill McCormick, Harry S. New, Lawrence C. Phipps, Reed Smoot, Seldon P. Spencer, James W. Wadsworth, Jr., and James E. Watson.[2] The main reason given for Harding's selection by the group is also worth mentioning. One of the senators said that they wanted a man in the White House who would defer to them, someone who was by nature disposed to seek counsel.[3]

This evaluation of Harding is consistent with contemporary perceptions of him as compliant, humble, affable, kindly, and conciliatory.[4] Affection and approval meant a good deal to him. Soon after his election to the nation's highest office, he said he would probably not be the best President the country had had, but he hoped he would be its best-loved President.[5] The need for affection and approval had not always been a Harding trait. Before he entered politics, he was not above the use of invective, or even coarse ridicule, if it served his purpose. But in his early thirties, just before his election to the Ohio Senate, there was a marked change in his behavior. He began to cultivate popularity, check aggressive impulses, and withhold frankness except with those he trusted.[6] He was quick to praise, slow to condemn, and prone to compromise. In conflict situations he deferred to power. His approach to politics is illustrated by a statement he made in 1920. If he wanted a measure adopted in a town meeting, he said, the first thing he would do would be to discuss it with three or four of the most influential men in the community, make whatever concessions were necessary, and then go to the meeting confident his plan would carry. "Well," he concluded, "it's the same in the nation as in the town meeting, or in the whole world, if you will. I should always go first to the three or four leading men."[7]

Harding, for the most part, received the affection he

sought; few, if any, regarded him as an enemy.* He saw himself as a person who naturally loved his fellow human beings and believed they, especially his friends, were trustworthy and deserving of his affection. He admitted that before his election he thought one of the chief pleasures of being President "would be to give honors and offices to old friends." [8] As President, he said he knew better than to give in to that impulse, yet he did not always act that way. Aware of his inability to say no to "deserving" friends, he even joked about it. In an off-the-record speech at the National Press Club dinner in 1922, he said that when he was a youngster his father told him it was a good thing he was not born a girl. When he asked why, the elder Harding responded: "Because you'd be in the family way all the time. You can't say No." [9]

Anticipation of possible personal rejection depressed Harding. Partly for that reason he was reluctant to seek political office, often consenting to do so only after being assured that victory was a practical certainty.[10] Sometimes he became despondent in the middle of a political campaign and wanted to quit because he felt sure he could not win.[11] This occurred in his bid for the Senate in 1914 and again at the Republican convention that nominated him for the Presidency in 1920. At the very moment the convention was moving toward his candidacy, he was in a state of depression. William Allen White, who saw him about that time, said he looked like "the wreck of the *Hesperus*"—unshaven, disheveled, eyes bloodshot.[12] An Ohio newspaperman described him in these terms: "He showed great mental distress. . . . Discouragement hung about him like a cloud. He was not interested in anything." [13] Yet only a few hours later the same newspaperman saw him emerge from a hotel, "jaunty, beaming,

* Cf. the opening lines of E. E. Cummings' poem on Harding:

> the first president to be loved by his
> bitterest enemies is dead

Quoted in Frederick J. Hoffman, *The Twenties* (New York: Collier Books, 1962), p. 350.

chipper." The press was then informed that Senator Harding would be nominated on the first ballot the next day.[14]

What some perceived as humility in Harding might have been seen by others as a sense of inferiority. He readily admitted that he was neither an "outstanding" nor a "dominant" individual. When his candidacy for the Presidency was first suggested, his immediate response was: "Am I a big enough man for the race?"[15] When he accepted the presidential nomination, he confessed, "I would not be my natural self if I did not utter my consciousness of my limited ability to meet your full expectations. . . ."[16] And in the White House his aides were shocked by his admissions of ignorance. They saw him as a frightened man who often did not know which way to turn, a man who at such times could only exclaim in despair: "My God, but this is a hell of a place for a man like me to be!"[17] To his friends he admitted that the Presidency was too much for him.[18] Yet not all shared Harding's perception of himself. For instance, Harry S. New, his Senate colleague and later Postmaster General, said: "He was a much abler man than he thought himself."[19]

When Harding was elected to the Presidency, he faced a dilemma: on one hand, he was inclined to reward friends with offices; on the other, mistrusting his own ability, he knew he needed competent men in his administration. Soon after his election, he announced his Cabinet would be composed of the "best minds" in the country. To some extent he followed through in this resolve: Charles Evans Hughes was made Secretary of State, Herbert Hoover became Secretary of Commerce, and Andrew Mellon took over the Treasury Department. But, again, Harding compromised. Friends were not forgotten, and though most were clearly not in the "best mind" category, they, too, were appointed to high office.

The compliant, affable Harding was drawn to more aggressive personalities. One such person was his wife, Florence Kling Harding, a firm-principled woman five years his senior. Another was Albert Fall, his seatmate in the Senate and a worldly-wise, tough cynic. Perhaps the most important person of this type was Harry Daugherty, the hard-boiled Ohio politician whose avowed political ambition was to put Harding in the White House.

II

Daugherty was a lawyer who operated in the penumbra of law and politics; lobbying for corporations and securing pardons were among his specialties. His talent was knowing the right man to see, the right wire to pull, the right time to move. He was as much a politician in the legal process as he was a lawyer in politics. He saw politics as a dog-eat-dog game, and loved it. Viewed by his contemporaries as shrewd, suspicious, and aggressive, he would rather fight than compromise; and when he fought, few holds were barred. Affection and approval were not his goals; his only goal was victory, and the more humiliating the defeat of his opponent the better. Since he was confident he was on the right side, it made no difference to him if the whole country were against him.[20] His enemies were legion, and they went to great lengths to keep him from public office. The attorney generalship of Ohio, the governor's office, the United States Senate—all were denied him.* Yet he rolled with the punches and did not complain. "If a man in politics complains about the way the wind blows," he said, "he had better stay out of politics and out of the wind."[21] † Defeat, like victory, was a part of the great game.

But a lifetime of defeat was offset by a single victory—the nomination of Warren G. Harding for the Presidency. The relationship between Harding and Daugherty began at the turn of the century when the two men spoke at a Republican rally in a small Ohio town. Impressed by the strik-

---

* For example, Mark Hanna wrote to George B. Cox on May 22, 1899: "I will tell you frankly that I am not pledged to anyone for governor, but I am opposed to Mr. Daugherty from a party standpoint, and I understand we agree in that position." Quoted in Herbert Croly, *Marcus Alonzo Hanna* (New York: Macmillan Co., 1912), p. 295.

† Daugherty's statement is a variation of the Russian proverb: "If you are afraid of wolves, do not go into the forest." Being a wolf himself, Daugherty, of course, was unafraid.

ingly handsome young editor of the *Marion Star,* Daugherty marked him for better things. The men became acquainted, and in time acquaintance ripened into friendship. Daugherty saw great potential in Harding; he thought he looked like a President and swore that some day he would "put it over." [22] No man, said Daugherty, knew Harding as well as he did: "He was like a younger brother to me. . . . He appealed to me for advice more than any other or all other men put together in the more than twenty years of our intimate acquaintance and association." [23] During that time, Daugherty acted as Harding's political manager, adviser, and protector. When Harding was reluctant to seek office, it was Daugherty who would persuade him to run. When Harding was despondent in the middle of a campaign, it was Daugherty who would tell him to buck up, for victory would surely be theirs.[24] When Harding was trusting of ostensible political allies, it was Daugherty who would laugh and say: "Yes—you *would* think that! You're too straight and genial and kind to believe in treachery. I've met traitors face to face. I've met them in battle many a dark night. They can't fool me with smiles and promises." [25] When Harding protested that perhaps he was not qualified for high political office, it was Daugherty who would reassure him he was—even for the Presidency. And Harding's response to Daugherty would be: "You know me better than any man in the world. Your opinion inspires me." [26]

Daugherty's grooming of Harding for the Presidency began a decade before his nomination. An unsuccessful bid for the Ohio governorship in 1910 was a false start. But in 1912, when Harding nominated Taft at the Republican convention, Daugherty watched his protégé with satisfaction. Two years later he persuaded the small-town editor to run for the United States Senate, and Harding won. In 1916 Daugherty pulled wires for Harding's selection as keynote speaker of the Republican convention. Accomplishing that, Daugherty counseled his friend to ignore any demonstration in his behalf for the Presidency, for his time had not yet come. Three years later, when Daugherty read of Theodore

Roosevelt's death, he knew it was time to move. Foreseeing a deadlock among the top Republican candidates in 1920, he thought Harding had more than a fair chance of receiving the nomination. But there was much planning and work to be done. Daugherty's first task was to persuade his perennially reluctant candidate to enter the race, and, for this office, Florence Kling Harding would also have to be convinced. Both finally agreed, but Harding really did not have his heart in it; he preferred to remain where he was—in the Senate. Daugherty, nevertheless, enthusiastically went to work, and it was his show from the beginning. Harding was unaware of the extent and precision of Daugherty's pre-convention work; even at Chicago the future President was not privy to much of the strategy of his own campaign. Daugherty said he called the shots without discussing them; Harding was told what to do, and invariably, according to Daugherty, he complied.[27] No fifteen men in a smoke-filled room nominated Warren G. Harding for the Presidency, maintained Daugherty; Harding was nominated because he—Daugherty—planned, organized, and fought for the nomination.[28]

Unquestionably, Harding perceived Daugherty as the man to whom he owed most credit for his nomination. After he was elected, he felt he would be an ingrate if Daugherty were not appropriately rewarded, and the only "appropriate" reward was the Attorney General's office. When that was suggested publicly, Daugherty's enemies and others raised a hue and cry; some of them would have preferred the Devil himself as Attorney General. Harding faced his usual dilemma: he wanted the approval of the press and of his party and at the same time he wanted to nominate Daugherty because he felt friendship and loyalty demanded it.[29]

But more than friendship and loyalty were involved; Harding felt he needed Daugherty in Washington with him. When Harding first offered the attorney generalship, Daugherty claimed he refused it, suggesting it be given to George Sutherland—Harding's friend, former Senate colleague, and adviser during the presidential campaign.[30] But Harding insisted that Daugherty take it, saying Sutherland would make a good Supreme Court Justice. Daugherty again demurred, asserting he had too many enemies who would make it difficult for the new administration. "Your enemies are mine," was Harding's rejoinder. Then Daugherty asked whether Harding was willing to risk nominating a corporation lawyer like himself. Harding said he would not appoint any other kind, for the capable lawyers in the country were all corporation lawyers. Although Daugherty asserted he still did not consent, Harding, piqued by reporters' comments about his friend, announced his nomination anyway. He then told Daugherty what he had done and asked: "Are you going to continue to stand by me, or desert me after all these years? I've never needed you in my life as I do today."[31] Daugherty accepted, later referring to his acceptance as "the tragic blunder of my life."[32] Yet, at the time, he was not unhappy about it and looked forward to playing the great game in Washington. Besides, he felt Harding really needed him.

Just as Harding saw the Presidency was too much for him, Daugherty saw he was not cut out to be Attorney General. The office itself was demanding and required a good administrator. It also required extensive knowledge of federal law and of the bar of the nation, as well as politics at both the national and state levels, for an important part of the Attorney General's job was the recommendation of nominees for the federal courts and legislation concerning the administration of federal justice. In all of this, Daugherty was doubly handicapped. He not only lacked the requisite background (some of his predecessors had also lacked such background), but, given his many enemies, most things he did were viewed with suspicion and attacked. Thus he spent considerable time and energy defending himself. He knew he needed reliable help and advice, particularly in such matters as judicial nominations, and he readily turned to a man who was regarded as an expert—former President William Howard Taft.

III

Both Daugherty and Harding highly respected Taft. While they were still working their way up the state political ladder, he was already President. Being an Ohio man himself, he knew them casually and manifested high regard for Harding. In 1910 Taft personally contributed $5,000 to Harding's unsuccessful campaign for governor and referred to him as a "man of clean life, of great force as a public speaker and attractive in many ways."[33] In 1912 Taft selected Harding to renominate him for the Presidency, and when Harding ran for the Senate in 1914, Taft declared him "a man of marked ability, of sanity, of much legislative experience . . . a regular Republican of principle, and not a 'trimmer.'" After Harding was elected, Taft congratulated him, prophesying, "You will have a great future before you."[34]

Daugherty exaggerated his acquaintance with President Taft into friendship, and unscrupulous men like the Atlanta lawyer Thomas B. Felder saw Daugherty's "friendship" with the President as most useful. Seeking to obtain a pardon for Charles W. Morse, a former banker who was serving a prison sentence for swindling, Felder asked Daugherty to act as co-counsel. Morse gave the lawyers a retainer of $5,000 and promised to pay an additional $25,000 when pardoned. Daugherty then went into action and, disclaiming any intention to influence Taft, interceded in behalf of the convict. While Morse was apparently feigning serious illness in the penitentiary, Daugherty asserted to Taft's aides that the ex-financier was "liable to die any day" and that he was confident Taft would do "the humane thing."[35] Whether Daugherty knew the truth concerning Morse's state of health is not known, but President Taft, Attorney General Wickersham, and several army doctors were taken in by the ruse; and Morse, who had been given no more than six months to live, received his pardon and went on to live for more than a decade.[36]

The same year Morse was pardoned, 1912, Taft, fighting for his political life, welcomed Daugherty's support at the

Republican convention. Daugherty, not one to let a "friend" like Taft down, was one of his strongest supporters. In fact, when Taft received the nomination, Daugherty felt his support justified his selection as National Committee chairman. Taft listened to the objections of various Republicans against Daugherty's appointment—that he was a lobbyist, that he had a weak record, and so forth—and then decided against him "on the ground that he was not well enough known."[37] After making the decision, Taft, characteristically, apologized to Daugherty, saying that he had been entirely willing to have Daugherty as chairman, "had it met with the views of those with whom [Taft] had to consult in making the selection."[38] Daugherty took the blow stoically (it was all a part of the great game) and settled for the job of Taft's campaign manager in Ohio.

The year 1912 was Taft's Waterloo. The help of all the Daughertys in the nation was not enough to win the election. Thus Taft retired to a professorship at Yale University, where he reflected upon his experiences as President. He was convinced that he had been deceived in the Morse case, but apparently he did not believe that Daugherty influenced him in the matter.[39] In 1920, when Daugherty and Harding emerged victorious at Chicago, the former President entered the campaign in Harding's behalf. Among other things, he wrote an article for the *Yale Review,* criticizing Wilson's appointment of Louis D. Brandeis and John H. Clarke to the Supreme Court and pointing out that, with four of the incumbent Justices beyond retirement age, the most important domestic issue in the election was "the maintenance of the Supreme Court as the bulwark to enforce the guaranty that no man shall be deprived of his property without due process of law." Only Harding, Taft argued, could be trusted to make the appropriate appointments.[40] Such loyalty did not escape the notice of Daugherty and Harding. To them, Taft was almost unique—a "best mind" who, at the same time, was a loyal Ohio Republican eminently worthy of political preferment.

Soon after Harding's election, Taft was invited to Marion,

Ohio, to discuss the forthcoming administration. Harding's candor nonplussed Taft. He reviewed his intended Cabinet nominations, including Harry Daugherty's, which had not yet been announced. He told Taft that he could see through Harry when he did not suspect it, but he was loyal and a good lawyer. Taft agreed that Harding was "entitled to have such a friend in the Cabinet." "Sutherland," said Harding, "wants the Supreme Bench, and I am going to put him there." Taft agreed that he would make a fine judge. "By the way," Harding began offhandedly, "I want to ask you, would you accept a position on the Supreme Bench? Because if you would, I'll put you on that Court." Taft, in his words, "was nearly struck dumb." Of course he wanted a place on the Court; that, not the Presidency, had been his life's ambition. But now it was not simply the Court that he wanted; his ambition centered on the Court's first position, the Chief Justiceship. With Chief Justice White ailing (both his sight and hearing were defective) the Chief Justiceship might well be within the gift of Harding. At any rate, Taft decided to make a try for it. He explained to Harding that the Court had been his lifetime ambition and why on two previous occasions he had declined to accept nominations. He then ventured this statement: "I [am] obliged to say that now under the circumstances of having been President, and having appointed three of the present Bench and three others, and having protested against Brandeis, I could not accept any place but the Chief Justiceship." When Taft finished, Harding was curiously silent, and there was no further discussion of the matter at Marion. Before Taft left, he sent a note to Harding stating that Chief Justice White had said many times he was holding the Chief Justiceship for Taft and would give it back to a Republican administration. The note added that Harding was, of course, free to nominate anyone he pleased for the office and that Taft was grateful for the honor of Harding's offer of a Justiceship.[41]

Before 1920 ended, Taft's friends were pressing his candidacy for the Chief Justiceship. He was delighted with every bit of favorable gossip reported to him. Senator Brandegee approached Harding on the matter, and the President-elect seemed favorable. Taft was encouraged in early January by a cordial note from Harding, which promised nothing. Later that month he heard that Harding definitely told Daugherty he was going to name him (Taft) Chief Justice. Charles D. Hilles,* a close friend of Taft and a New York politician, doubted that Daugherty was telling the truth. Yet Hilles believed Taft's appointment possible and told Harding he wanted nothing from the new administration, except the appointment of Taft as Chief Justice.[42]

Taft regarded Daugherty as important to the realization of his ambition. Late in February, when Harding named Daugherty Attorney General, Taft wired his congratulations, saying he was confident Daugherty would give the country "an able, efficient, and courageous administration." He added it was good that Harding would have "in a constant close relation an intimate, wise, frank, disinterested friend and counselor to help him in the arduous task he faces."[43]

If Chief Justice White were holding the Chief Justiceship for Taft, he made no move to relinquish it. When Max Pam, a Chicago lawyer and close friend of both Taft and White, told the Chief Justice in February that Taft's friends were talking about his coming to the Court, White replied, "But there is no vacancy." Though Taft found this discouraging, he was consoled by the fact that his stock was still high in the White House. In early April, Hilles discussed the matter with Harding again and reported he was "satisfied that the Chief Justiceship is in hand."[44]

In mid-April Jacob M. Dickinson, Taft's former Secretary of War, called on Chief Justice White to discuss the possibility of his retirement. White said he planned to retire, then quickly changed the subject. Dickinson did not pursue the matter; after talking to Justice McReynolds about it, he concluded that though White at times had an impulse to re-

---

* During Taft's administration Hilles was personal secretary to the President and also served as Assistant Secretary of the Treasury. In the 1920's he was chairman of the Finance Committee of the Republican party, and it was rumored that Harding was going to appoint him Secretary of the Treasury.

sign, he could not bring himself to do so. This news depressed Taft. Earlier, when he had heard of White's reluctance to leave the Court, Taft had told his wife that "we may as well possess our souls with humility and suppress our ambitions." But for Taft that was easier said than done. Now, with Harding apparently willing to name him Chief Justice, Taft felt it was not fair of White to cling to the office. As Taft saw it, it was now or never for him. "You see," he explained to Dickinson, "I am growing old myself. I shall be sixty-four . . . in September." Those had been sixty-four good years for Taft, as he well knew. Since his graduation from Yale as salutatorian in 1878 his rise had been phenomenal—assistant prosecutor, trial judge, United States Solicitor General, federal circuit judge, governor general of the Philippines, Secretary of War, President, and professor of law at Yale. "Considering everything I have had to be grateful for to God and to the American people," he said, "it is absurd for me to be thinking of something else, and I suppress ambitious thoughts, which thrust themselves on me uninvited. From a selfish point of view, there is nothing so mind and soul disturbing as waiting for other men's shoes." And yet Taft eagerly waited. As his friend, the reporter Gus J. Karger, put it: "The situation seems to rest in the lap of the gods, or in the lap of Mr. White."[45]

On May 19, 1921 the situation was in the lap of the gods: Chief Justice White had died. What many assumed would happen did not occur: Taft's name was not forthwith sent to the Senate. The hitch was Harding's pledge to put ex-Senator Sutherland on the Court. Harding believed Sutherland expected to be appointed to the first vacancy; that the vacancy was the Chief Justiceship complicated matters. Harding toyed with the idea of satisfying both Taft and Sutherland by persuading one of the older Justices to retire and then nominating Taft and Sutherland together, or by promoting one of the older Justices to the Chief Justiceship and appointing Sutherland Associate Justice immediately and Taft Chief Justice later. For his part, Taft declined to have anything to do with such an arrangement. Harding, nevertheless, sent intermediaries to Justices Day and Holmes, but no agreement could be reached. Meanwhile friends of Taft, including his former Attorney General, George W. Wickersham, conferred with Daugherty, who said he was still for Taft as he had been all along. He agreed the appointment should be made as soon as possible and promised to take up the matter with Harding. A week later Harding agreed that Taft's name should be sent to the Senate alone and Sutherland should fill the next vacancy. On June 30 the Senate received Taft's nomination and confirmed it without reference to committee, an honor probably accorded him because he had been President. Four senators, however, voted against confirmation. They were Borah, Johnson, LaFollette, and Watson of Georgia.[46]*

Daugherty's interest in Taft's appointment was revealed by Harding when the nomination was announced. "The courts are congested," said the President, "and the Chief Justice will be a factor in bringing on a better situation. Additional judges will be needed; there may be need of authorization of commissioners. . . . The courts are all clogged up. It is a problem of the Department of Justice to work this out, and the Attorney General wants the Chief Justice to help work it out." [47]

Taft was more than willing to help Daugherty in this and other aspects of his work, especially in making judicial nominations. Nominating judges was what Taft liked about being President (he believed it to be one of the President's most difficult and important duties†), and when his party came back to power, he found it difficult not to volunteer advice. "If you don't mind it," he told Daugherty, "my in-

* From Montreal, where he was still working on the Grand Trunk Arbitration, Taft wrote to Sutherland: "Conundrum—If you have to have opposition, whose would you rather have than Borah, Johnson, LaFollette, and Watson? That composite is a 'Daisy.'" July 2, 1921, Sutherland Papers.

† On December 6, 1909 Taft bared his soul on the subject of judicial appointments to his friend Judge Warrington: "Oh, John! you don't know—you can't know—the difficulties of such responsibility as I have to exercise, and how they burden a man's heart with conflicting feelings prompted by duty and personal affection." Taft Papers.

terests in the Federal Judiciary, where I know something of the situation, makes me anxious to give you benefit of what I have learned from considerable experience. I am not butting in, but I am only testifying, without any personal slant, and only with a view of helping if I can." Daugherty's response in 1921 was to go ahead: "I want you at all times to feel free to make suggestions." [48]

A mutually agreeable working relationship developed between Taft and Daugherty. Daugherty and Harding were happy to get Taft's advice, for when they followed it, they seldom ran into difficulty. And giving such advice was a labor of love for Taft. Neither Harding nor Daugherty imposed it on him. He took it upon himself voluntarily, he said, because of his sense of duty to the judicial branch of government he headed.[49]

To Taft, despite the Morse pardon case, Daugherty was not the Devil incarnate. He saw him as a fighter, a bitter hater, a suspicious man, a man who lacked real ability, but nevertheless an honest man.[50] When enemies were attacking Daugherty, which was practically all of the time, there were often sympathetic words from the Chief Justice. "My dear Harry," wrote Taft in June 1922, "you want to refute your enemies, and you are going to do it, but one of the chief opportunities is through the selection of the highest standard of men for these twenty-five additional judgeships. I hope you will appoint some Democrats, in spite of the partisan bitterness of the attacks on you. . . . I am concerned in your welfare and in your success, and that of the Administration, and what I have written is out of a full heart and with a fairly competent knowledge and experience in a particular field." [51] Daugherty generally followed Taft's advice. About a month after Harding's death, Taft said of Daugherty: "Harry is a good man about Judges and loyally stands for the best men and rarely acts without invoking my assistance in getting at the truth." [52] Later he said: "But for [Daugherty], Harding would have made a wreck of it [nominating judges], I fear, because he was not a lawyer and did not appreciate the importance of the selections." [53] More than one historian has remarked that the judicial appointments of the Harding administration were regarded as being of strikingly high quality.[54]

IV

In many ways Taft's personality was like Harding's. He, too, was perceived as humble, affable, kindly, and conciliatory. He, too, wanted affection and approval. And, like Harding, he was sensitive about the feelings of those around him and suspected that others had greater ability and could do his job better. On the Court he regarded his appointee, Willis Van Devanter, as his intellectual superior, and in some ways Van Devanter's personality complemented Taft's as Daugherty's complemented Harding's.[55]

Van Devanter was a Wyoming frontier lawyer in the 1880's and 1890's who rose rapidly in politics. At twenty-seven, he was city attorney of Cheyenne; at twenty-eight, a member of the territorial legislature; and at thirty, chief justice of the Wyoming Supreme Court. In 1898 he went to Washington as an Assistant Attorney General assigned to the Interior Department. There he acquired enough visibility and support to be appointed to the Eighth Circuit bench in 1903, joining Judge Walter H. Sanborn. His duties often brought him to St. Paul where he developed a friendship with one of the state's leading practitioners—Pierce Butler. In 1910 Van Devanter was appointed to the Supreme Court by President Taft.[56]

Contemporaries saw Van Devanter as a man of "great physical vigor, a powerful intellect and driving and dominant personality."[57] In conference, Taft described him as "an antagonist who generally wins against all opposition."[58] When Taft came to the Court, he established close ties with Van Devanter; the two men became intimate friends and worked in coalition, not only in regard to cases before the Court but in all matters in which Taft was interested, such as legislation concerning the judiciary (Van Devanter was chief draftsman of such legislation) and judicial appointments, including appointments to the Supreme Court. Van

Devanter advised Taft so much that the Chief Justice was said to refer to him as his "lord chancellor," [59] and at times he acted as Taft's alter ego. For instance, in 1922, when Taft left for England to receive an honorary degree from Oxford, he wrote Daugherty that he had discussed all pending judicial nominations with Van Devanter: "he will be at your service where you desire it. He could make investigation that you possibly could not through sources peculiarly open to him." [60]

The President and his Attorney General, the Chief Justice and one of his associates—they were the top tier of Harding and Company, the men who would nominate Pierce Butler to the Supreme Court. If constitutional doctrines like separation of powers are taken seriously, the combination was unusual—indeed, unconstitutional—for members of the Supreme Court are to have nothing to do with the appointment of colleagues. But then there is more to politics and law than constitutional doctrines.[61]

Part Two: How

Chapter 3

CHOOSING A CANDIDATE

As he surveyed his Court in 1922, Chief Justice Taft saw that in the near future, perhaps within the year, age and sickness would claim or force the retirement of as many as four of his brethren. Justice Holmes, the Magnificent Yankee, was now eighty-one. Though still one of the most agile minds in the Court, he appeared to be breaking physically. An operation had left him a shadow of his former self; his jauntiness was gone, he would fall asleep in conference, and at times he had difficulty breathing. Two years his junior was Justice McKenna, McKinley's former Attorney General. In his case, age had taken a greater toll on the mind than on the body; the old Justice was well on his way to senility. To the embarrassment of his colleagues, in case after case assigned to him for opinion, he would miss the point of the Court's decision, and in one case he wrote an opinion sustaining the opposite conclusion to that voted by the entire Court, including himself. Then there was Justice Day, who was seventy-three. After suffering through ten days of high fever early in 1922, he told Taft he intended to follow his doctor's recommendation that he retire soon. The saddest case was Justice Pitney, one of Taft's own appointees. Though only in his early sixties, he had suffered a serious stroke late in 1921, which was diagnosed as progressive arteriosclerosis affecting the blood vessels of the brain and Bright's disease. When Taft heard this, he said: "Poor Pitney is completely gone." [1]

Nevertheless, Taft believed Providence had been kind. At least these men had lived long enough to deliver their places to a Republican administration. Unlike Wilson, Harding—with a little help from the right people—could be counted on to name Justices who would preserve the Constitution. Taft, of course, expected to be consulted. He had, in fact, given more thought to the matter than either Harding or Daugherty. The first vacancy, he knew, would be filled by Harding's friend and former Senate colleague, George Sutherland. That was agreeable to Taft; he felt Sutherland would be an excellent appointment. But good men would have to be found for the remaining vacancies.[2]

I

Believing Nathan L. Miller, the Governor of New York, to be of Supreme Court caliber, Taft wrote and told him so in May of 1922: "How I would like to have you on our Court! I don't know whether this is in the line of your ambition, but I need not say to you we need the highest courage and the highest ability and judicial experience. There are no vacancies, of course, but I have dreams." [3] Though flattered, Miller replied he did not think he could accept an appointment to the Court because the salary was insufficient to provide for his large family. But, he added, New York was entitled to the next vacancy and Judge Frank H. Hiscock of the State Court of Appeals should be given first chance. Despite Miller's lack of enthusiasm for appointment to the Court, Taft believed that when the offer was actually made, he would accept. Hence, in June, though there was no vacancy clearly in sight, Taft strongly urged Miller upon Harding, who seemed interested.[4]

Later that month there were signs of a vacancy in the making. Harding had a conference with Justice Day's son in which he intimated that if the Justice would retire in the next few months he would be appointed chairman of the German-American Mixed Claims Commission then being created. When Day heard this, he wrote the President that if the matter could be worked out along the lines suggested, he would submit his resignation, to take effect early in October. Taft was delighted by the news, but by late August he was troubled because Day had made no further move toward resignation. The Chief Justice was well aware that old justices sometimes change their minds about retiring, even after indicating an intention to do so; thus he wanted Day to commit himself to a definite retirement date.* That date, Taft felt, had to be after the Court term began because Day's vote was needed in some closely divided cases carried over from the previous term; but it had to be before the end of October, for Taft wanted Day's successor—presumably Sutherland—nominated and confirmed before Congress adjourned for the coming elections. Taft had in mind the 10th or 15th of October.

Tactfully he suggested that Harding and Daugherty work out this arrangement with Day. Characteristically, Harding said he could not for fear of wounding Day's feelings, but if Taft wanted to broach the subject with Day, he had no objection. Immediately Taft and Van Devanter took up the matter with Day. Thus matters stood at the beginning of September.[5]

Then there was a surprising development: Justice Clarke, who was the same age as Taft, sixty-five, and apparently

* Taft's suspicions about Day's reluctance to retire were well founded. On November 5, 1922 Day wrote to former Justice Clarke: "I am free to admit that it has been a wrench for me to quit the work, hard as it is, and ready as I am to avail myself of the right to retire. I have been at it so long that it seems like second nature to keep doing the work." Clarke Papers.

in good health, said he intended to resign from the Court. Though surprised, Taft could understand why Clarke would want to resign. Justice McReynolds had made life in the Court almost unbearable for him by his incessant insolence and personal insults; beyond that, Clarke was, at the time, beside himself with grief over the death of a sister, his only close relative. Taft was genuinely sympathetic; nevertheless, he felt Harding should make the most of the situation and accept Clarke's resignation before his friends could induce him to withdraw it. After all, Clarke was a Wilson appointee whose voting record in the 1921 term was even more liberal than Brandeis'.[6] Reading of Clarke's resignation, Harold Laski wrote Holmes: "If God is good, you will have Learned Hand; but I fear . . . you are more likely to have some such person as Senator Sutherland." [7] * Laski's fear was justified; at the time he wrote Holmes, Sutherland was already a Supreme Court Justice. Harding had nominated him upon receipt of Clarke's resignation, and the Senate, according Sutherland an honor reserved usually only for senators, confirmed his nomination without reference to committee.[8] †

With Sutherland "taken care of," Taft's thoughts turned

---

* Three months later, Judge Hand was considered and rejected for the vacancy created by Pitney's retirement. On December 4, 1922 Taft wrote to Harding: "There is a United States District Judge of proper age, Learned Hand. He is an able Judge and a hard worker. I appointed him on Wickersham's recommendation, but he turned out to be a wild Roosevelt man and a progressive, and though on the Bench, he went into the campaign. If promoted to our Bench, he would most certainly herd with Brandeis and be a dissenter. I think it would be risking too much to appoint him." Taft Papers.

† Taft's comments on Sutherland's appointment indicated the sort of man he desired on the Court. "Yes," the Chief Justice wrote, "I am very glad to have Sutherland substituted for Clarke in the Court. I like Clarke—he is a good fellow—but I don't like his legal politico-economic views. Sutherland is a much abler man and a much sounder lawyer and not a hidebound conservative but a reasonable one. He has tempered his views by long political experience—a process which makes him a much more useful Judge than one who, like Holmes, has had no political experience and proceeds as if the American Constitution were as malleable as the British Constitution." Taft to Horace D. Taft, Sept. 13, 1922, Taft Papers.

to the anticipated Day vacancy. He found a comment from Harding especially reassuring. "I assume," said Harding right after the Sutherland appointment, "that we shall have other vacancies to fill, but we can meet that situation when it is developed." [9] Taft had no intention of waiting for the situation to develop. Already he and Van Devanter had reached an understanding with Day as to the approximate date of his retirement and were sizing up candidates to succeed him. Solicitor General James M. Beck would probably want the place; so would Senator Frank B. Kellogg of Minnesota. Both were quickly eliminated: Beck was "a lightweight"; Kellogg, at sixty-five, was too old. Governor Miller still seemed to be the best bet if he could only be convinced. If not, maybe his candidate, Hiscock, should be given the place. Van Devanter was unimpressed by Hiscock; Miller, he thought, was probably satisfactory. Since only two members of the Court were Democrats, Taft and Van Devanter agreed there was much to be said for the appointment of a Democrat of "sound" views. They had in mind Wilson's former Solicitor General and ambassador to England, John W. Davis—"a good lawyer and level-headed," a man who "does not run from work and . . . enjoys a good reputation all over the country." "If I were making the appointment," said Taft, "I would appoint John Davis." [10] *

Taft circulated these views to Charles D. Hilles, George W. Wickersham, Elihu Root, and other close friends. Hilles was especially interested. Since it was understood that New York was entitled to an appointment and a Democrat would be acceptable, the New York politician suggested a shrewd scheme to kill several political pigeons with a single stone. This was the heart of the plan:

> Justice McKenna is the only Roman Catholic on the Court. Chief Justice White was a member of that church.

* In time, Harding too came to accept the view that the appointment of a Democrat was appropriate. On October 19, 1922 he wrote to Nicholas Murray Butler: "I very much wish to avoid the accusation of being unduly partisan, and am considering a Democrat for the next vacancy in view of the fact that I chose Sutherland, Republican, to succeed Justice Clarke." Harding Papers.

McKenna is fading and will disappear shortly, probably within a year. If with his disappearance there should be one Hebrew on the Court and no Catholic, there will be an insistent demand for a successor to McKenna who is of the faith he embraced. It would be an unfortunate thing and create an awkward predicament. Furthermore, there are few really able Catholic lawyers in the Republican party. If a Democrat should be appointed to succeed Day, it would be expected that the successor to McKenna would not also be a Democrat. Therefore, this would seem to be a propitious time to appoint a Democrat who is also a Roman Catholic. The question would not then arise upon the retirement of McKenna.

There are two Democratic jurists in New York who are Catholics. One is Mr. Victor Dowling of the Appellate [Division of the Supreme] Court and the other is Judge [Martin T.] Manton of the United States Circuit Court.* Good lawyers say both are proficient in the law and able on the bench. If Manton were appointed, the President would have a vacancy on the Circuit bench which he would fill from Vermont, Connecticut, or New York. If Dowling were appointed, Governor Miller would name his successor, but only until the next election. Possibly there are excellent Democrats in the Chicago circuit.[11]

Taft was shocked by the scheme. Did his old friend, Dewey Hilles, think that religion should be considered in this fashion in making a Supreme Court appointment? To be sure, said Taft, a man who is otherwise qualified should not be barred from the Court because of his religion, but religion should never be a reason *for* appointment. (It was Taft's belief that Brandeis would not have been confirmed by the Senate if he had not been a Jew and that Wilson had had that consideration in mind when he nominated him.) Hilles, Taft felt, must have been talking to their mutual friend, Max Pam, who earlier suggested the same scheme.

* Dowling was fifty-six years old. A graduate of New York University Law School in 1887, he was first elected to the New York Supreme Court in 1905. Manton was only forty-two. A graduate of Columbia University Law School in 1901, he was appointed by Woodrow Wilson to the federal district bench in 1916 and the circuit bench in 1918.

How either of them could suggest Dowling or Manton for the Supreme Court was beyond Taft. Neither judge, he felt, was worthy of the place. Although Taft knew Dowling, and liked him, he felt the man did not have the eminence to commend him for appointment to the Court. Manton was another matter: he was a "shrewd, cunning, political Judge." Worse, Taft felt that he was unethical and never should have been appointed to the bench in the first place—and would not have been if Wilson and Tammany Hall had not put him there.[12]

Hilles surrendered. Davis, he agreed, was "pre-eminently the man" because his appointment would strengthen Harding's hand with the Democrats in Congress and, at the same time, strengthen the Court. "But don't forget," he reminded the former President he once served, "that this is a practical world and that a great body of good citizens will be unwilling to concede that no one of their number could be found who was worthy and well qualified." [13] All Hilles was trying to do was to find a good candidate before the opposing forces were organized and plugging for their man. Hilles' switch to Davis did not eliminate Manton as a candidate. The wheels of the Manton band wagon in New York were already beginning to roll, and Hilles' early support probably helped. Toward the end of September, Daugherty heard from a friend in New York that there were reasons why Manton should receive Day's place on the Court which went beyond his being a Democrat, reasons he felt he could not very well write about but which he would be glad to come to Washington and disclose personally. Presumably he had information that the Roman Catholic Archbishop of New York, Patrick Hayes, desired Manton's appointment. Daugherty answered that a number of people were interested in seeing Manton appointed and that in due time his name would receive "careful consideration." [14]

Reverting to his former role as Taft's Attorney General, Wickersham surveyed the New York candidates more soberly than Hilles. Like Van Devanter, he rejected Hiscock. Though Hiscock was a sensible and learned judge, he had no experience in the federal field, and, at sixty-seven, Wickersham thought he was too old to make the transition. Another probable candidate was Hiscock's colleague, Frederick E. Crane. Wickersham believed Crane was a straightforward, competent state judge, but not Supreme Court material. Benjamin N. Cardozo, also of the Court of Appeals, was another matter. Wickersham felt he would make a superb candidate—"a man of sound learning and personally a very attractive character." But Cardozo was a Jew, and Wickersham did not believe "it would do to have two Jews on the Supreme Court." Thus Cardozo was eliminated.* Though Wickersham regarded Miller as a sound lawyer, he also saw some defects—an intolerance of difference of opinion and a dogmatism about his own views. If a Democrat was to be chosen, he agreed Davis would be ideal. But Wickersham's candidate was Federal Judge Charles M. Hough of the Second Circuit, whom he regarded as "far and away the best man available." He was afraid that Hough's age might be held against him and tried to gloss over and compensate for it. "He is only 63 years old," he told Taft, before describing him in terms of Taft's image of the ideal Supreme Court Justice: "experienced federal judge . . . great vigor of mind . . . a thoroughly trained lawyer . . . courageous, but judicial minded . . . universal respect of the bar . . . would step at once into the team and do teamwork." Obviously, answered Taft, Hough was a strong judge, though some of his opinions indicated he was a bit erratic. That, however, was not the problem:

* There was, however, other strong support for Cardozo. Nicholas Murray Butler, for example, wrote Harding that Cardozo was "universally regarded as one of the finest judicial minds and one of the finest natures of his generation. . . . I have never heard of him any criticism that was not so favorable as to be truly described as enthusiastic." Oct. 23, 1922, Harding Papers. And Dean Thomas Swan of the Yale Law School wrote Harding that it was the unanimous opinion of his faculty that Cardozo should be appointed. Nov. 3, 1922, File of Benjamin N. Cardozo, Record Group 60, Department of Justice Records. Later, in evaluating candidates for the next vacancy, Taft conceded that Cardozo was "the best judge in the State of New York" but pointed out he was a Jew, a Democrat, and "what they call a progressive judge." Taft to Harding, Dec. 4, 1922, Taft Papers.

Hough was more than sixty, and Taft felt that fact in itself would eliminate him.[15]

Taft specifically asked for Wickersham's opinion of William D. Guthrie, prominent New York lawyer, Republican, and Catholic. In an exchange of confidential notes, they agreed Guthrie's standing at the bar justified his appointment and that he could well afford to accept the place, but he, too, had defects—age (he was sixty-three) and a lack of a sense of humor, which, to Wickersham, meant "a lack of a just sense of proportion." [16]

By early October Miller definitely eliminated himself, leaving Davis as the only acceptable candidate. Davis, however, expressed little enthusiasm for the appointment. When Wickersham first approached him on the matter, he said he could not and would not consider it. Then he said if there were a definite offer, he might accept it; at any rate, he would give it "prayerful consideration." Wickersham's net impression was that Davis would accept the appointment if it was offered him, but for financial reasons would prefer to remain in practice with Stetson, Jennings, & Russell, the firm that represented J. P. Morgan.[17]

More important to Wickersham than Davis' decision was the possibility of Manton's appointment being pressured through the White House. "I understand Manton is pulling every wire he can," wrote Wickersham on October 10. And the next day, appalled by the English in one of Manton's opinions, he marked the poorly composed paragraphs and sent the opinion to Taft with the comment that such work would not "enhance the prestige of any judicial tribunal." [18] Taft did not have to be convinced. Harding and Daugherty were well aware of his objections to Manton. Now Taft's old friend Max Pam also registered his objections to Manton with the President and the Attorney General. And Senator William M. Calder of New York wrote Harding saying that he had known Manton for twenty-five years and that his appointment to the Supreme Court would be received unfavorably by leading members of the New York bench and bar. Nevertheless, Manton's strength was growing. Frank A.

Munsey, the publisher, came to his support and told Harding that the appointment of the New York judge "would be strategically wise." Senator Walter E. Edge of New Jersey wrote Harding that "friends of the party" in New York were highly favorable to Manton's appointment. Finally, it was now definitely known that Manton's chief support was coming from Archbishop Hayes.[19] If Davis would not accept the appointment, or if he delayed his decision much longer, another candidate would have to be found—and quickly—if only to head off Manton's nomination.

In New York, Hilles actively sought a suitable candidate to avert the Manton "disaster." A friend called his attention to Harlan F. Stone, then dean of the law school at Columbia University, as pre-eminently fit for the Supreme Court. Interested, Hilles wrote Nicholas Murray Butler, the president of Columbia, inquiring about Stone's "special qualifications" and "political predilections." Butler answered that Stone was about as good a man as could be found—for the post he had, but not for "the great office" mentioned by Hilles. "For highest success in that office," he added, "I think somewhat different characteristics of mind and temperament are required." New Yorkers possessing the requisite characteristics, in his opinion, were Cardozo and Guthrie.[20] One of these men, not Stone, he said, should be appointed. Thus Stone was eliminated.*

III

The quest for a candidate in New York had led to nothing but blind alleys. Now Taft was willing to look elsewhere.

---

* Hilles, nevertheless, raised Stone's name with Taft a few months later for the next vacancy, saying he wondered if it would be audacious to suggest the Columbia Law School Dean as "an entirely new possibility. . . . [It] would be a refreshing thing, and would be acclaimed by the honest struggling young men of this country, if the President were to depart somewhat from the beaten path and take a man of this type." Taft said he liked Stone and was sure he would make a good judge, but it was unlikely that Harding would appoint him. Hilles to Taft, Jan. 18, 1923; Taft to Hilles, Jan. 20, 1923, Taft Papers. Stone was later appointed to the Supreme Court by President Coolidge.

Hilles' early comment—"Possibly there are good Democrats in the Chicago circuit"—may have suggested the Midwest. At any rate, when Van Devanter mentioned Pierce Butler, Taft thought the idea worth pursuing—particularly in view of the growing strength of Manton's candidacy—for Butler, like Manton, was a Democrat and a Roman Catholic.

So Van Devanter wrote Judge Walter H. Sanborn, his good friend and former colleague on the Eighth Circuit bench. He said he was writing about a matter in which they might be able to work some "public good." He then explained that two or three vacancies on the Supreme Court were imminent, and, as he saw it, Democrats, Catholics, and Southerners would be demanding that one of their number be appointed, for each of those groups recently lost representation on the Court. Therefore, qualified men—such as John W. Davis, a Democrat from West Virginia—had a good chance of appointment. Van Devanter said he was disposed toward Davis, but he also thought their mutual friend Pierce Butler would make an excellent appointee. "You know him well, both as a man and as a lawyer," the Justice added, "and have known him all during his professional career. Won't you tell me what you think of him for the place?" [21]

A few days later Van Devanter received Sanborn's answer:

> I cannot think of anyone better qualified for such place by character, ability, learning, judgment and temperament than he. . . . His character is above reproach. . . . His intellect is clear, calm, analytic and unusually powerful. His mind is well stored with general information and with profound and accurate knowledge of the law; his industry is indefatigable; his knowledge and experience of business affairs involving interests great and small, public and private, have broadened, strengthened and ripened his judgment, originally well endowed with the saving gift of common sense. His temperament is even, calm and judicial. . . . Take him all in all, Pierce Butler is, in my opinion, one of the few great men of my acquaintance.[22]

The letter had a profound effect on Taft, who highly esteemed Sanborn and who at one time seriously considered appointing him to the Supreme Court. The recommendation was, moreover, one of the strongest Taft had ever read.[23]

If a Midwesterner was to be nominated, Taft knew that the New York bar would have to agree on the man. Hence, when Van Devanter wrote Sanborn, Taft asked Wickersham for his opinion about Butler, for the Minnesota lawyer had been retained by Wickersham to prosecute some antitrust cases during Taft's Presidency. Wickersham replied that he had not seen or heard from Butler in about ten years, but that he thought Butler had done good work in the antitrust litigation. So far so good, thought Taft.[24]

An important question yet to be answered was whether Pierce Butler was interested in becoming a Supreme Court Justice. Max Pam went to the Midwest to find out. Learning that Butler was in Toronto working on an important valuation case, Pam arranged a meeting in Minneapolis with Butler's son, Pierce, Jr., a recent graduate of the Harvard Law School. There he disclosed that the elder Butler was being seriously considered for appointment to the Supreme Court. The message was relayed immediately to Butler at the King Edward Hotel in Toronto. The news almost overwhelmed the St. Paul lawyer. Using hotel stationery, he immediately wrote to Taft. Yes, he was very much interested in the possibility of his going on the Court, but he assured the Chief Justice he "did nothing directly or indirectly to suggest the thought to anyone or in any way to reinforce the suggestion," nor would he countenance such activity on the part of his friends. Nevertheless, he wanted to know the true situation. If the President was really considering him, Butler wanted him to have the full facts. But how, he asked Taft, should he go about it? "You will understand about how I am feeling," he wrote, "and know how much I would like to have *information* and friendly advice."[25]

Taft was only too happy to give advice and encouragement. "My Dear Pierce," he responded in a letter marked

Very Confidential, "it would delight me to have you on our Bench, and I think it quite within the bounds of possibility. Of course, you would not countenance the activity of your friends at your invitation in such a matter." Taft told Butler that one of his strongest supporters was Van Devanter, but other support would have to be stimulated. The support of the Minnesota senators, Nelson and Kellogg, would be especially important. Perhaps Van Devanter could sound them out. Referring to the case Butler was working on in Toronto, Taft said: "I should think you would be tired of arbitrations of value. You would find my work much more interesting." [26]

Despite those encouraging words to Butler, Taft still preferred Davis. But he knew he could not wait much longer. On October 24 Day announced that he would retire as of November 14, and this made for increased activity in Manton's camp. In New York, Taft's brother, Harry, a partner of Wickersham, was leading the fight against the New York judge. He was amazed at the diversity of Manton's support—support that ran the gamut from Archbishop Hayes to the shady lawyer Thomas B. Felder, with whom Daugherty had been associated in the infamous Morse pardon case. In late October Harry came to Washington to present his case against Manton. He told Daugherty that his friend Felder was supporting Manton, and Daugherty responded: "Felder is no friend of mine." "Well," answered Harry, "he is exploiting your friendship and getting the same advantage as if the friendship existed." Daugherty agreed that Manton was unfit for the bench and said that he would advise Harding accordingly. He emphatically added that he would not approve of anyone for the Court who was not approved by the Chief Justice. Confident that Daugherty was telling the truth, Harry nevertheless felt that Manton might be nominated because of pressure brought directly on Harding, for even Daugherty admitted that the President was weakening.[27]

In reporting this conversation to the Chief Justice, Harry said he saw no good reason why there should be objection to a first-rate man just because he was sixty-three or sixty-four. Though he was probably referring to Hough, his brother thought he meant Wickersham. This was discomforting, for Taft himself came to the Court at sixty-four, and as President had appointed some Justices who were beyond the age of sixty. Further, he knew Wickersham well and liked him; he acknowledged he was bright, personable, a hard worker, and loyal—in short, Supreme Court caliber. Yet Taft felt he had to be realistic. Harding, he believed, would not appoint anyone who was more than sixty. No, said Taft, a man who was more than sixty had no chance. Then, said Harry, the best solution seemed to be the selection of Pierce Butler. "I base this," he added, "entirely upon what you say of him; but his being a Democrat and a Catholic make the suggestion of his name peculiarly appropriate at present." [28]

About the time Taft's attention shifted to Butler, Max Pam was surveying the entire country for available Catholic Democrats. He sent five names to Harding—Judge Victor J. Dowling, W. D. Guthrie, Pierce Butler, Federal District Judge Martin J. Wade of Iowa, and Senator Thomas J. Walsh of Montana. It was a peculiar list in one respect: all the men named except Dowling and Butler were more than sixty years old, and Pam knew that candidates beyond that age, as a practical matter, had no chance of appointment. As between Dowling and Butler, Pam apparently preferred the former. He described Dowling as "well and favorably known throughout the nation, especially among co-religionists." Butler, on the other hand, was described as "well-known to members of the American bar" but as not enjoying the same popularity among Catholics as Dowling. During the last week of October, Pam made a final effort in Dowling's behalf. He sent Taft and Daugherty a memorandum listing Dowling's important decisions and a biography emphasizing the judge's standing in Catholic circles. It indicated such honors as Knight of the Order of St. Gregory, conferred by Pope Benedict XV, and Commander of the Order of the Holy Sepulchre, conferred by the Latin Patriarch of Jerusalem. Taft, having rejected Dowling, paid little attention to the communication; Daugherty agreed to see Pam for a few minutes about the matter.[29]

On October 27 Taft was close to a decision. "I think Pierce Butler is our man," he wrote to Van Devanter.[30] The following day he told Pam that next to Davis, he felt Butler the most qualified candidate.[31] Yet hopeless as the Davis candidacy seemed, Taft and Van Devanter had not completely given up. On October 28 Van Devanter wrote Davis telling him point-blank that he and the Chief Justice were interested in his appointment to the Court. "While recognizing that you are not seeking the preferment," he wrote, "we conceive you would deem it a patriotic duty to accept, if the place were tendered." He then asked Davis to communicate his "real attitude" concerning the possibility of his appointment.[32]

For two days and two nights Davis pondered the problem. He knew what Van Devanter's communication meant—a place on the Court if he wanted it. Such an honor was difficult to turn down, and the mention of patriotic duty touched him. Yet had he not given himself fully and unselfishly to his country for the past ten years as Congressman, Solicitor General, and ambassador to Great Britain? He was not a wealthy man, and his governmental service, especially his two years as ambassador, had depleted his savings. Now had he not the right to think of his family—and his law partners, who had been generous to him and expected him to remain with them? It was not that he wanted a fortune ("in these income-tax days," he said, that was impossible anyway), but surely he was entitled to acquire a measure of economic independence and to make provision for those dependent upon him. And yet, could he bring himself to say he did not want to go on the Supreme Court? Yes, he could. Maybe later he could answer the question otherwise, but not now. "All I ask is a breathing spell" was his final plea.[33] Davis was now definitely out of the running.*

---

* Thomas W. Shelton, a mutual friend of Davis and Taft, pleaded with Davis to accept the proffered Justiceship: "When the names of

While Davis was still in the throes of decision, Taft decided he could wait no longer. On October 30, the day before Davis made his decision, Taft, with Sanborn's recommendation of Butler before him, penned the following letter to President Harding:

> In your consideration of candidates for the Supreme Bench, I think I spoke to you of Pierce Butler of Minnesota. I have known him for a number of years very well indeed. He was counsel for the Government of Canada in the arbitration of the Grand Trunk valuation, in which I was one of the arbitrators, and heard him in trial and in argument for months together. He builded himself up from the bottom. He has a family of a wife and eight children. He is one of the trustees or Regents of the Minnesota University of which he is a graduate. He is a Catholic and was a great friend of Archbishop Ireland. Justice Van Devanter knows him well. He has heard him argue one hundred cases in the Circuit Court of Appeals of the Eighth Circuit. He is the head of one of the largest firms in St. Paul. He is a Democrat of the Cleveland type, but really one I think who would make a great Justice of our Court, such a man of rugged character and force as Justice Miller was. Van Devanter thinks so but wrote to Sanborn, the oldest and strongest of our Circuit Judges, who presides in the Eighth Circuit, and lives in St. Paul. As between him and John Davis, it would be hard to choose as to ability, qualifications and judicial temperament. Butler is about fifty-four, I think, certainly under sixty. I enclose the letter Van Devanter received from Sanborn, who has no motive in the matter other than getting a good man and who knows Butler as few members do.[34]

J. P. Morgan or Carnegie have been forgotten," he wrote, "when Choate and Carter will be meaningless, the words of Mr. Justice Davis will be fresh in mind; will be educating coming generations in fundamental principles and will be measuring civil liberty and property rights amongst millions." The eloquence was wasted; by the time Davis received the letter, his mind was made up. Taft told Van Devanter that Davis would live to regret his decision. "He has made his choice now, and I don't see quite how the opportunity can come to him again, because while he is young enough to wait some years, by that time he will become so identified with the Morgan interests that no President would feel like taking him from the center of Wall Street and putting him on the Bench." Shelton to Davis, Oct. 30, 1922; Taft to Van Devanter, Nov. 2, 1922, Taft Papers.

The next day, a messenger brought Harding's reply:

> I have been giving some little attention to an appraisal of Mr. Butler myself. What you write concerning him fully confirms all I have been able to learn. I am convinced he is in every way worthy of consideration. I am returning herewith the letter to Justice Van Devanter.[35]

Taft was delighted. He sent Harding's letter to Van Devanter, who answered: "Am glad to see this. This is good as far as it goes and I hope it will continue in that line."[36]

Chapter 4

CAMPAIGNING

If Butler was to be nominated, Taft knew there had to be a strong show of support for him. Endorsement by the Minnesota senators was seen as crucial. Recommendations also had to come from other men of substance, men whose names and positions would impress Harding—corporate executives, leaders of the bar, judges, college and university presidents, bishops and archbishops. All of that could be arranged, but mobilizing the Catholic hierarchy presented difficulties. If Taft's friend Archbishop John Ireland of St. Paul were alive in 1922, it would have been a relatively easy task. Taft would have explained Archbishop Hayes's misguided support of Manton, and thereupon Ireland, who in political matters usually had not seen eye to eye with the eastern hierarchy anyway, could have been relied upon to mobilize the archbishops and bishops of the Mississippi Valley and the West in support of Butler. But without Ireland, Taft did not know how the hierarchy could be reached.[1]

I

Van Devanter thought Judge Sanborn might be able to help in regard to the Catholic hierarchy. In a letter to the circuit judge at the end of October, he said that it would have given Archbishop Ireland great satisfaction to inform the President of Butler's "splendid qualifications" and of the enthusiasm with which his appointment would be received. If Ireland's successor wrote to Harding, Van Devanter continued, his recommendation would naturally carry much weight, because men in such positions are known to have the interests of the entire country at heart. Only the day before, Van Devanter and Taft heard that a Roman Catholic cardinal (presumably William Cardinal O'Connell of Boston) was asked for his opinion of Manton and Butler for the Supreme Court; the prelate said he had a low opinion of Manton and would not support him, and though he had heard that Butler was "a high-type man," he did not know him. "We could not help regretting," concluded Van Devanter, "that the Cardinal did not personally know Butler as well as we do." In view of these remarks, it was perhaps no coincidence that on the same day Harding wrote Cardinal O'Connell asking for information about Butler.[2]

Two days later Taft wrote Butler about the same matter. "I think you are quite mistaken in supposing that letters do not do any good," he said. "I think you ought to advise your son [Pierce, Jr.] and Mr. Mitchell [Butler's law partner] that personal letters written directly to the President on the subject, especially by such men as Governor Preus, and by the people whom the President is likely to know, like the Archbishop of your Diocese, and the head of the University of Minnesota, would be of the utmost of value, and the sooner they are sent the better." [3]

Sanborn checked on Ireland's successor, Archbishop Austin Dowling, and found that he was not known to have the political finesse of his predecessor. Yet the prelate would probably cooperate and could be educated to write the right kind of letter to Harding. There was even a good chance that he might be induced to write other Church officials, assuring them of Butler's fitness for the Court. Sanborn strongly impressed upon Mitchell the necessity of Dowling's support, and soon thereafter the Archbishop was approached. He manifested "favorable interest and desire to help." Butler was confident that Dowling would write to the President and that "the attitude of other prominent churchmen [would be] the same." [4]

Although all was going according to plan, Taft was doing some soul-searching. He believed he had been justified in asking Butler to seek Church support, and he knew that he wanted Butler on the Court because he would make a good Justice and not simply because he was a Catholic. Yet the fact that Butler was a Catholic was not unimportant. Since the appointment of Manton was something to be genuinely feared, and since he had the support of the eastern hierarchy, there seemed to be no choice but to enlist the support of the western hierarchy for Butler. Would Butler understand he was wanted on the Court for his own sake and not because he was a Catholic? Would others understand that Taft was acting to preserve the integrity of the Court he loved so much, and not utilizing a man's religion to boost him to the Supreme Court? Perhaps to assure himself as much as his candidate, Taft expressed his innermost thoughts on the subject to Butler on November 7.

"[Y]ou know I want you on the Bench," Taft wrote, "because I believe you to be eminently fitted to render great public service there." Few men are qualified for the Supreme Court, and members of the Court share a heavy responsibility; for that reason, Taft said, he had a personal interest in the character of each of his associates. It was "of the utmost importance to every other member of the crew" that each man "pull his weight in the boat." Because Taft was sure that Butler could do this, he was supporting him. How, then, did Butler's Catholicism enter the picture, if at all? This was Taft's answer:

> Now I am for you whether you are a Unitarian, a Catholic, a Presbyterian, an Agnostic, or a Mormon, and I resent the suggestion that a man's religion should play any part in the primary reasons for selecting him for our Court. A man who does not at once commend himself as eligible for the place, without thought of his religion, should certainly not be able to make up for his lack of eminent capacity by his

> being a member of one church or another, and the Church or the candidate who seeks to do the latter thing, ought not to receive the slightest encouragement, but should be condemned for the attempt. In spite of this view, however, which I believe sincerely to be the proper one—and any other demeans the Court—politicians refuse to adopt it, and are quite willing to piece out a man's indifferent qualifications for our Bench by the pleas that we need a Catholic or a Jew, and that therefore we should take one or the other, with mediocre qualifications, just because he is one or the other. The reason for my elaborating this view of mine is that there has been a conspiracy, which includes some of the Hierarchy of the Catholic Church in New York, to induce the President to appoint an utterly unfit man for our Court who has so many political and other associations that he has been able to mass a formidable amount of influence to be brought to bear upon a President, who is not a lawyer, to induce him to make an appointment which I think would be deplorable, not only for the country but for the Catholic Church, some of whose representatives are active in promoting it.[5]

Taft, of course, was referring to Manton. Bluntly he explained why Manton's appointment would be a disaster. Manton had been "an ambulance chaser" before he became a judge. He had been a partner of the New York politician W. Bourke Cockran* and a confidant and political ally of Boss John McCooey, Brooklyn Tammany leader. He was a warm friend of wealthy men who played the role of king-makers in politics; his consultation room was always full of such men. Politics had made him rich; he was, perhaps, the only judge on the federal bench who owned eight or nine laundries. In short, he lacked the moral qualities a judge should have and would never have reached the bench had it not been for men like Boss McCooey.[6]

"Archbishop Hayes," said Taft, "should be ashamed of

* Cockran, who had been periodically in and out of grace with Tammany Hall, returned to Congress in 1921 as Tammany's representative. He was a leading Catholic layman. When he died in 1923, Archbishop Hayes celebrated the funeral mass, and the Reverend John J. Wynne, S.J., editor of *America,* delivered the eulogy.

himself for pressing Manton." The Chief Justice thought that Hayes probably did not know how unfit Manton was. Really, Taft said, "the Church should be saved from the responsibility" of Manton's appointment. With that as a preface, Taft gave his justification for asking Butler to seek clerical support:

> In view of this, and to neutralize that influence, it is fortunate that it is possible to secure, as a candidate, you, who are so eminently qualified for the place, and who are a Catholic, so that the Church may do itself credit in recommending you and avoid the condemnation it ought to have were it to be successful in procuring the appointment of a man like Manton. This is the reason why, when I wrote you, I suggested that you should secure a letter directly to the President from Archbishop Dowling and such others of the Hierarchy as can be properly approached and shown the danger the Church is in and the necessity for their uniting their efforts in behalf of one of their co-religionists whose well-deserved promotion to the Bench may naturally give them pride.[7]

Butler answered that he did not want to be appointed because of his religion and would not accept a place on the Court "as a representative of any creed, class, party, or group." On the other hand, he did not want to be turned down because of his religion. As for politics on the part of the clergy, he deplored it. "Naturally they prefer to keep out and they ought not to be induced or forced into the struggle in that field. I would not have any feeling or rivalry arise among them in any matter in which I am concerned." But he felt that all the archbishops and bishops who knew him would speak favorably of him "if asked or if proper occasion arises." Friends in St. Paul would judiciously take care of the matter. Cardinal O'Connell, Butler reported, was making inquiries about him, and it was certain that the Cardinal did not favor Manton. Bishop Turner of Buffalo, "an old and very dear friend" of Butler, would be glad to help. Bishop Carroll of Helena, another friend, would also give his support, unless someone like Senator Walsh of Montana was being considered.[8]

Among Butler's friends who were "judiciously" approaching the hierarchy in his behalf was John Twohy, with whom he had studied law some thirty-four years before. Twohy, out of paternalistic affection for his former law clerk, embarked on a cross-country campaign in Butler's behalf. Accompanied by his son, James, he called on Senators William E. Borah of Idaho, Charles L. McNary of Oregon, Hiram W. Johnson of California, and several western congressmen. His primary target, however, was Catholic support, both lay and clerical. A fairly well-known Catholic layman himself, Twohy had little difficulty in establishing contact with important persons in the Church. His campaign carried him to the offices of some of the foremost clergymen in the nation —Archbishops Christie of Oregon and Hayes of New York; Bishops Carroll of Helena, Cantwell of Los Angeles, and Granjon of Tucson; and the Reverend Zachaeus J. Maher, S.J., president of the University of Santa Clara. He personally urged each of these men to support Butler's candidacy and make their support known. Among the prominent Catholic laymen whose support he solicited were John D. Ryan, chairman of the Anaconda Copper Mining Company; John S. Drum, president of the Mercantile Trust Company of San Francisco and immediate past president of the American Bankers' Association; James D. Phelan, former United States Senator from California who had served with Harding in the upper house; Senator Henry F. Ashurst of Arizona; and Congressman N. J. Sinnott of The Dalles, Oregon. These contacts by Twohy and similar contacts by other friends of Butler had immediate consequences.[9]

On November 6 Archbishop Dowling, in a handwritten letter to Harding, endorsed Pierce Butler—"my friend & counsellor . . . a big, wholesome, capable man without fear and without bias"—for the Supreme Court. He stressed Butler's ability as a lawyer in the intricacies of railroad valuation and also his interest in public education. "No member of the board of Regents of our State University has had a stronger or more beneficent influence than he has had." From experience, said Dowling, he knew the wisdom of

Butler's counsel, the sanity and tolerance of his outlook, and the soundness of his judgment. "Sincerely religious & courageous in the profession of his convictions," the Archbishop concluded, "he has gone his way without offense & enjoys the esteem & confidence of the whole community." Whether or not Dowling was "educated" to write the letter, Taft and Van Devanter agreed it was eminently satisfactory; indeed Archbishop Ireland could not have done better.[10] *

On the following day Archbishop John J. Glennon of St. Louis wrote Harding assuring him that Butler, as a Supreme Court Justice, would "face the vexed problems of the day, seeking with American genius and courage, 'to mete the bounds of hate and love' and 'reach the law within the law.' "[11] In the next fifteen days, the Archbishops of Oregon (Christie), San Francisco (Hanna), and Dubuque (Keane) and the Bishops of Pittsburgh (Boyle), Harrisburg (McDevitt), and Helena (Carroll) went on record for Butler.[12] Father Maher of the University of Santa Clara also endorsed Butler, and Bishop Thomas J. Shahan of Catholic University called on the President for the same purpose. Shahan had acted at the request of Dowling, and the St. Paul Archbishop had been in contact with Archbishop Hanna.[13] The letter of Bishop Carroll is illustrative of the communications sent to Harding by the higher clergy. Butler, he wrote, was one of the ablest lawyers, not only in the Midwest, but in the entire country. "His patriotism," the letter continued, "is sincere and without alloy. He believes in only one flag—the Stars and Stripes. He is, moreover, a man of judicial temperament and of deep religious convictions. I believe his appointment would give genuine pleasure not only to the West but the country at large." The Bishop added he would loyally accept whomever Harding appointed,

---

* Archbishop Dowling, uncertain that he had sent his letter in such a way that it would come to Harding's attention immediately, dispatched a copy of it to the President two days later, so that, in his words, "I may not fall short of what I owe my friend and through my faith in his high merits owe to the country which, I hope, it will be in your power to make the beneficiary of his services." Nov. 8, 1922, Harding Papers.

but he would be especially pleased if Butler was named.[14]

Despite Archbishop Hayes's reported commitment to Manton, Butler's friends solicited the prelate's support. John and James Twohy had two sessions with him on the matter, and they were accompanied by John D. Ryan of Anaconda Copper on the second occasion. The Archbishop indicated that though he had already gone on record in Manton's behalf, if a midwestern Catholic had a chance of receiving the nomination, he would be well disposed toward Butler. Butler was happy to hear this report, which he interpreted to mean that if the New York judges, Manton and Dowling, were out of the running, he would receive Hayes's support.[15]

Bringing in the clergy for Butler had been a delicate undertaking, but it was worthwhile, for by mid-November it was apparent that Manton's clerical support had been neutralized. If Taft needed any assurance that he was justified in his actions, he received it from Elihu Root, who said that Manton was one of Wilson's worst appointments. Manton's career did not justify his selection, for, Root added, Manton had neither the respect of the bar nor the confidence of the public. "He is purely a product of intrigue & if the people get that idea of the Supreme Court they will smash the whole outfit." So that all points of view might be represented, Root conceded there was some basis for the appointment of a Catholic. "But the appointment would have to be based primarily on high character, ability & standing of the man. If he has no substantial qualification except Church favor, the appointment would be regarded as a surrender & there would be the devil to pay." [16] Taft agreed, but he was not worried; he believed Butler had the requisite character, ability, and standing for the Supreme Court.

II

While the clergy were being approached, the support of others was actively sought. Taft and Van Devanter were especially concerned about the attitude of the Minnesota senators, Frank Kellogg and Knute Nelson. The earnest good will and active endorsement of both, Van Devanter felt, would probably be more helpful than any other support. Yet they were Republicans and for that reason might be less than enthusiastic about a Democrat. Taft, projecting his own former inordinate ambition for the High Bench to Kellogg, feared the Senator wanted the appointment himself. But "with one eye, his age, and his Senatorial position," Kellogg, Taft felt, should consider himself out of the running. Even if he did, there was another disturbing possibility: Kellogg might press the candidacy of his law partner, Cordenio A. Severance—a recent president of the American Bar Association and a close friend of Harding.[17]

Senator Nelson presented a different problem. As chairman of the Judiciary Committee, he was one of the most powerful men in the Senate, and he had his own ideas about the kind of men who should be appointed to the Supreme Court. Taft thought Nelson had disapproved of his own appointment as Chief Justice the year before, and he also thought the old Minnesota Senator had never forgiven him for appointing Edward D. White, a Confederate and a Democrat, to the Chief Justiceship. If Nelson opposed Butler on the ground that he was a Democrat, there was good reason to believe Harding would not consider him further, for when Taft mentioned the fact that he had appointed some Democrats, Harding remarked: "But, Mr. Chief Justice, I haven't seen evidence of any marked approval by the country of what you did in that regard." Yet all hope was not lost, for Taft knew Nelson looked for conservatives, not just Republicans.[18]

Taft had been mistaken about Kellogg: even if he was not returned to the Senate, he did not want to go to the Court. Moreover, he had gone on record for Butler about the same time as Taft. On October 25, at the request of the Chicago bar leader, Silas Strawn, Kellogg endorsed Judge Baker over Senator Shields. Later the same day he received a letter from Harding in which Butler's name was mentioned. He immediately wired Harding that Butler was "the very best you could appoint. . . . He would be my preference as against Baker." After giving the matter further thought,

Kellogg sent a third wire to Harding, this time recommending his law partner, Severance—"the most eminent lawyer in the Northwest, and the best qualified man I know for the position. . . ." Severance, however, disclaiming any aspiration to the High Bench, indicated that he supported the candidacy of his old friend, Butler. Kellogg then reaffirmed his support of Butler.* Other prominent Minnesota Republicans followed Kellogg's lead. Governor Preus, at the request of Pierce, Jr., went to Alexandria, Minnesota to seek Senator Nelson's support. Nelson said he was *"very well satisfied"* with the prospect of Butler's nomination, and the next day Preus wired Daugherty: "[Senator Nelson] and I both believe that Butler's appointment would be splendid. I will leave here the day after the election and if nothing is done before that time, will come at once to see you and the president in regard to the matter." [19]

Democrats, too, were going on record for Butler. A Democratic national committeeman, the Democratic candidate for Congress in Butler's district, the Ramsey County Attorney, and other ranking Minnesota Democrats wrote in behalf of Butler. Two federal district judges appointed by Wilson, Charles C. Haupt and James E. Michael, assured Harding in similarly worded messages that Democrats of the Northwest welcomed Butler's nomination.[20]

Three members of Congress who were in some way connected with the Twohys endorsed Butler in telegrams to Harding. Two were Roman Catholics—Senator Henry F. Ashurst, Democrat of Arizona, and Congressman N. J. Sinnott, Republican from The Dalles, Oregon. The non-Catholic was Congressman J. Stanley Webster, Republican from Spokane, Washington.[21]

Butler himself sought the support of his friend Congressman Carmi Thompson of Ohio, who had formerly been an associate of the railroad giant, James J. Hill. Thompson's

* It appears that Kellogg's support of Butler was given with at least a slight reservation. In making his recommendation to Harding, Kellogg mentioned in passing that Butler's law partner was William D. Mitchell, a lawyer not as well known as Butler but "of even better judicial timber. . . ." Oct. 30, 1922, Harding Papers.

support was regarded as important because he knew Harding intimately and had been picked by the President as the Republican candidate for the Ohio governorship. Thompson wrote Harding strongly urging Butler's nomination. If a Democrat was to be chosen, he said, Butler was "about as mild a Democrat" as he knew. Further, Thompson declared that he was "under lasting obligation to the Butler family for their great help to me and to the Republican Party in its fight this year." [22]

It was Mitchell who solicited the support of the federal judges, Haupt and Michael. At his request, Judge Sanborn wrote another letter in behalf of Butler—this time to Harding directly. But the most important support stimulated by Mitchell came from the Minnesota Supreme Court. Every justice and commissioner of the court signed the following letter to Harding:

> It gives us, the judges of the supreme court of the state of Minnesota, great pleasure to certify to the high character and brilliant legal attainments of the Honorable Pierce Butler of St. Paul.
>
> During the time he has been a member of the bar of this court he has conducted himself so as to merit the respect and approval of the entire bench and bar of Minnesota. He is in our opinion eminently qualified for the position of associate justice of the supreme court of the United States.[23]

In addition, the Minnesota chief justice wired Harding his personal recommendation.[24]

There was no attempt to deluge Harding and Daugherty with recommendations from members of the Minnesota bar. Only a few lawyers from Minneapolis and St. Paul, among them the vice-president of the Minnesota Bar Association, Royal A. Stone, and Thomas D. O'Brien, former Ramsey County Attorney under whom Butler had served thirty-two years before, sent telegrams urging Butler's nomination. Taft was more concerned about Butler's national reputation at the bar. He believed that unless a lawyer held some national office, his reputation was generally confined to a city, a state, or an area of the country. That presented a problem in Butler's case because leaders of the New York bar were not likely to know Butler, and since they felt one of their own number was entitled to the nomination, they might oppose Butler.[25]

To avoid that possibility, Taft, his brother Harry, and Wickersham were doing all they could for Butler in New York. Taft's inquiries to members of the New York bar indicated that Butler was known but had not the stature of a lawyer like Paul D. Cravath.* Taft discussed the matter with Nathaniel T. Guernsey, general counsel of the American Telegraph and Telephone Company. On November 1 Guernsey said he would make some inquiries, and the next day he wrote to Taft that it was "conservative to say that for many years he [Butler] has been recognized in the West as a man of high ideals, great industry, broad experience, much learning, and outstanding ability." Then he added what Taft wanted: "I think it may be justly said that his reputation is national." [26] †

The Chicago bar was also taken into account. Taft wrote to his former Secretary of War, Jacob M. Dickinson, a Chicago bar leader, asking him about Butler's reputation in the Chicago area. Dickinson answered that he knew Butler only generally as a railroad lawyer but would check with others who knew him better. Responses to his inquiries, he said, showed that Butler's professional standing and personal character qualified him for the Supreme Court.[27]

Because of his judicial office, Taft felt handicapped in seeking support for his candidate. Friends like Pam, Wickersham, and Dickinson were therefore invaluable, but Pam was now in Europe and there were limits as to what the

* Cravath was the senior partner of Cravath, Henderson, Leffingwell & DeGersdorff, the leading law firm in New York at the time. See Robert T. Swaine, *The Cravath Firm and Its Predecessors, 1819–1948* (2 vols.; New York: privately printed, 1946, 1948).

† There seems to be no question that Butler was generally known in railroad circles throughout the nation. When George Stuart Patterson, general solicitor of the Pennsylvania Railroad, heard of Butler's candidacy, for example, he asked the St. Paul lawyer's permission to talk to Justice McReynolds about the matter. Butler consented. Butler to Taft, Nov. 9, 1922, Taft Papers.

Chief Justice could expect of busy practicing lawyers. Thus he gladly accepted the aid of Thomas W. Bowers, son of his former Solicitor General, Lloyd W. Bowers. At the time, Tom Bowers was a vice-president of the National Bank of Commerce of New York, but until the spring of 1922 he had been an associate in Cravath's law firm. He had contacts in Chicago as well as New York and acted as Taft's lieutenant in working up support for Butler in both cities.

A canvass of New York bar leaders by Bowers showed that attitudes toward Butler were mixed. James Byrne, president of the Association of the Bar of the City of New York and a Catholic, was inclined to be favorable because he felt a Catholic should be appointed. Yet he would not write President Harding because he believed it would be improper for him to volunteer a letter in his capacity of bar president. Moreover, he thought that if a Catholic was to be chosen, William D. Guthrie was the best man. The attitude of F. W. M. Cutcheon, another well-known New York lawyer, was important because he had practiced in St. Paul and knew Butler well. He told Bowers he would not support Butler because he did not think he was "temperamentally fitted" for the Court, nor did he believe Butler possessed "sufficient erudition." But he admitted, nevertheless, that Butler was a man of "very great ability." Cravath told his former junior associate that he knew Butler only slightly, whereupon Bowers did his best to tell him "what a splendid fellow Butler was." Cravath manifested interest and said he would make some inquiries. Bowers was confident that in view of the difficulties between Cravath and Guthrie when they dissolved their partnership some years before, it was unlikely that Cravath would support Guthrie. A week later, Cravath, having made his inquiries, told Bowers that he was satisfied with Butler and would personally make his support known to Daugherty.[28]

Bowers was unable to secure similar support among Chicago bar leaders. He contacted Jacob Dickinson, but Dickinson, not knowing Butler well, was disinclined to conduct a campaign for him among Chicago lawyers. Even if he had been so inclined, he probably would have had little success, for before Bowers' arrival in Chicago several important members of the bar had already gone on record for Judge Francis E. Baker of the Court of Appeals for the Seventh Circuit. Among them were Carl Meyer of Mayer, Meyer, Austrian & Platt; Silas H. Strawn of Winston, Strawn & Shaw, and the senior partners of McCormick, Kirkland, Patterson & Fleming.* In 1922 these firms stood, as they do today, at the very top of the legal profession.[29]

Bowers' contacts with the midwestern business community were more successful. Before leaving for Chicago he wrote to Marvin Hughitt, former head of the Chicago Northwestern Railroad, and Charles W. Bunn, general counsel of the Northern Pacific Railroad. He told them what he was trying to do and suggested that Bunn line up prominent Minnesota Catholics in support of Butler. He planned to see these men, as well as Hale Holden, president of the Chicago, Burlington & Quincy Railroad, when he came to Chicago. Since both Bunn and Holden worked with Butler in the *Minnesota Rate Cases,* Bowers was confident that they would do what they could for Butler.† Hughitt's view on Butler's candidacy surprised Bowers: the railroad man said he believed Butler's railroad connections would stand in the way of his appointment. Nevertheless, he highly approved of Butler and said he would do what he could to help him.

* On October 26, 1922 A. D. Lasker, head of the Shipping Board, wrote to Carl Meyer: "I have your telegram regarding Judge Baker. It was only last night I was talking the matter over with the Attorney General. I will write him immediately to-day to let him know of your interest in Judge Baker. How the matter came up was that someone had brought up that a New Yorker ought to have the position, and I asked why the Middle West should not be represented." File of Francis E. Baker, U.S. Supreme Court Personnel, Series 82, Department of Justice Records.

† Bunn was in England at the time. When he landed in New York on November 17, Bowers met him and explained the situation regarding Butler. Bunn promised to do what he could when he went to Washington the next day. On his return to St. Paul, he wrote a warm letter of recommendation to Harding in behalf of Butler. Bowers to Taft, Nov. 17, 1922, Taft Papers; Bunn to Harding, Nov. 21, 1922, File of Pierce Butler, Record Group 60, Department of Justice Records.

Although Dickinson had been disinclined to conduct a campaign for Butler among Chicago lawyers, he promised to call on E. F. Carry, president of the Pullman Company and a Catholic, to see whether he could write to Harding in behalf of Butler. Bowers reported all of this to Taft and also a telephone conversation he had had with James C. Davis, the federal director of railroads, in which Davis said he had a high opinion of Butler and would talk to the President about him. Taft was pleased with Bowers' work. "I think," he wrote his lieutenant on November 13, "the case of Pierce Butler is being worked up pretty well." [30]*

The work of Taft, Bowers, Mitchell, Pierce, Jr., and the Twohys in behalf of Butler was fruitful. Support from the business community was strong and well-selected. The president of the Merchants Loan & Trust Company in Chicago was one of Butler's early backers. Both the president and the editor-in-chief of the West Publishing Company—probably the richest and most powerful law publishing house in the world—warmly recommended Butler to Harding. O. H. Spencer, general counsel of the Chicago, Burlington, & Quincy Railroad, wrote Daugherty endorsing Butler, and his superior, Hale Holden, wrote the President that he knew of no man in the Midwest who had better qualifications for the Supreme Court than Butler. "Mr. Butler," Holden went on, "has that deep reverence for country and constitution so essential to true citizenship; his habit of practice as a lawyer has been as an upright officer of the Court—high-minded, capable and independent in his professional life. . . . He is not of your political party, nor of my own, but my belief and admiration for him leads me to bring him to your attention, knowing that party affiliations are of no

* Bowers also toyed with the idea of seeking the support of the James J. Hill family because it was Catholic. When he found out, however, that the entire Hill family, except Louis Hill, was bitterly against Butler because of his representation of Louis in a family fight, Bowers abandoned the idea and wondered whether that ill feeling might be adverse to Butler's appointment. Taft thought the Hill fight would not play any part in the appointment.

consequence whatsoever in your consideration of the right man for this great office."[31]

From the Twin Cities, two of the leading bankers urged Butler's selection, as did the timber tycoon F. E. Weyerhaeuser, who told Harding his "appointment would be favorably received by businessmen as well as by those in his own profession." John R. Mitchell, a native of Minnesota and a member of the Federal Reserve Board, wired Secretary of the Treasury Mellon that Butler was a man who could be recommended without qualification and asked the Secretary to do what he could to further the appointment. Mellon sent the wire to Daugherty.[32]

From San Francisco support stimulated by John Twohy was manifested in communications to Harding. The prominent Catholic banker, John S. Drum, wired his recommendation of Butler; so did the vice-president of Drum's bank, T. S. Montgomery. Former Senator James D. Phelan, another prominent San Francisco Catholic, also went on record for Butler. And from Spokane, Washington, Daniel W. Twohy, John's brother and chairman of the Old National Bank of Spokane, wrote the President asking him to nominate the man who studied law in his brother's office back in 1887 and 1888.[33]

Lotus D. Coffman, president of the University of Minnesota, wrote Harding that Butler had few equals in the legal fraternity. He lauded Butler's twelve years of service as regent as well as his intellectual and physical vigor. Although Butler was a Democrat, said Coffman, he was not "hidebound" and stood well with both Republicans and Democrats. Everett Fraser, the highly respected dean of the University of Minnesota Law School, vouched for Butler's legal knowledge and concluded with the statement that he knew of no lawyer in the Midwest "better qualified intellectually and physically for the position." John G. Williams, a lawyer and regent of the University, assured Harding that Butler intensely loved the Constitution and that, on the bench, his natural bent on policy issues would be conservative, but not reactionary. Dr. Charles H. Mayo of Rochester, another regent of the University, promised to contact Harding, as did President Donald J. Cowling of Carleton College, Butler's alma mater. Butler thought Cowling's support especially important because he was "a Protestant D.D." When Cowling wrote the President, he mentioned that he was a Congregational minister and that Butler was a Catholic. From his association with Butler, he said, he was convinced that the lawyer's basic convictions were thoroughly sound and that he was "deeply interested in the fundamentals of religion as the only lasting foundation for our social, industrial and political institutions." Cowling, however, had delayed writing his letter, and by the time it reached the White House, the decision to nominate Butler had already been made.[34]

The Catholic hierarchy, the bench, the bar, the business and academic communities—all had come to Butler's support, as Taft hoped they would. There were some doubters—the New York lawyer Cutcheon, who believed Butler was not "temperamentally fitted" for the Court, and the railroad man Hughitt, who believed Butler was too closely identified with the railroads to be appointed—but these perceptions of Butler were not reported to Harding. The campaign for Butler had moved quietly and discreetly—and with impressive results. Chief Justice Taft was impressed, and he believed that Harding, with his Main-Street view of the world, would also be impressed. But would Harding be impressed enough not to waver in the face of strong simultaneous pressure on behalf of other candidates? Even Taft could not answer that question.

Chapter 5

NOMINATION

While Taft and Butler were discussing strategy, rivals were already in the field, their campaigns well under way. In New York the steel magnates, Judge Elbert H. Gary and Charles M. Schwab, both friends of Harding, had come to the aid of Judge Manton with strong recommendations. In Illinois Judge Baker had acquired the support of Senator William B. McKinley and Congressman "Uncle Joe" Cannon. And in Pennsylvania Senators George Wharton Pepper and David A. Reed had gone on record for Robert von Moschzisker, chief justice of the Pennsylvania Supreme Court. Taft felt that neither Baker nor von Moschzisker (the candidate with "an unpronounceable Polish name") had a chance,* but Manton was another matter. Despite Daugherty's assurances that Manton would not be named, Taft remained uneasy.[1]

* Francis Rawle, a leader of the Philadelphia bar, opposed von Moschzisker's appointment on the ground that he lacked the experience necessary for the Supreme Court. In a letter to George W. Wickersham, Rawle said that he had not written to Daugherty because he did not know him and that he had not written Senators Pepper and Reed because they were still in practice and might feel an obligation to support Chief Justice von Moschzisker. Wickersham to Taft, Nov. 3, 1922, Taft Papers.

I

On November 3 Harry Taft reported to his brother that the Judiciary Committee of the Association of the Bar of the City of New York met at his home and voted unanimously to do all in its power to stop Manton's drive for the Court. Harry told the committee that the appointment of someone else now seemed likely, so there was probably not much that the committee would have to do. The Chief Justice did not share his brother's optimism; on the very next day Hilles came to Washington to tell Taft that Manton's candidacy was growing stronger. Hilles described an incident involving ex-Postmaster General Will Hays and some senators that Taft found almost incredible. Taft did not disclose the nature of the incident when he mentioned it to his brother on November 4, but three days later he again referred to Hays and Manton. The Postmaster and the circuit judge were linked, Taft said, through a New York insurance man named Rosen, who was "a warm friend" of Manton. Rosen, according to the Chief Justice, was influential in certain Republican circles because he had collected considerable sums of money for the party war chest. Further, he was the principal backer of a Hollywood movie venture in which Hays had an interest. This, Taft believed, was connected with Hays's pressing "Manton on the President as a fine political appointment." Taft undoubtedly knew more of the Hays-Manton relationship than his correspondence indicates, for he insisted that Manton's friends were "misrepresent[ing] the situation" and for that reason they had to be closely watched. Harry Taft agreed, saying that it was a "part of the game" for Manton's friends and characteristic of all the moves they had made.[2]

On November 10 the *Chicago Tribune* published Manton's photograph with the statement that he "has been mentioned as a likely successor of Justice Day on the United States Supreme Court." The next day the Reverend John J. Wynne, S.J., editor of *America,* called at Taft's home in Washington to vouch for Manton's fitness for the High Court. Taft's absence at the time of the call spared both men an embarrassing encounter. Two days later the Jesuit wrote Taft from New York urging Manton's appointment to the Court, "a matter which I have much at heart." He assured Taft that Manton not only had the esteem and confidence of Catholics, "but of all who know him." "It is, in fact, singular," concluded the cleric, "how one who is by nature retiring has won such good and wide repute." "Singular" was indeed the right word for Manton's reputation, thought Taft; he answered Father Wynne's letter with a single sentence: "I have yours of November 13th, and note what you say about Judge Manton." [3]

II

Unknown to Taft, scattered letters in behalf of Ohio candidates had been coming to the White House during October and early November. Most of them were written apparently in the belief that Harding would be partial to the appointment of a native son of Ohio. One such letter, which Harding probably never saw, was written by the wife of a Columbus politician. "[W]ould it be presuming, my dear Mr. President," she wrote, "to ask consideration of the appointment of my worthy husband, Timothy S. Hogan, of Columbus, Ohio? My ambition for him has always been the United States Supreme Court, and now can it be that it may be realized?" As tactfully as he could, Harding's secretary explained to Mrs. Hogan that though the President held her husband in high esteem, "appointments to the Supreme Court may not be personal in character and that very many public and national viewpoints have to be considered." In other words, there was no chance that Mrs. Hogan's ambition would be realized.[4]

The strongest Ohio candidate was Federal Judge Maurice H. Donahue of the Sixth Circuit, who like Butler was a Democrat and a Catholic. Archbishop Henry Moeller of Cincinnati strongly urged his appointment in a letter to Harding dated October 13. Within ten days similar letters were written by Bishop James J. Hartley of Columbus and Bishop Joseph Schrembs of Cleveland. "We see him every

Sunday in the Cathedral," wrote Bishop Hartley, "and always think that because he had been true to the faith of his fathers, God has blessed him and helped him to win success that has come to him thus far in life." The Bishop's final comment on Judge Donahue was: "It would give us all great joy to see you place him in the sanctuary of the greatest civil tribunal in the world today." Harding, of course, answered each of the prelates personally. But Donahue had little chance of appointment. On the same day that Harding received Taft's endorsement of Butler he wrote to a friend in Ohio: "There has been a good deal of insistence on behalf of Donahue, but I have never appraised him as an outstanding figure for a place on the Supreme Bench." [5]

There was also some support for Senator Atlee Pomerene of Ohio, but by the time the movement in his behalf got under way—after his defeat in the November election—it was too late for him to be considered for the Day vacancy.[6]

III

Meanwhile, campaigns on behalf of southern candidates had reached huge proportions. These campaigns followed a similar pattern: a native son would be selected as the candidate by state political leaders; then the governor, usually both senators, and a number of congressmen would write Harding; then would follow a strong show of support from judges, lawyers, businessmen, and citizens. In quantitative terms the southern campaigns outstripped Butler's. For example, the campaign for the Georgia candidate, Robert C. Alston—who was described by the *Atlanta Constitution* as a prominent attorney and vice-president of the local chamber of commerce—resulted in hundreds of letters and telegrams to Harding and in petitions containing hundreds of signatures.[7]

Alabama had two candidates, Federal District Judges Henry D. Clayton and William I. Grubb.* The former's sup-

* Grubb, a former Yale classmate of Taft's brother Horace, was appointed to the federal bench during the Taft administration. The Chief Justice agreed with his brother that Grubb was worthy of considera-

port came mainly from the Montgomery area and included Dr. Luther L. Hill, father of the present Senator Lister Hill, and President George Denny of the University of Alabama. The latter's support came mainly from the Birmingham area and included a strong endorsement from Senator Oscar W. Underwood. Florida's candidate was Federal Circuit Judge Nathan D. Bryan; Virginia supported Congressman Andrew D. Montague; West Virginia's choice was Guy D. Goff, one of Daugherty's top assistants in the Justice Department and later United States Senator; Senator John K. Shields of Tennessee was his state's candidate; and both political parties in Texas agreed to back Nelson Phillips, former chief justice of the Texas Supreme Court. Of these candidates only Phillips and Shields received serious consideration.[8]

Senator Shields had been chief justice of the Tennessee Supreme Court and let it be known that he was interested in the Day vacancy. Thereupon his Senate colleagues Edwin S. Broussard of Louisiana, Lee S. Overman and Furnifold M. Simmons of North Carolina, James A. Reed of Missouri, Joe T. Robinson of Arkansas, Augustus O. Stanley of Kentucky, and Oscar W. Underwood of Alabama came to his support, asking Harding to appoint their "mutual friend." Governor A. A. Taylor of Tennessee and former Senator Hoke Smith of Georgia were also strong Shields supporters. Although some regarded Shields' appointment as a definite possibility because of his personal relationship with Harding and his Senate support, Taft did not give him the slightest chance. The movement in behalf of Shields in the Senate, said Taft, was only formal and would be unsuccessful. And it should be, he added, for Shields "is narrow, obstinate, and

---

tion for the Day vacancy and promised to keep him in mind for a future vacancy. Grubb was one of the few southerners who had Negro support. The president of the Negro Republican Club of Jefferson City, Alabama wrote Harding: "The Negroes of Alabama take this method of making their first request of their beloved President to do them a favor, and that favor is to have Judge Grubb appointed to the Supreme Court." W. B. Driver to Harding, Nov. 16, 1922, File of William Grubb, U.S. Supreme Court Personnel, Series 82, Department of Justice Records; Taft to Horace D. Taft, Oct. 30, 1922; Horace D. Taft to Taft, Nov. 7, 1922, Taft Papers.

partisan, and very much opposed to the Federal Courts." Taft was thankful that Shields was sixty-four, for that in itself would eliminate him.[9] *

Nelson Phillips† was not so easily eliminated. Noting the letters coming to the White House in Phillips' behalf, Harding wrote his close friend, R. B. Creager, who was head of the Texas Republican organization, inquiring about the former Texas judge. Creager enthusiastically endorsed Phillips. "If a Southern Democrat is to be appointed to succeed Judge Day (and the proprieties seem to require this)," he wrote, "you cannot possibly select an abler man than Judge Nelson Phillips of Dallas. His personal character is without blemish. His legal ability and attainments are recognized, not only throughout Texas, but throughout the Nation." Impressed with Creager's report, Harding sent it to Daugherty on October 30, the same day Taft decided to go on record for

---

* Taft was not the only one who believed Shields was unworthy of the Supreme Court. Mrs. Harriet Stanton Blanch quoted the Senator as opposed to giving the ballot to "nigger women" and stating, "You see, we couldn't treat the wenches as we do the men; we just club the 'niggers' if they come to the polls." This was reported in the *New York Call* on October 28, 1922 and brought sharp protests against Shields' candidacy for the Court from the National Association for the Advancement of Colored People and other Negro organizations. Mary White Ovington to Harding, October 31, 1922; Carl Murphy to Harding, Nov. 10, 1922; J. W. McIntyre to Harding, Nov. 15, 1922; Protest File of John Knight Shields, U.S. Supreme Court Personnel, Series 82, Department of Justice Records. Wayne B. Wheeler of the Anti-Saloon League also went on record against Shields, stating that his appointment would be "one of the hardest blows to prohibition that could be struck. . . ." Wheeler to Harding, Sept. 16, 1922, Harding Papers. There were also southerners opposed to Shields. Justice Thomas C. McClellan of the Alabama Supreme Court said that the only ground he could see for Shields' appointment was " 'personal pull' by reason of his service in the Senate with the President." McClellan to Thomas W. Shelton, Nov. 1, 1922, Taft Papers.

† Phillips was forty-nine years old in 1922. He attended Bingham's Military Academy at Melbane, North Carolina, and then prepared for the bar in a law office while working in his father's bank. Admitted to practice in 1895, he became a trial judge ten years later. In 1912 he was elected to the Supreme Court of Texas and became its chief justice in 1915. In 1921 he left the court to return to the practice of law.

Butler. Daugherty answered: "It would be hard to conceive a more fortunate endorsement, more forcibly put, than Mr. Creager's letter. The composition of the letter itself is a compliment to the author." The Attorney General added that he was familiar with Phillips' work as a judge and was much impressed by the principles laid down in one of his cases.[10]

The show of support for Phillips was remarkable. Hundreds of lawyers, scores of judges, and dozens of businessmen wrote Harding and Daugherty endorsing his candidacy. Both Texas senators, Charles A. Culberson and Morris Sheppard, went on record for him, as did Senators John W. Harreld of Oklahoma and Holm O. Bursum of New Mexico. At least five Texas congressmen, including Hatton W. Sumners, Tom Connally, and Sam Rayburn, declared their support of Phillips. A nonpartisan citizens committee headed by John H. Kirby, a wealthy lumberman and a friend of Harding and Creager, journeyed from Texas to present personally the name of Judge Phillips to the President. Jesse H. Jones, a former neighbor and golf partner of Harding, expressly invoked his personal friendship in recommending Phillips to the President. And, in a long-distance phone call to Harding on October 31, the editor-in-chief of the West Publishing Company, Harry E. Randall, highly praised the quality of the ex-chief justice's work on the Texas Supreme Court.[11]*

IV

The Phillips campaign was at its peak when Taft entered the picture. Toward the end of October the United States Marshal at Paris, Texas called on the Chief Justice and told him of the ground swell for Phillips. Taft learned that Phillips was a friend and supporter of former Senator Joe Bailey, a staunch Democrat for whom Taft had little love. Taft also learned that Phillips had been twice elected to the Supreme

* Later, when Randall was informed that Pierce Butler of his own city was a candidate for the same vacancy, he wired Harding indicating a preference for Butler, explaining he had not been aware of the St. Paul lawyer's candidacy when he had called him in late October. Randall to Harding, Nov. 18, 1922. File of Pierce Butler, Record Group 60, General Records of the Department of Justice.

Court of Texas and was its chief justice when he resigned to become general counsel for Texas of the Southwestern Bell Telephone Company, a subsidiary of the American Telephone and Telegraph Company. Taft decided to check on Phillips through his old Yale friend Nathaniel T. Guernsey, general counsel of A.T.&T., and arranged to meet him in New York on November 1.

Guernsey told Taft that Phillips was one of his men in Texas, but he was no more fitted for the Supreme Court than "he [Guernsey] was fitted to be a vestal virgin," and in the Court's conference Phillips would not weigh a feather. In fact, the work done by the former Texas judge for the company, said Guernsey, had been disappointing; in brief writing he "scattered" and lacked cogency and force. Since Phillips had argued a case before the Supreme Court during the 1921 term, Guernsey was surprised that Taft did not know of him. Only when the Texan was described as "a small man with grey hair that came down toward his shoulders" and as a "silver-tongued orator" did Taft remember such a man, but he had made no impression.

Van Devanter also checked on Phillips. His source was Wilson's former Attorney General, Thomas W. Gregory, who referred to Phillips as "an active little henchman of Jo[e] Bailey" and "a poetical, oratorical kind of a man" whom the Wilson administration would never have thought of putting on the Supreme Court. Of course, Gregory added, the Harding administration could do worse.

Taft sent this information to Harding. Anticipating Harding's reaction, the Chief Justice began his letter by saying: "I hope you do not object to my sending such information as comes to me which I hope may be of assistance to your consideration of candidates for our Court." Then, without mincing words or sparing Phillips, he detailed what he had heard. Having done what he conceived to be his duty, Taft concluded his communication rather sheepishly: "I hope you feel that I am only trying to help." Feeling that perhaps he should in some way soften the impact of his letter, Taft added the following postscript:

> It is an awful and nerve-straining hunt you are engaged in. A man's name is suggested with glowing praise and he seems just the man, and then first one thing and then another turns up that shakes one's first conclusion. I only succeeded in securing a man such as I wanted in the South by going down South and staying there for several vacations. This enabled me to know him. I mean Lamar.[12]

Harding, responding the same day, agreed that it was difficult to obtain reliable information about Supreme Court candidates. The appraisal he had received of Phillips earlier was rather different from the one Taft sent. Nevertheless, the President said he was glad to have whatever information came Taft's way: "I am anxious, of course, to make a thoroughly high-grade and satisfactory nomination." [13]

Though Taft's letter to Harding jolted Phillips' candidacy, it did not end it. So Taft continued his investigation of the Texan. He asked his brother Harry, Guernsey, Dickinson, and Gardiner Lathrop of the Santa Fe Railroad to make the appropriate contacts and report back to him. He also wrote to Federal District Judge Edward R. Meek of Dallas for a confidential evaluation of Phillips:

> Ex-Chief Justice Nelson Phillips of your state is being seriously considered for our Court to succeed Justice Day. The Republican organization with Creager at its head, expecting a Democrat to be appointed, is pressing him. Jo[e] Bailey is doing the same thing. Texas Pride (with the big P) is prompting very strong letters in his behalf. Now I know well how such a thing can be worked up. I would like to get a real opinion of Phillips' capacity, of his learning as a lawyer, of his courage as a judge, of his industry and power of decision. You are where you can find out the real opinion of lawyers who know and who would tell you confidentially their judgment. I don't know that I shall have any influence in the matter but I should like to have light. It is a serious matter for us as well as for the country, because we are deeply interested to know whether the new man will pull his weight in our boat. If you could kindly and quietly make these inquiries at once and advise me promptly, I would greatly appreciate it.[14]

Harry Taft was the first to respond. He had talked to Judge Robert S. Lovett of the Union Pacific Railroad, who had known Phillips some years before. His view of Phillips was similar to Guernsey's, but he admitted he was prejudiced against the Texan because of his appearance—"long hair, long Prince Albert coat, bulging shirt front with one button of the vest buttoned, and broad-brimmed felt hat." In fairness to Phillips, Lovett said he would like to check with someone who had first-hand, up-to-date, reliable information. Lovett also suggested that Judge Edwin D. Parker be contacted because he had been one of the leading members of the Texas bar before he became a member of the German Mixed Claims Commission. Since Justice Day was chairman of the commission, Harry thought that perhaps Day might ask Parker about Phillips.

Taft thought it was a good idea, and at his request Day called Parker in New York. Parker said Phillips would make an excellent judge and was as qualified for the Supreme Court as John W. Davis—high praise indeed. Though the estimate came as a surprise to Taft, he immediately relayed it to Harding on November 4 with some letters in behalf of Butler, knowing full well that what he wrote might be crucial in a decision between Butler and Phillips. Taft apparently meant what he said in his letter to Harding conveying Parker's appraisal of Phillips: "I want to submit to you all the evidence that comes to me, so as to enable you to make your independent judgment on the subject." [15]

The following day, November 5, Parker called on Taft to say his "conscience stirred him" because his statement about Phillips needed amplification. He explained that he was embarrassed to say anything else over the telephone to Day because Phillips had been a friend for many years. Yet he felt the "appointing power" should have a full statement. There was no question as to the Texas judge's honesty or integrity, but it was true that Phillips had a flowery, oratorical, diffusive manner of address, and "his forte was in advocacy rather than in close judicial reasoning." Taft made the most of the disclosure, reporting it to Harding right after

Parker left. "This statement from Mr. Parker," Taft wrote, "given as it is only from a strong sense of duty, and with pain at having to tell a somewhat unfavorable truth about a friend, is most convincing." [16]

Harding answered Taft the next day, saying it was interesting to note that all the reports concerning Butler were exceedingly favorable and the only unfavorable reports concerning Phillips were confidential reports to Taft. And even those reports, Harding added, amounted only to criticism of Phillips' taste in clothing and style of speech, things not "highly essential to eminent services on the Bench." "Please know," he concluded, "that I appreciate your disposition toward helpfulness in this matter. I do want to make nominations which will appeal to the approval of the country. I think I ought to say, in more intimate acknowledgment of your letter, that I think so well of Judge Parker that I am bound to respect his opinion of Judge Phillips." [17]

Since Harding's letter made no mention of Parker's retraction, Taft wrote saying that he hoped Harding had received the letter. "It is not an easy thing," the Chief Justice added, "to get an opinion about a Texan from a Texan when state pride and friendship play a part." He suggested that Harding ask Secretary Mellon to ask one of his Texas lawyers to check on Phillips, and also that Harding send for Parker and have him give his deliberate judgment. "I fully agree," Taft concluded, "that Mr. Parker is a witness whose statement should be given great weight." [18]

By this time Taft had also received the reports on Phillips that he requested of Guernsey. Though Guernsey stood by his original position, his respondents were more favorable to Phillips. When one in Texas was asked to name three or four men in the state who were of Supreme Court caliber, only Phillips was named. Taft sent these reports to Harding on November 8 with this comment: "My own judgment about the matter is that Mr. Guernsey is perhaps a little extreme in his views, but Judge Phillips would not make more than a mediocre member of our Court; but he is rather of an indolent mental tendency, and that the pressure for him is largely due to state pride, and that it does not prove his eminent qualities for our Bench." The same day Harding wrote that he did not see important differences of opinion about Phillips and that he seemed worthy of consideration. "At the moment," he added, "there is not much drift of preference in that direction." The Phillips candidacy, it seemed, was dead.[19]

Soon thereafter the rest of the reports on Phillips came in. Taft was surprised that they were uniformly good. Judge Lovett's correspondent described Phillips as a man of courage who had the "caliber and capacity suitable for a Justice of the United States Supreme Court." Dickinson's and Lathrop's contacts in Texas made the same report. Judge Meek wrote three letters to Taft about Phillips, all favorable. The Texas bar, he said, felt that Phillips was "a lawyer and judge of marked ability and that he is in all ways fitted for a place on your bench," a judgment in which he concurred. An analysis of Phillips' recent Texas Supreme Court opinions by Taft's law clerk revealed that some of Phillips' opinions disclosed "legal attainments of high order, and that all of his opinions show[ed] him to be painstaking, accurate, concise and thorough." Taft apparently did not relay this information to Harding, but even if he had, the Phillips candidacy probably could not have been revived, for by that time Harding, unknown to Taft, was pursuing another idea.[20] *

V

The day after Taft wrote Harding of Parker's reservations concerning Phillips, the President dispatched the following letter to Senator Underwood of Alabama:

THE WHITE HOUSE
WASHINGTON

November 6, 1922

(PERSONAL AND CONFIDENTIAL)

My dear Oscar:

I am wondering if you would like to be appointed to the

* Apparently the Chief Justice felt he unwittingly did Phillips an injustice. After Butler was nominated, Taft indicated he had no opposition to Phillips for the next vacancy. Taft to Harding, Dec. 4, 1922, Taft Papers.

Supreme Court. I have such personal affection and such a high regard for your abilities that if you entertain such an ambition I would like to consider you for nomination. Somehow I have the feeling that service on the Bench would not be in harmony with your preference for a public career. I suspect you of preferring to remain in the big political contest and nurturing an ambition to be a candidate for President. Of course, I would like to see you the Democratic nominee, though I probably would not be as favorable to your election as I am for your nomination. I am quite sincere about the matter first referred to in this letter. Please let me have a personal and confidential note as to your feelings.

With very best regards, I am,

Very truly yours,
Warren G. Harding[21]

What Harding hoped to accomplish by this quasi-offer of a Justiceship is not clear. Perhaps it was a gesture to southern Democrats before naming a northern Democrat, or perhaps it had something to do with Harding's personal relationship with "Oscar." Harding, of course, assumed Underwood's answer would be negative, which was a fair assumption. Even the *Birmingham Age–Herald* stated editorially that though the Court would be suited to Underwood's taste and inclination, "the state and nation can ill spare him from legislative duties." Yet if perchance Underwood said he were interested, he might be safely appointed to the Court, for Democrats like Jacob M. Dickinson took the view that "if a Southern Democrat must be appointed, Davis & Underwood would be better appointments than Shields." [22]

Underwood, resting after the 1922 elections at Pass Christian, Mississippi, received Harding's letter on November 10. His answer, as expected, was that although the suggestion concerning the Court gave him much pleasure, he could not consider it. The reason he gave for declining was ill health. "The man who goes on the Supreme Court," he said, "must make a contract with himself to work hard—that I cannot do at this time." Harding did not see Underwood's reply until the 13th of November. By that time the Butler campaign was in high gear.[23]

VI

Harding's time for decision was drawing near, and it was a bad time for him. The 1922 elections, held on November 7, were almost disastrous for Republicans. Though they retained control of Congress by a slim margin, they lost seventy seats in the House, and their margin fell from sixty to fifty-three in the Senate. Senator LaFollette, the chief critic of the administration, was re-elected in Wisconsin by a quarter of a million votes. Not only that, his campaigning on behalf of Henrik Shipstead, the Farmer-Labor candidate in Minnesota, was instrumental in unseating Senator Kellogg, who had defended the record of the Harding administration. Other defenders of the administration, including Carmi Thompson, Harding's friend and candidate for the Ohio governorship, were also defeated. In Washington, D.C., on election night, crowds cheered the Democratic victory. "When one newspaper threw the picture of ex-President Wilson on the screen," reported the *New York Times,* "the cheers were hearty and long. Only dignified cheers were given when this was quickly followed by the smiling face of the President." So bad was the Republican defeat, added the *Times,* that informed political opinion was that Harding could not be a candidate to succeed himself.[24]

The extent to which the election results, indicating the waning of Harding's popularity, affected his thoughts about the Supreme Court appointment is not known. Obviously it was important to make an appointment that would be popular, and the election results indicated that there was much to be said for the appointment of a Democrat. But which Democrat? By mid-November the only ones in the running were Butler and Manton.

About November 15, the day after Justice Day's retirement became effective, Harding invited Senator Nelson to the White House and asked him what he thought of Pierce Butler for the Supreme Court. "Well," said Nelson, "if you want a Democrat and a Catholic, you could not get a better lawyer, and he is a very fine man."

"[T]hose qualities of being a Democrat and a Catholic," answered Harding, "in addition to others, are just what I do want." [25]

When Nelson reported this conversation to Taft on November 16, the Chief Justice was elated. The following day he sent a memorandum to Harding setting forth Butler's record as a Democrat, which he said he had secured "from the best source possible." By this time, Taft was sure that when Congress convened in special session on November 20 to consider Harding's ship subsidy bill, Butler's name would go to the Senate, for already he was discussing strategy to insure confirmation.[26]

On November 18 a final and forcible attempt to secure Manton's nomination was made. Alfred E. Smith, who had just returned to power as governor of New York, wired Daugherty: "IT WOULD BE MOST GRATIFYING TO ME IF JUDGE MARTIN T. MANTON WAS APPOINTED TO THE SUPREME BENCH." [27] Daugherty did not answer Smith until November 21. But before he wrote the governor-elect, he sent the following message to Harding:

> I am transmitting herewith for your consideration the nomination of Pierce Butler, of Minnesota, to be Associate Justice of the Supreme Court of the United States, vice William R. Day, resigned. Mr. Butler is endorsed by the Minnesota State Bar Association as being eminently well qualified by experience, learning and temperament for this position. He is also endorsed by many of the leading citizens of the Northwest recommending him as a lawyer of wide experience and great ability.
>
> I am pleased to join in recommending Mr. Butler to you for this appointment.[28]

Daugherty then wrote Smith telling him that he informed the President of his wire the previous day. "As I write this letter," Daugherty continued, "the matter has not been determined finally, but it now is entirely in the hands of the President and before you receive this the President may have decided who shall receive the appointment. I can assure you that Judge Manton is held in high esteem by this Department and the President."[29] Thus Manton's 1922 campaign for the Court ended.

On November 22 Justice Van Devanter wrote to Federal District Judge John C. Pollock about Day's successor. "At this writing," said Van Devanter, "I think Pierce Butler, of St. Paul, will be appointed to succeed Justice Day, and that the nomination is likely to go to the Senate very soon, possibly tomorrow. Butler is a fine lawyer, a broad-gauged, red-blooded man and in every way fitted for the place." The same day, while Senator Thomas J. Walsh of Montana was asking his colleagues for authority to investigate government oil leases at Teapot Dome, Harding signed Butler's nomination. And the next day, among the nominations received by the Senate for confirmation was "Pierce Butler, to be Associate Justice of the Supreme Court, vice William R. Day, resigned."[30]

Chapter 6

REACTION

A week before his name went to the Senate, Butler warned Taft that leftists and former University of Minnesota professors would protest his nomination. "Of course the socialists will oppose you," the Chief Justice answered, "and the Nonpartisan Leaguers perhaps. If they don't, I don't know whether I should be in favor of you." Undoubtedly Butler's corporate connections would be made an issue by the progressives, but, as Taft explained it to his brother, Butler was a Catholic and that would "make the Catholics unite on him to meet any attack that may come from Borah and LaFollette and the Nonpartisan Leaguers in the Senate."[1]

I

The typical insider's reaction to Butler's nomination was relief, for it meant Manton's drive for the Court had been frustrated. As Charles C. Burlingham put it: "We New Yorkers are all much pleased with the appointment of Butler and the elimination of 'M'." Wickersham was jubilant. "I congratulate *you* on the President's selection of Pierce Butler," he wrote Taft. With characteristic modesty, Taft answered it was the bar that deserved congratulations.[2]

Justice Van Devanter was deeply gratified by the nomination. On the day it was made, he wrote Butler that for several weeks he had been "striving and hoping for this result in a very modest way—not as a matter of friendship for you, but to promote the public good and maintain the high reputation and traditions of the greatest institution established by the Constitution." Judge Sanborn's activity in securing the nomination received special mention: "[H]is discreet suggestions, friendly acts and deep interest have contributed much to the proper presentation of a splendid cause." If things took their natural course, as Van Devanter believed they would, there would be neither controversy nor delay in the confirmation. Yet, in order to be sure, Thomas D. O'Brien, William G. Brantley, and other friends and former associates were already attending to the confirmation. Van Devanter was confident. "I anticipate great pleasure and satisfaction," he wrote his colleague-to-be, "from having you with us." [3]

II

The typical outsider's reaction was surprise. Editorial writers were asking: "Who is Pierce Butler?" "No man," said the *New York World,* "has probably ever been appointed to the United States Supreme Court about whom the general public knew less than it does about Pierce Butler of Minnesota. His nomination . . . came as a complete surprise." [4] Nevertheless, editorials published soon after the nomination indicated their writers learned a great deal about Butler in a short time.

"He is a lawyer, not a politician," said the *New York Times,* "one of those lawyers whose natural bent is the study of legal principles and whose devotion to the profession has screened him from wide public fame." The *Times* pointed out that Butler was a railroad lawyer, "like Abraham Lincoln," adding that perhaps Senator LaFollette might find it difficult "to pardon that crime." It noted that Butler was a Democrat and that it pleased the public sense of fair play to see a Republican nominate a member of the opposite party. Finally it mentioned Butler was a Catholic, "like Chief Justice Taney, Chief Justice White, and Associate Justice McKenna." "The fact is worth mentioning," it concluded, "only because certain belated bigots in various parts of the country are trying to proscribe many millions of our citizens on account of their race or their religion." [5]

Other newspapers were, on the whole, favorable, or at least neutral. The *New York World,* a critic of the Harding administration, took the position it would withhold judgment, for, as matters stood then, Butler appeared to be committed neither to liberal nor reactionary views. Since he served corporations and the government with equal fidelity, said the *Milwaukee Journal,* there was every indication he would faithfully serve the people. At least Butler was not a lame duck and the Northwest would be represented, commented the *Philadelphia Evening Bulletin,* and on that score alone Harding's choice ought to be commended. The *Cleveland Plain Dealer* agreed, and added that Butler was "a man of parts; of conservative tendencies, it appears, who in spite of his lack of judicial experience, will go on the supreme bench well qualified for service." [6]

The *Boston Pilot,* the organ of Cardinal O'Connell's archdiocese, began its editorial with this statement: "The appointment of Mr. Pierce Butler to the Supreme Court of the United States is a magnificent tribute on the part of President Harding to legal genius, high statesmanship, and sterling Americanism." Since Catholics, the editorial continued, had attained prominence by increase in numbers and service to the nation, especially during the World War, it was only just that Harding nominate a Catholic to the bench. Harding—"our kindly and noble Chief Executive"—deserves universal commendation, Catholic readers were told; for in a time when bitterness was rife and religious animosities were being stirred up, it took "unfailing strength of character," "clear vision," and "patriotic devotion" to nominate Pierce Butler.[7]

At least one Catholic newspaper, the *Michigan Catholic,* was less sanguine about Butler's nomination. Like the *New York Times,* it noted Butler was a railroad lawyer, but added that sentiment in Minnesota and other states where people suffered because of exorbitant rates was against railroads. "A railroad lawyer may be as honest as Abe Lincoln," it conceded, "but some corporation attorneys are standpatters opposed to public welfare. We prefer to reserve our jubilation until it has been shown that the appointee is solidly progressive as well as Catholic." [8]

III

Butler's Catholicism was in itself enough for some persons to protest his nomination. They wanted to know how a Mason like Harding could nominate a fourth-degree Knight of Columbus like Butler. "When you became president of these United States," wrote a lawyer in Birmingham, "we understood . . . you would not appoint Roman Catholics to places of trust in this nation." A Minneapolis citizen vigorously protested: "The appointment of Butler would tighten the papal noose around the neck of America almost to the strangulation point." Harding even received a protest from the Women's Auxiliary of the Ohio State Good Government Association. The ladies were at a loss to understand how the President could appoint to the Supreme Court a member of an "un-American" organization like the Roman Catholic Church. They said they were "extremely sorry" and hoped it would not happen again.[9]

Senators received similar protests. Butler's appointment, one man wrote to Senator Nelson, would only "create happiness in Tammany and other Pope domains in the U.S." Another wrote that Butler was "a rank Roman Catholic" too dangerous to appoint to the Supreme Court. With the Oregon public school law coming to the Supreme Court, a constituent asked Senator Jones of Washington, "do you think it is safe to trust a Catholic judge?" Turning over the government to the Catholics was poor politics, he pointed out, for in four states in which governors joined "the R.C.'s to fight K.K.K.'s," the incumbents lost the election. There were also reports that an eleventh-hour drive by the Ku Klux Klan flooded the Senate mail with protests against Butler.[10]

Butler's corporate affiliations rather than his religion were the basis of other protests. "Big business fanatic," "reactionary," "enemy of the common man," "tool of the vested interests"—these were the terms used to describe him.[11] "The people are sick and tired of men of the stamp of Butler," a small businessman wrote to Senator Norris, "being put into these high offices to further the interests that he has so long served."[12] Samuel Gompers, A.F. of L. president, took a similar view. "When a man whose whole life has been marked by corporation leanings and sympathies and alliances," he wrote, "takes to the study of railroad valuation or railroad rate-making, it is fair to suspect that his conclusions in his favored field will be tinged with the point of view of the corporations in that field." Noting that the Interstate Commerce Commission would soon complete its valuation of railroad properties and that its action was sure to be contested in the courts, the union leader suggested there was perhaps something "forehanded" about Butler's nomination.[13]

Members of state railroad commissions shared Gompers' concern. J. H. Henderson, transportation counsel for the Iowa commission, asked the Senate Judiciary Committee to delay its decision on confirming Butler until some of the commissioners from the western states could meet and determine whether the National Association of Railroad Commissioners would formally oppose the nomination; and Senators Capper, Curtis, and Norris received protests against Butler from individual members of the association.[14]

Butler's record as a corporation lawyer was also the basis of a protest by the Minneapolis City Council. On November 24 the Socialist majority of the council passed a resolution condemning Butler's nomination as "a crime against the people." As far as the people were concerned, the resolution stated, the Supreme Court could be dispensed with, for the presidents of the railroads would now act as the judicial branch of government.[15]

There was also a lone dissent from the legal academic community. Professor Hugh E. Willis of the Indiana University Law School wrote President Harding that the fact that Butler had been a successful trial lawyer did not mean he was fitted for a place on the Supreme Court. "It seems to me," Willis continued, "that he is unfitted for judicial duties by the very characteristics by which he has won his success as a trial lawyer, as well as by the fact that he lacks the wide legal scholarship which a jurist should possess. Is it not his forte to win cases rather than administer justice?" The professor's advice to Harding was to withdraw Butler's name and send to the Senate the name of Dean Roscoe Pound of the Harvard Law School, Charles Evans Hughes, or Benjamin N. Cardozo of the New York Court of Appeals.[16]

IV

Six men, in various parts of the country, reacted intensely to Butler's nomination. Five of them believed that they had suffered injustice because of him. All of them wanted to prevent his confirmation, and one of them planned to come to Washington and fight it to the bitter end.

In Butte, Montana, on November 25, D. J. Leary, an elderly crippled man, reading of the nomination, remembered Butler as the man who prosecuted him in St. Paul in the early 1890's. Immediately he wired the chairman of the Senate Judiciary Committee asking to be heard in opposition to confirmation. The telegram, in part, stated: "THE PROMINENT MEN WHO HAVE ENDORSED HIS NOMINATION DO NOT KNOW THE REAL PIERCE BUTLER. I CAN SHOW HIM A CRIMINAL CONSPIRATOR. MEMBER OF THE INFAMOUS BUTLER–O'BRIEN GANG WHO HAVE ENCOURAGED AND PROTECTED VICE AND PROSTITUTED JUSTICE IN THE CITY OF ST PAUL FOR MORE THAN TWENTY FIVE YEARS." He added that though he was not wealthy, he would put up one thousand dollars that the committee could turn over to the Salvation Army if he did not make a case. About two weeks later he wired again, this time referring to Butler as an "ARCH-SCOUNDREL, A DR JECKYL (*sic*) AND MR HYDE," and assuring the committee: "I DO NOT OPPOSE BUTLER ON POLITICAL OR RELIGIOUS GROUNDS. HE IS OF IRISH EXTRACTION AND A CATHOLIC. I AM OF IRISH EXTRACTION AND NOT AN ENEMY OF THE CATHOLIC CHURCH."[17]

From Minneapolis, a University of Minnesota professor,

apparently feeling it was useless to protest to either Nelson or Kellogg, wrote Senator Edwin F. Ladd of North Dakota, a former professor who was known as a progressive, protesting Butler's nomination. Ladd, without disclosing the identity of the writer, released the letter to the press on November 26. It conceded Butler was an able lawyer but maintained he lacked a judicial temperament. In support of this, the following "facts" were cited:

1. His aggressive behavior earned him the nickname "Fierce" Butler.
2. Lawyers regarded him as a bully in the courtroom.
3. During public hearings of the Board of Regents of the University, he attacked those whose causes he disliked in a manner that was disgraceful and ungentlemanly; even those who otherwise sympathized with his views conceded this.
4. Former President Folwell once feelingly referred to him as a "huge bully."
5. When A. W. Rankin, a retired professor of education, attacked Butler in the press, former President Northrop profusely thanked Rankin—and Northrop was a conservative.
6. At times Butler's domineering attitude brought President Coffman to the brink of resignation.

The professor also denied press reports that Butler was a man of broad liberal views, citing Butler's representation of the Minneapolis Steel and Machinery Company in its fight against the wage standards set up by the War Labor Board and his defense of the kidnappers of Nonpartisan Leaguer John Meints. "I am not a lawyer," wrote the professor, "but to a layman it seems that the presentation of such a plea argues a suspicious lack of devotion to the law, if not, also, a lack of moral integrity." [18] *

From Urbana, Illinois, Gerhard Dietrichson, a chemistry professor at the University of Illinois, also wrote Senator

* When asked about the letter, Butler told reporters that he was not anxious to know who wrote it and had no feelings about it. "Whether the book of my life is a 'red book' or a 'white book' or a 'blue book,' " he said, "it is written up to this point; nothing I could say would change it in any way. Nor would it be in good taste for me to say anything." Quoted in the *St. Paul Dispatch,* Dec. 1, 1922.

Ladd protesting Butler's nomination. Five years earlier, when Dietrichson was an instructor at the University of Minnesota, he had charged the dean of the chemistry school with maladministration. Dietrichson's appointment was then not renewed, and he took his case to the regents, laying before them the following charges:

1. No reliance could be placed on the word of the dean of the chemistry school.
2. There was a misappropriation of resources (time and equipment) in the school.
3. Administration of the school was inefficient.
4. As a result of the above, the work done in the classrooms and laboratories was unsatisfactory to students and instructors.
5. Dietrichson's dismissal was arbitrary.

The charges went to the regents' executive committee, which Butler headed, and were investigated by two professors from the law school, E. M. Morgan and E. G. Lorenzen, who made a confidential report to the regents. After receiving the report, the regents unanimously found there was no support for any charges of dishonesty, lack of veracity, or misappropriation of money and that Dietrichson's relations with the University were properly terminated. The next day, when Dietrichson called at the president's office to receive the regents' official action in his case, he was mistakenly given the report made by Morgan and Lorenzen. With dismay he read that the law professors found that charges 1, 3, 4, and 5 were true. The finding that the dismissal of Dietrichson was arbitrary, however, had been qualified with the statement that at the time of the dismissal such friction existed between the dean and Dietrichson that both could not remain. Shocked at what he believed to be proof of a grave injustice to him, he released the contents of the report to the press. The regents made no rejoinder, and Dietrichson sought another job. As the years went on, his sense of injustice continued to rankle. News of Butler's nomination to the Supreme Court greatly disturbed him. No honest man with a sense of justice, Dietrichson felt, could have stood by and permitted his dismissal in view of the Morgan-Lorenzen report. And Butler, in his opinion, bore a heavier responsibility for the action than the rest of the regents, for he was chairman of the executive committee and one of the dominant members of the board. Such a man, Dietrichson believed, was unfit for the Supreme Court.[19]

Dietrichson discussed the matter with Clarence A. Berdahl, a colleague in the political science department at Illinois. Berdahl, a native of South Dakota, appealed to Senator Thomas Sterling of that state, asking him to use his influence to prevent Butler's confirmation. The political science professor said that certain facts were brought to his attention by Dietrichson, "whose word [could] be relied upon absolutely," that showed Butler was "utterly unfit" for the Supreme Court. Berdahl said he himself had seen the evidence, and the confirmation of Butler in the face of such facts "would surely arouse contempt for the Senate and suspicion of the Court." [20]

"My dear Clarence," Sterling answered, "let me say that Mr. Butler comes very highly recommended as a lawyer. I have some recommendations from members of the bar of South Dakota. There are members of the Senate Judiciary Committee who know Mr. Butler personally, and speak very highly of his attainments." Sterling added that, in justice to Butler, charges would have to be specific and substantiated by facts. He assured Berdahl that there would be ample opportunity for Dietrichson to furnish the facts and even appear before the Judiciary Committee.[21]

From San Francisco, Stanley I. Rypins, a former instructor in rhetoric at the University of Minnesota, wired Senator-elect Henrik Shipstead that Butler's appointment would be a "national calamity" because of his "prejudiced and domineering mind." As in Dietrichson's case, Rypins' appointment at the university had not been renewed during Butler's tenure as regent. A Rhodes Scholar with a Ph.D. from Harvard, Rypins came to Minnesota in 1919. Unlike most of his colleagues, he was a political activist. He was active in the

American Civil Liberties Union and the Committee of Forty-eight, a political-action group that had as its purpose the establishment of a third political party. He lectured at the Workers' College in Minneapolis, spoke publicly on a number of issues, such as censorship during the war, and was one of the speakers at a meeting celebrating the release of A. C. Townley, a Nonpartisan League leader who had been convicted of conspiring to make disloyal statements during the war. Rypins' speeches, to the consternation of certain individuals in Minnesota, received considerable publicity in the *Chicago Tribune* and the *Chicago Daily News*. After reading about one of those speeches, a lawyer wrote Butler protesting Rypins' employment by the university. He said that if Rypins was going to act as the spokesman of the "radical Reds," they, not the state, should pay him. Butler wrote President Burton about Rypins, and subsequently the instructor's contract was not renewed.[22] Rypins blamed Butler for the regents' action, claiming Butler had asked for his "decapitation." Referring to Butler's letter to Burton—which, oddly enough, as in Dietrichson's case, somehow fell into the instructor's hands—Rypins said that it was "the neatest thing you ever saw—not a direct order, and not even a request for my dismissal, but a carefully worded statement to the effect that it seemed to him (Butler) regrettable that the name of the university had been linked up in the press with the name of myself. That was all. But Burton sent it down the line of officials as a positive decree and my fate at Minnesota was settled."[23]

At Northfield, Minnesota, John H. Gray, an economics professor at Carleton College, was also troubled by Butler's nomination. He, too, felt Butler was responsible for his leaving Minnesota. Behind him was a distinguished career: president of the American Economic Association, twelve years as head of the economics department at the University of Minnesota, and fifteen years in a comparable position at Northwestern University. But he was not held in high esteem by the Minnesota regents, especially Butler—or so Gray believed.

In 1917, while on leave of absence with the Interstate Commerce Commission, Gray acted as examiner in a valuation case involving the Texas Midland Railroad, a case in which Butler was chief counsel of record. Although Butler never appeared before Gray, the professor heard that Butler had been unhappy with his handling of the Texas Midland case and personally complained about him to members of the commission. Also, while the case was in progress, Gray was requested to resign as head of the Minnesota economics department. President Vincent made the request, saying only that in view of the war and the requirements of business education, the administration wanted to reorganize the economics department and hoped Gray would cooperate by resigning. Gray quickly contacted his colleagues and learned that not only had they not been consulted, but they disapproved of his resignation. In view of this and the fact that he had come to Minnesota in the dual capacity of professor of economics and head of the department—both positions having been offered as specific and separate considerations for his move from Northwestern—Gray felt that his loss of the headship, in addition to being humiliating, would be a violation of the agreement the university had made with him. Hence he asked President Vincent to withdraw his request for the resignation. Gray remained head of the department, but two years later the regents created a business school that absorbed the economics department, and though Gray retained his professorship, he was not put in charge of the new school.

Returning from leave in 1920, Gray was unhappy with what he considered a demotion and also with the fact that during his entire teaching career at Minnesota he had never received a salary increase. Thus, at the age of sixty-three, he resigned his post at Minnesota to go to Carleton College. Although he had no proof that Butler interfered in any way with his career at the University of Minnesota, his suspicions led him to consider a course of action that conceivably might prevent Butler's confirmation.[24]

V

The man who had the most serious grievance against Butler was William A. Schaper, former chairman of the Department of Political Science at the University of Minnesota, who in 1922 was an unsuccessful manufacturer of laundry appliances. He had already decided to do what Gray was considering. For Schaper the announcement of Butler's nomination recalled bitter memories of September 13, 1917—the day he was dismissed from the University of Minnesota for disloyalty. That day he received a telephone call asking him to appear before the Board of Regents. Upon his appearance, the president of the board, Fred B. Snyder, told him the regents had received a letter from a member of the Public Safety Commission containing a list of professors whose loyalty was suspect, and that Schaper's name was on it. Schaper asked if there were any charges against him, and, if so, who was making them. Snyder said there were none and that all the board wanted to know was Schaper's position on the war.

Schaper told the regents he opposed the United States' entry into the war and his efforts in this direction were well known, but once war was declared, he took the position that it was his duty, and the duty of every citizen, "to abide by the law and not hinder in any manner the government's conduct of the war." He said he advised students that all peace movements would have to be dropped, and even told his student assistant that since war had been declared he should enlist. He concluded by saying he had met every call made on him thus far and was presently considering a request to address the soldiers at Fort Snelling.[25]

This statement the board deemed insufficient; the regents wanted Schaper to discuss in detail his personal opinions and attitudes concerning the war. "Well," said Schaper, "in that respect I am in a delicate position. I have four nephews who have been drafted and are going into our army, and I have first cousins in the German army. Under the circumstances I feel that I cannot go out and boost for the war." President

Burton, trying to help Schaper, asked whether he was not boosting for the war when he advised his students to enlist. "Perhaps," was the professor's answer; by boosting for the war he had in mind haranguing public meetings for the purpose of stirring up war hysteria. "That," he said, "I could not do. It would be revolting to my conscience." He was not just against the war with Germany, he explained, but all war, because it was an utterly wrong method of settling disputes. "But," he added, "I stand ready to defend this country against attack or aggression from any quarter."[26]

At this point Butler began his cross-examination of Schaper, during which both men lost their tempers.[27] This is how Schaper remembered the exchange:

BUTLER: That is the kind of patriotism Pfaender* was advocating. You believe in obeying the law to keep out of jail, don't you?

SCHAPER: I obey the law out of a sense of duty as a citizen.

BUTLER: Don't you believe the Kaiser, the Crown Prince, and the Hohenzollerns should be wiped out, root and branch, and that the government of Germany should be destroyed?

SCHAPER: It would be an unwise policy to go that far. It would be dictating to another nation what its form of government shall be. That would be contrary to our national traditions and would certainly cause trouble for us.

BUTLER: Is the purpose I stated not the very object for which we entered the war?

SCHAPER: I do not think so. President Wilson has not set that as our object, in my judgment. In his reply to the Pope's peace message, he did not commit us to such a policy, necessarily. I have noticed that the editors of the *New Republic* and of some other periodicals understand the President's re-

* The following day one of the regents, probably Butler, told newspapermen: "Instead of coming out with a ringing statement of love for this country and of support of its government, he [Schaper] said he had been advising students to abide by the situation and comply with the laws. That's the kind of loyalty recently preached by Albert Pfaender of New Ulm, a kind that hurts the cause of America, that gives aid and comfort to our enemies. . . ." Quoted in the *Minneapolis Tribune,* Sept. 14, 1917. Ironically twenty-one years later, when the Board of Regents reconsidered the Schaper case, Pfaender was himself a regent. See below, pp. 199.

ply the same way. I agree with those editors. Even the press hints at such an interpretation.

BURTON: President Wilson has insisted on the establishment of a representative government in Germany, has he not?

SCHAPER: Yes, but that does not require the destruction of royalty or monarchy.

BUTLER: You are the Kaiser's man. You want the Kaiser and the Crown Prince to dominate the world, don't you?

SCHAPER: That is an accusation, not a question. It is absurd.

BUTLER: It is the truth, is it not?

SCHAPER: It is utterly absurd. . . .

BUTLER: What would you teach regarding the Belgian question?

SCHAPER: I would see that all the students read all sides of the question and drew their own conclusions. That is the only way a scientific man can deal with a controverted question.

BUTLER: How long have you held your position?

SCHAPER: For sixteen years.

BUTLER: For sixteen years you have lived off the public money of this State. It was practically your only source of income, was it not?

SCHAPER: Gentlemen, I was not aware that this Board was dispensing a charity. I had supposed that I held an honorable position in this University. I earned every dollar I ever received from the State.

BUTLER: Why are you not in a training camp?

SCHAPER: I am not in the military years.

BUTLER: You say you're not of the military age, but you are physically fit. Why don't you go out and do something for your country?

SCHAPER: I am beyond the military age desired by the government. Mr. Butler, you assume the role of prosecuting attorney, and assign to me the position of prisoner at the bar. I desire to remind you that our relations are very different. I am the Professor of Political Science in this University and you, Sir, are a member of the Board of Regents.

And so the questioning continued. Other regents asked a few questions, but, in Schaper's recollection, Butler dominated the interrogation.[28]

Later that day Schaper was recalled by the board, informed that it had voted unanimously that he was a disloyal

American citizen, and asked to resign. His response was that if the board had any charges against him, they should be reduced to writing so that he might be in a position to answer them. The president of the board turned to his fellow members and said, "Gentlemen, you hear the request. What is your pleasure?"

"His answer is in," shouted Butler. "His answer is in." [29] No other regent spoke.

"You heard the reply of the board," said President Snyder. "Have you anything further to say?" Schaper reiterated his request of a statement of charges and was then excused. That night a telegram was delivered to his home informing him of the regents' action. The board found that an informant of the Public Safety Commission claimed Schaper was "a rabid pro-German"; that the board's interrogation of him concerning his loyalty satisfied it that his "attitude of mind" and "unwillingness to aid the United States in the present war" rendered him unfit and unable to perform his duties as a professor of political science; and that the best interests of the university, state, and nation required on the part of university teachers "unqualified loyalty" and a "willingness" and ability to further the national purpose by precept and example. "Therefore," it concluded, "be it resolved, the relations existing between W. A. Schaper and this University be, and same are, hereby terminated." [30]

In a single day Schaper saw his career smashed. He could not believe it. He felt that Butler and the other regents had done him a great injustice, and he questioned their good faith. Doubting that they had ever received a letter about him from the Commission of Public Safety, he wrote a letter of inquiry to John Lind, a member of the commission and a former governor and congressman. Lind answered that at no meeting that he attended was any charge considered against Schaper, and checking the minutes of the meetings he did not attend, Lind said he was unable to find any mention of Schaper's name.[31] Now Schaper was absolutely sure he was a victim of an unjust act and began his fight for reinstatement. The American Association of University Professors conducted an investigation; so did Max Lowenthal, one of Schaper's former students, for the Federal Labor Conciliation Commission; and Felix Frankfurter, the commission's legal adviser, also looked into the case. But, as matters stood in 1922, Schaper had neither been reinstated nor given an appointment at another school.

Dissatisfied with his laundry-appliance business, Schaper yearned to return to the classroom where he believed he would have been but for Pierce Butler. As soon as he heard of Butler's nomination to the Supreme Court, he decided to take the first train to Washington and do all in his power to prevent the confirmation of his enemy. "The chance," he said, "was too good to miss." [32]

Arriving in Washington on November 26, Schaper called on the progressive Senators—LaFollette, Norris, Brookhart, and Ladd—and also on Senator Nelson of his own state. Immediately rapport was established between Schaper and LaFollette. Schaper told the Senator his entire story—his education, which began in Wisconsin, his attempt to establish a state tax commission in Minnesota, his work in drafting city charters, his dismissal from the university during the war, Butler's behavior during the dismissal proceedings, and all the rest. The Senator listened sympathetically, and when Schaper finished, LaFollette was "full of fight." Schaper, deeply pleased, thanked LaFollette for his time and patience. "Not at all," said the Senator. "You have given me one of the most interesting hours of my life." Schaper's discussion of the Butler nomination evoked similar responses in Norris and Brookhart. Although Ladd had appeared sympathetic, Schaper doubted that the Senator would fight in earnest when the chips were down. Senator Nelson was rather gruff with Schaper, but when the former professor got up to leave, his feelings obviously hurt, the old Senator called him back and, in Schaper's words, "placed his arm about me and talked to me in a manner that would be a credit to any father." [33]

Schaper felt he was making progress. He wrote Max Lowenthal, who was still trying to get him reinstated at Minnesota, asking for help. Lowenthal contacted liberal friends in New York suggesting that the *New Republic* and *The Nation* go on record against Butler's appointment. Some of the liberals said they were hesitant to do so because the Ku Klux Klan, which they abhorred, was also attacking Butler.[34] Nonetheless both journals published editorials and articles opposing Butler's confirmation. "There seems to be no excuse for Mr. Butler's nomination," said a *Nation* editorial, "unless, as some charge, Mr. Harding is trying to pack the Supreme Court with friends of the railroads in view of the vital questions in regard to them which are expected to come before the tribunal in the next few years." The *New Republic* used even stronger language. It said that Butler as regent of the University of Minnesota behaved "in the manner of a blind and bumptious bigot." His appointment "is a piece of crass stupidity," it added, "because he is the kind of man who would assuredly use a warped or doubtful interpretation of a phrase in the Constitution to prevent needed experiments in economics and government." [35]

Schaper also interested William Hard, a Washington political correspondent, in his attempt to prevent Butler's confirmation. Hard interviewed Schaper at length and wrote a series of five articles for the *Washington Times* on the fight over Butler's confirmation.[36]

VI

Meanwhile, Senator LaFollette was gathering information about Butler. He wired William A. DeFord, William Randolph Hearst's attorney, asking him to use his contacts in the newspaper world to find out what he could about Butler's fitness for the Supreme Court. In a few days, DeFord had several reports. They came from men like Delos F. Wilcox, a political scientist who had recently investigated improper expenditures of the Twin City Transit Company, which Butler represented; Edward W. Bemis, liberal economist and rate expert, and Oliver Morris of the *Minneapolis Star*. Though Bemis reported that Butler would be a dangerous man on monopoly questions and should be defeated at all costs, DeFord received no information touching Butler's ability or character, and in relaying the reports to LaFollette, he said they fell short of furnishing what would be needed to block confirmation. To indicate his own opinion, DeFord enclosed a carbon copy of an editorial he wrote opposing Butler, adding that it would probably soon appear in some of the Hearst papers.[37]

LaFollette saw that if Butler's confirmation were to be blocked, action by the Senate on the nomination would have to be delayed. But events were moving quickly. By November 28 the Senate Judiciary Committee recommended that the nomination be confirmed, and it was assumed that confirmation would come before the special session of Congress adjourned on December 4. LaFollette considered a filibuster, then decided upon another maneuver. At the time there were about 1700 nominations before the Senate awaiting confirmation, and LaFollette, in order to get the time he needed, notified the Senate leadership that unless Butler's name was excluded from the list, he would ask that each nomination be confirmed separately. The maneuver was successful. Congress adjourned on December 4 without confirming the Butler nomination; the next day Harding renominated Butler.[38]

VII

Soon after Schaper arrived in Washington, he began drafting charges against Butler that he planned to present to the Senate Judiciary Committee. The early drafts of the charges were over his own signature as member of the Central Committee of the Farmer-Labor Party of Minnesota, but when Senator-elect Shipstead arrived in Washington, Schaper rewrote the charges for presentation by Shipstead.

On December 5 Schaper and Shipstead requested a hearing before the Senate Judiciary Committee, and on December 7 Shipstead filed the following charges with the committee:

1. That because of his long service as counsel for corporations, Butler was imbued with their views and therefore could not objectively decide cases. In this regard, the ap-

pointment of Judge Gary of U.S. Steel would not be more improper.

2. That by virtue of his past employment as counsel for railroads and public utilities, Butler would be disqualified in a large number of rate cases soon to come before the Court. Such cases should be decided by a full Court; moreover, since the theories of valuation advocated by Butler as counsel were "utterly incompatible with the public interest," his daily association with the other Justices would, as it were, contaminate the decisional process.

3. That as counsel for the Twin City Rapid Transit Company, Butler was presently using his legal talents "to defeat the ends of justice" by opposing inspection of the company's corporate books.

4. That in cases in which he sat in a quasi-judicial capacity, such as Board of Regents hearings at the University of Minnesota, Butler was swayed by prejudice and ignored the most fundamental principles of justice, thereby showing he was "not judicial in mind or attitude."

A hearing on the charges was requested and the committee was asked to summon as witnesses Delos F. Wilcox, Stanley I. Rypins, Gerhard Dietrichson, Max Lowenthal, Felix Frankfurter, and William A. Schaper.[39]

Chapter 7

IN COMMITTEE

Even before Butler was nominated, Taft was planning strategy to ensure his candidate's confirmation by the Senate. He knew from experience that in matters as important as the appointment of a Supreme Court Justice nothing should be left to chance. "The minute that your name goes in," he wrote Butler, ". . . you ought to have all your friends in St. Paul, Minneapolis and elsewhere center their attention on the Senate, both Republicans and Democrats, and have personal letters written to the Senators by men who know you and can speak with confidence." [1]

Members of the Judiciary Committee and senators from the Midwest were singled out by Taft as special targets. Kellogg and Nelson, Taft knew, would do what they could, but that might not be enough. Two committee members, Walsh and Shields, had been mentioned for the vacancy; hence they would probably be less than enthusiastic about Butler's nomination. Taft wanted to know what sort of relationship Butler had with Walsh. If necessary, would Bishop Carroll intercede with the Montana senator in Butler's behalf? Could someone write Senator Cummins of Iowa? Taft believed he was the most effective man on the committee. And there was Senator Sterling of South Dakota. Could

Butler see that he was "properly primed"? Did Butler know Norbeck, the other senator from South Dakota? Could Butler's friends in Illinois take up the matter with Senator McCormick? Taft himself would attend to McCormick's colleague, McKinley. LaFollette could be written off; he would probably honor Butler as he did Taft—by opposing him. But the other Wisconsin senator, Lenroot, probably could be counted on to help. Would Butler get someone to write him? "Many other avenues of communication with the Senators will occur to you," Taft counseled Butler, "and I think it is important that you should neglect nothing." [2]

I

When the special session of Congress adjourned without confirming Butler's nomination, Taft was surprised. Yet in view of the importance of the nomination, he felt that it was just as well that the Senate did not act in haste. Besides, he was confident of the result. The radicals might be able to delay confirmation, he told Butler, but they could not defeat it. The Chief Justice's thoughts then returned to strategy:

> I think what you ought to do, or what your friends ought to do, is to keep in touch with Nelson and then select a representative body of the leading men of Saint Paul, Minneapolis, Chicago, South Dakota and North Dakota who know you and who will come before the Committee and testify to your high standing at the bar and your influence as a professional man and barrister in the practice of law. I think, too, it might be well if you can arrange to have the President of the University come down to rebut these attacks that are prompted by those disloyal traitors whom you assisted in kicking out of the University. Uncle Knute is a bit slow in pressing matters, and Norris is an ugly kind of individual, at odds with the world generally, and he would be glad to exploit himself in this case.* But your nomination has

* Earlier in 1922, when Norris criticized the Chief Justice for dining frequently with "the idle rich," Taft wrote to his brother Horace: "I suppose you have seen Norris' attack on me in a wild speech he made in the Senate against all Federal Judges in which he urged all Federal

been received with such wide approval that I think their effort will recoil on themselves.[3]

"Uncle Knute" Nelson, contrary to Taft's statement, was not in the least slow. The seventy-nine-year-old viking—five months from his death—was girding for his last important battle in the Senate. Butler had not been his choice for the Court, but Nelson had endorsed him and would see the matter through to victory.[4]

Nelson's twenty-seven years in the Senate gave him some decided advantages. Long before he had learned that facts were weapons in such battles; thus, no matter how absurd the charge against Butler, Nelson had it investigated. Pierce, Jr. and Mitchell made elaborate investigations of some of the charges; the Bureau of Investigation, predecessor of the F.B.I., sent an agent to Minnesota to gather information; and Nelson himself made extensive inquiries. As chairman of the Senate Judiciary Committee, he selected a subcommittee consisting of himself and two progressive senators—Thomas J. Walsh, Democrat of Montana, and Albert B. Cummins, Republican of Iowa—to hear the charges against Butler. In choosing Walsh and Cummins, the old Minnesota Senator knew precisely what he was doing, for, before the completion of the hearings, Taft could confidently write that the subcommittee members were "all for Butler." [5]

Nelson agreed to an early hearing of the charges brought by Schaper and Shipstead, scheduling the first subcommittee meeting for December 7, only two days after the Minnesotans requested a hearing. Senators Walsh and Cummins, however, were unable to adjust their schedules on such short notice,

---

Courts but the Supreme Court be abolished. Norris and I are old enemies. He is as bad as LaFollette." April 9, 1922, Taft Papers. Commenting on the same subject, Norris told a correspondent that he was glad she approved of his remark about Chief Justice Taft. "I am inclined to think," Norris added, "that the man who is attending society dinners nearly every night cannot be a good public servant. *Continual association with the over-rich will cause men to forget those who toil and suffer*." Norris to Mrs. Virginia Laurenson, April 22, 1922, Norris Papers. (Emphasis added.) Compare this statement with Norris' remarks in the struggle over Hugh's confirmation, quoted below, p. 193.

so the hearing was postponed until the following day. At 2:30 P.M. on December 8 Senators Nelson, Walsh, and Cummins entered the Judiciary Committeeroom. Waiting for them were Senator-elect Shipstead and Professor Schaper. The doors were closed; hearings on the confirmation of Pierce Butler were ready to begin.

II

Senator Nelson called the meeting to order and said that Senator-elect Shipstead would be heard first. Before Shipstead spoke, Nelson told him that Butler had filed a statement with the subcommittee acknowledging his representation of railroads in valuation matters and hence there was no need to present evidence on that point. Shipstead's charges, which had been sent to each member of the subcommittee the day before, were then put into the record.[6]

Senator Walsh began by questioning Shipstead about the charge that Butler had used his legal skill to prevent examination of the Twin City Rapid Transit Company books. Walsh asked whether the matter was relevant to Butler's confirmation.

MR. SHIPSTEAD: I thought it proper to call the attention of the committee to it, and let the committee decide it.

SENATOR WALSH: Let us suppose that the facts are just as you have stated; that they have been spending this money in an improper way, and all that. Mr. Butler is employed by them. What is the difference between defending that, and defending a murderer? You certainly would not want to have him disbarred, or his confirmation defeated, because once on a time he was employed to defend a murderer, would you? In other words, is not this mere professional employment?

MR. SHIPSTEAD: I think it is. I see your point.[7]

Walsh then shifted to the charge that Butler's long service for corporations biased him in their favor. He read the following paragraph from Shipstead's statement of charges:

> It is not merely that Mr. Butler has been under retainer by these corporations, but he has for many years been one

> of the principal advocates and spokesmen of a large number of corporations in their attempt to secure for themselves special privileges incompatible with the public interest. His advocacy of the claims of these corporations has not been limited to professional appearance in court, but he has also been their constant and partisan advocate as a citizen.

"Now, that part of this charge is of interest to me," said Walsh. He asked Shipstead to go into greater detail on this point and asked whether any of the witnesses named would testify concerning it. Shipstead replied that he understood Butler had strong views on these matters of public interest, views that he expressed in places other than the courtroom. When asked if he could testify on the matter himself, Shipstead said he could not; he was only before the subcommittee on behalf of citizens who wanted to be heard. Further, he admitted that he did not know Butler personally and in fact had no personal knowledge of the charges. "This nomination came in quite awhile ago, you know, Senator," said Walsh. Shipstead responded that he was not fully aware of the matter until he came to Washington and discussed it with Schaper.[8]

Senator Cummins asked Shipstead whether Butler was a lobbyist in behalf of railroad interests or whether Butler was attempting to influence public opinion. Shipstead felt it was safe to say that Butler was attempting to do the latter. "Of course," said Cummins, "sometimes such an operation can be right. . . ." He wanted to know whether Butler was doing anything wrong in attempting to influence public opinion. Instead of answering the question directly, Shipstead said that big men could represent corporations and still maintain an unbiased and judicial mind, but Butler had not done so. In other words, he asserted, Butler lacked a judicial temperament.[9]

"That comes under another branch of this statement, Senator Shipstead," Walsh pointed out. That charge referred to Butler's activity as a regent of the University of Minnesota, about which, Walsh gathered, most of the witnesses listed were to testify. "Are we to try the issue whether the

Board of Regents acted properly?" asked Senator Nelson. "No, I should say not," answered Senator Walsh.[10]

Returning to Butler's railroad affiliations, Senator Cummins said he had read Butler's briefs on railroad valuation and frankly he completely disagreed with them. "[B]ut," he added, "I have not supposed the fact that I do not agree with him would disqualify him as a proposed member of the Supreme Court, because I assume in the first place that he would not sit in those cases in which he was engaged." Walsh tried to explain to Shipstead that they could not expect President Harding to name to the Supreme Court a man whose views on political and economic questions approximated theirs; after all, the President was of another political party and of another economic school. Shipstead said he understood that; yet he could not help believing that there were men available, like Dean Roscoe Pound of the Harvard Law School, who had not the disadvantage of Butler's corporate environment, and "for the good of the country" one of those men should have been chosen.[11]

Senator Walsh wanted Shipstead to discuss Butler's role in the dismissal of the professors at the University of Minnesota. Beginning with Dietrichson, Shipstead outlined the circumstances surrounding the chemistry instructor's dismissal and stressed as especially significant the regents' suppression of the report that vindicated him. Senator Nelson immediately questioned the propriety of the subcommittee's investigating the management of the University of Minnesota. "Unless Mr. Butler was guilty of some specific wrong, why," he asked, "can you charge him more than the other members of the Board?"[12] Shipstead turned to Professor Schaper and asked him whether Butler was a member of the committee that recommended the firing of Dietrichson. Schaper said that Butler was the committee's chairman, adding with feeling that so far as Butler's acts could be shown "to have been involved in this injustice . . . he acted not as a man should who wanted to be fair, who wanted to see justice done [but] . . . let his bias and his prejudice rule his reason." Nelson's rejoinder took the form of two questions: "But was not the whole action ratified by the Board? Did not the Board, as a board, act unanimously on that?" Schaper said he was unable to answer those questions.[13]

Senator Walsh then asked Schaper to discuss his own dismissal for the purpose of illustrating the charge that Butler acted in an unfair and unjudicial manner in his capacity as regent. The request apparently caught Schaper by surprise, for he had not planned to testify about his case at this stage in the hearings. Briefly he told of the circumstances of his dismissal, stressing that he had neither been informed of charges against him nor given a fair hearing. But most important in the matter, he added, was that after his dismissal he learned from former Governor John Lind, who had been a member of the Minnesota Public Safety Commission, that, contrary to the public statement of the regents at the time of the dismissal, the commission had not informed the regents that it received a report accusing Schaper of being "a rabid pro-German." To prove his assertion, Schaper submitted to the subcommittee the letter of dismissal from President Burton and the letter from Lind that said he knew of no charge against Schaper emanating from the Public Safety Commission. Senator Walsh now thought that perhaps there was something in the charges against Butler after all, and he, for one, wanted to hear more about the matter. Schaper, it appeared, had made a prima-facie case, and there was no doubt that there would be further hearings.[14]

Just before the meeting adjourned, a Senate clerk handed a memorandum to Shipstead and said: "It is a brief by Mr. John H. Gray for the Committee." Shipstead glanced at the memorandum and, seeing that it was another charge against Butler, handed it to Nelson. The "brief" charged that Butler appeared before Professor Gray when he was acting as an I.C.C. examiner in a valuation case involving the Texas Midland Railroad in 1917. Gray, according to the memorandum, ruled adversely to Butler's contentions several times, and Butler, annoyed by these rulings, left the hearings at

Texas and went to Washington, D.C., where he "made the rounds of the offices of members of the Interstate Commerce Commission and lodged personal complaints among these members against Dr. Gray. . . ." About this time, the memorandum continued, Professor Gray's difficulties began at the University of Minnesota: his resignation as head of the economics department was requested, and when he refused to resign, his position as head of the department was abolished; he received no salary increase during all of his years at Minnesota; and finally he was virtually forced to leave the university—all of which, he believed, was due to a "feeling" against him on the Board of Regents. The Gray charge was serious. Like Schaper's charge, it would have to be carefully examined. Senator Nelson scheduled the next meeting of the subcommittee for December 13.[15]

III

As Senator Nelson prepared for the December 13 hearing, he noted the letters and telegrams he had received concerning Butler's nomination. Congressman Oscar Keller of St. Paul, an ally of Samuel Gompers in the movement to impeach Attorney General Daugherty, transmitted a resolution passed by the Working People's Nonpartisan Political League of Ramsey County urging the Senate to reject Butler's nomination on the ground that he had served the rich so long he could not serve the common people. There were similar protests from the Wisconsin Women's Progressive Association of Superior, Wisconsin and the Chicago Federation of Labor. A member of the Minnesota Railroad and Warehouse Commission said he personally opposed Butler's confirmation because of his work on behalf of railroads in valuation cases. And there were other miscellaneous objections to Butler—that he was Irish, a Catholic, a Democrat, and a "wet." [16]

Letters to Nelson also indicated a counter-reaction to the charges of Butler's opponents.* John F. McGee, a member

* One of the most extreme counter-reactions came from Minnesota

of the Minnesota Commission of Public Safety who had figured in Schaper's case, wrote Nelson that the Socialists on the Minneapolis City Council, who had adopted the resolution opposing Butler's confirmation, were the same people who had given the state so much trouble during the war. In fact, he asserted, the alderman who had led the movement against Butler was an admitted member of the I.W.W. "The appointment," McGee assured Nelson, "is applauded by all law-abiding people." Strong letters supporting Butler came from persons who had known him as regent of the University of Minnesota—Presidents Coffman and Burton, Board President Fred B. Snyder, Regents John G. Williams and George H. Partridge, and ex-Governor J. A. A. Burnquist. Governor Preus also sent a telegram, saying that there was never any objection to Butler's work as regent and that the charges against him were "groundless and made for delay." Seven Ramsey County judges vouched for Butler's upright character and integrity, as did some Minnesota lawyers.[17]

The commander of the Minnesota Department of the American Legion and the executive committee of the St. Paul chapter of the Disabled American Veterans urged Butler's confirmation, describing him as the "best type of citizen" and a "patriot . . . of great human sympathies." Pierce, Jr. sent Nelson a clipping of a letter to the editors of the *St. Paul Dispatch* written by a legionnaire who said he had been a student in Schaper's classes and could testify to Schaper's pro-German attitude. Schaper was now seeking

---

Republican Elmer E. Adams, who sent his views to Butler and Nelson. With an apparent attempt at humor, he wrote to Butler:

"You know that during the past few years, nearly all of our illnesses have been attributed to defective teeth and it is unlikely that in the pursuance of this policy, Senator Shipstead [who was by profession a dentist] is of the opinion that your health would be better if he removed your teeth. Whether this doctor of dental surgery is correct . . . or not, I do not know, but we have too many men on the bench and other places with false teeth.

"I have only one hope and that is that you will be able to fire a few more professors before you leave for the East." Adams to Butler, Dec. 13, 1922, copy to Nelson, Nelson Papers.

revenge against Butler, wrote the legionnaire, and trying "to punish Pierce Butler for being loyal to his country during a crisis." [18]

Nelson regarded a letter from H. R. Leonard, manager of the Twin Cities Milk Producers Association, as especially important. Leonard said he did not feel that the criticism of Butler's nomination should be given much consideration, for Butler had been in close touch with the cooperative movement in Minnesota for many years, and at the time he was retained by three cooperative companies, representing more than 70,000 farmers. "Our farmer officers," wrote Leonard, "are very much pleased to learn of the appointment, as they feel that Mr. Butler is capable, absolutely sincere, and that he thoroughly understands the farmers' position." [19]

Butler's former colleague on the railroads' Committee of Counsel, former Congressman W. G. Brantley, testified to Butler's "great ability and splendid character." And from Princeton University a chemistry professor, George Halett, who had worked with Butler in the *Bleached Flour Cases* in 1910, wrote that he believed the St. Paul lawyer "possessed one of the ablest minds in this country. His ability to grasp the fundamental points in the technical questions involved was remarkable." [20]

Most of Nelson's correspondence, both for and against Butler, was from Minnesota. Apparently there were no objections to Butler arising from the fact that the nomination had not gone to someone from the South or from New York, Pennsylvania, or one of the other large states. Perhaps the retirement of Justice Pitney just before the December 8 hearing had something to do with this, for a senator whose candidate had been passed over in favor of Butler might still hope that his man would yet be appointed to the Supreme Court by Harding.[21]

Despite the strong support for Butler, Nelson felt that there were a few things that would have to be cleared up before the subcommittee met again on December 13. Right after the subcommittee adjourned on December 8, Nelson telegraphed the University of Minnesota, requesting a copy of the letter from the Commission of Public Safety that charged Schaper with being a rabid pro-German. Nelson also wired President Burton of the University of Michigan, who had been president at Minnesota when Schaper was dismissed, asking him to appear before the subcommittee on December 13. At Minnesota the documents requested by Nelson could not be located immediately because Pierce, Jr. had the University's file on Schaper at his office. It was assumed that John McGee had the documents, and this was communicated to Nelson, who immediately wired McGee. On the 11th of December, Nelson still had not received the documents he requested and again asked the university to send them. By that time Pierce, Jr. had returned the Schaper file to the university and indicated which documents should be sent to Nelson. On the 12th Nelson received a night letter from the university quoting the requested documents. The same day an affidavit by McGee dealing with the matter arrived.[22]

Nelson also contacted Butler and asked him for a statement concerning the Gray charges. Before Nelson received an answer, two letters came from Shipstead on December 9 indicating that perhaps these charges were spurious. Shipstead admitted he was mistaken when he said the memorandum given the subcommittee was Gray's; someone else had written it for Shipstead's personal use. On the 12th Butler's statement arrived; the same day Nelson made further inquiries at the Interstate Commerce Commission concerning the Texas Midland case and Butler's role in it. Senator Nelson, armed with facts, was now ready for the second round of hearings.[23]

IV

Pierce Butler was not shaken by the charges against him; he felt that when the full facts were known, there would be no question about his confirmation. As for the charges concerning Professors Schaper, Dietrichson, Rypins, and Gray, these were the facts as Butler reported them to Chief Justice Taft:

William A. Schaper was the only professor in the group who was dismissed by the Board of Regents because of disloyalty. The case began during the war with a report from the Commission of Public Safety that it had information that Schaper was "a rabid pro-German." When the board invited Schaper to explain his position, he "admitted that he was opposed to the war and that he could not do anything to help the United States in that crisis." When the board heard this, it promptly adopted a resolution terminating his relationship with the university. The newspapers and alumni strongly supported the regents, and their action served as an example to other disloyal persons in the University.

Gerhard Dietrichson, the chemistry instructor, had quarreled with his dean and preferred charges against him. The charges were investigated by two law professors, whose report was modified somewhat by the regents before they voted unanimously to drop Dietrichson.

Stanley I. Rypins, the rhetoric instructor, was "very radical" and active in the "Seekers," an organization that advocated the I.W.W., free love, and atheism. His contract for a second year was renewed over Butler's objection, and when the president refused to recommend his appointment for a third year, Rypins left the university and became active in agitation and third-party movements.[24]

The charges concerning Professor Gray were simply false. Butler said he never appeared in a case before Gray in Texas or any other place. Nor did he ever complain about Gray to the Interstate Commerce Commissioners. It was true that Gray was not selected as head of the newly established business school at the University of Minnesota, that Gray ceased to be head of his department when it was merged into the new business school, and that he never received a salary increase at the university, but Butler said the regents were unanimous in all of their decisions affecting Gray; there was nothing personal, certainly not on his part, in those decisions. On the contrary, Butler said he had recommended Gray to Carleton College when President Cowling was considering offering him a professorship.* Gray, Butler believed, had nothing to do with making the charge; LaFollette and Shipstead wanted him to take an active part in opposing the confirmation, but Butler understood that Gray refused to do so.[25]

Of particular concern to Butler was possible opposition from the National Association of Railroad Commissioners. He reported that Charles E. Elmquist, formerly a member of the Minnesota Railroad and Warehouse Commission, was strongly in favor of his confirmation and was coming to Washington to confer with the executive committee of the Association about the matter. Charles F. Staples, acting head of the Bureau of Valuation of the I.C.C., and P. J. Farrell, chief counsel of the Association, also favored Butler's appointment. Thomas D. O'Brien, Butler's old friend and former associate, was doing his best to keep the Association out of the fight. Yet Butler was not sure what the group would do. Since it was powerful, he felt its opposition would affect the votes of some senators.[26]

Butler saw opposition to his confirmation as part of a radical plot. In support of his thesis, he cited the editorials in the *New Republic;* the denunciation of his nomination by the Socialist majority of the Minneapolis City Council, which was led by an I.W.W. alderman; the attitude of the Nonpartisan League, which was represented by Shipstead; and the attitude of disloyal and socialist elements at the University of Minnesota.[27]

Taft agreed with Butler. It was simply Butler's misfortune to be nominated at a time when there was a "radical flareback" and a movement attacking Harding and the Supreme Court. "To this extent," he told Butler, "you are the goat." He felt that the attack raising the pro-German issue strengthened Butler's position with many senators, certainly with the

* Cowling told Fred B. Snyder that if Butler had not endorsed Gray's appointment, Carleton would not have hired him. Snyder to Nelson, Dec. 12, 1922, Butler Confirmation Papers.

public. The possibility that the National Association of Railroad Commissioners would oppose Butler's confirmation irked Taft; he regarded its interference as "dangerous." "I have no respect for the body," he said. "It is a very cantankerous and bumptious lot of people. If members of our Court are to be subjected to a civil service examination by them, we have reached a pretty pass."

And as always with Taft, there was the human touch—now sympathy for the assailed Butler. The Chief Justice said he did not know what the *New Republic* wrote about Butler's nomination because he did not read the magazine, but he had no doubt that it said everything it ought not to have said; after all, Frankfurter was one of its contributors. Taft said it had attacked even his nomination, and he felt that men whom it did not attack were of questionable reputation as to loyalty and sound constitutional views. "A situation like this is always very hard for the person most involved," he reassured his candidate, "because he is not permitted to come before the committee himself, and everybody that has any grievance against him may go there and be heard, if he can only get some loud-mouthed senator to demand it." [28]

V

When Schaper left the Judiciary Committeeroom on December 8, he felt he had made progress. The subcommittee had been unreceptive at first, but he knew what he had said about his case had impressed the senators. Now there was at least a chance of preventing Butler's confirmation. Schaper took some comfort in the fact that two members of the Iowa State Railroad Commission had asked to be heard in opposition to the confirmation and were waiting outside the committeeroom while he and Shipstead presented their charges. There must be others, Schaper felt, who would also be willing to testify against Butler. Bill Hard's articles in the *Washington Times* dealing with various aspects of the Butler charges were also heartening. Yet things could be better. To Schaper's surprise, Shipstead returned to Minnesota on December 9 to attend to "private business matters" and would not return in time for the hearing on the 13th. Further, a number of Minnesotans Schaper had approached to testify against Butler now refused to do so on the ground that they might jeopardize their own causes. Still, Schaper found some comfort in the fact that LaFollette and Norris were still staunchly with him.[29]

In true academic fashion, Schaper spent many hours drafting and redrafting his statement, editing and polishing it. And the statement showed it: parts of it were eloquent. One of Schaper's main points was that he had been deprived of his position at the University of Minnesota without being given due process. "Permit me to point out to this committee," he wrote, "that in one afternoon, on 15 minutes notice, I was deprived of my position, barred from my profession and branded a disloyal American, all without a hearing." Then the statement continued:

> The proceedings before the Board of Regents did not constitute a hearing. Those proceedings lacked every essential of a hearing as recognized by our law.
>
> What constitutes a hearing?
>
> First, notice of time set for appearance.
>
> Second, privilege of being represented by counsel.
>
> Third, right to have accusation stated in writing and be confronted by accusers.
>
> Fourth, right to subpoena witnesses and submit testimony.
>
> Not one of these privileges was accorded me.[30]

Near the end of the statement, Schaper made his accusation against Butler. "There is but one conclusion to draw from this case," he wrote, "that it was a travesty on American principles of justice and right and that the action was taken on the direct advice of Pierce Butler, who dominated the Board, took the leading part in hurling unfounded accusations at me, and finally advised the regents to refuse the hearing I demanded. . . ." In his final paragraph Schaper said that it must be plain to the subcommittee that Butler lacked "those fine qualities of even-tempered sense of justice that we look for in a Justice of the Supreme Court." Because of that, the former professor concluded, he felt it was his "duty as an American citizen, interested in the correct functioning of the courts and in the protection of defenseless individuals as well as the safeguarding of the great public interests, to take the time and trouble to come to Washington to lay this before the Senate. For on you now rests the grave responsibility of giving your advice and consent to the President in the pending appointment." [31]

Schaper thought he had written a good statement, yet he was apprehensive about going to the subcommittee hearing by himself. He wished that Senator-elect Shipstead were in Washington to accompany him. A little before 2:00 P.M. on December 13 Schaper entered the Senate Judiciary Committeeroom alone. The white-goateed Senator Nelson nodded to him. Senators Walsh and Cummins were also there. The hearings on the confirmation of Pierce Butler were ready to resume.

VI

Senator Nelson called the meeting to order. Senator Walsh asked Schaper if he had the statement he had released to the press right after his dismissal in 1917. Schaper produced the release, and it was made a part of the record. Walsh then asked if Schaper had anything further to offer. "Yes," said the former professor as he took out his prepared statement, "I desire to submit a brief statement if I may have the privilege of reading it to the committee. It is a few pages." Walsh said that Schaper had better just leave it with the committee, unless he had something further to add.[32]

Schaper was struck by Walsh's words; he would not get to read the statement he had so laboriously prepared. He felt angry and very much alone. The senators, he felt, were hostile to him. Yes, he had something further to add. He wanted to say:

> I would not be human if I could entirely overlook the fact that this man [Butler] dealt me a cruel, crushing blow, in an irregular and unfair manner. However, I hope that I am man enough, and a good enough American to be able to discriminate between injury he did me personally, and the deeper significance to the nation of the elevation of this

man to the high office and sacred trust of an Associate Justice of the Supreme Court.

It is evident that an impossible struggle is now going on in this country for economic power. On one side stands the amassed corporate wealth of the nation backed by the best brains, enlisted in its service and enjoying its bounties. On the other side are the great toiling masses, the workers in the tenements or small cottages, the farmers on their limited acres, the small business man in his store, bank, shop or factory. The question is who shall control the government and enjoy its fostering care and its special privileges? Shall corporate wealth and its beneficiaries control the government and use that power largely for their own benefit or shall the masses regain that control and use it largely in their interest?

This question was eliminated from the campaign of 1920 by the adroit manipulation of the nominating conventions and selection of candidates. In 1922 the struggle was precipitated in some of the western states and its results are so plain that only the politically blind can fail to see them. In 1924 the issue will have become nation-wide.[33]

All this and more he wanted to say. But, he thought, what was the use? These men were not in the proper frame of mind to listen to what he had to offer, much less heed it. Besides, there was no one there to support him. So Schaper stiffly said to Walsh: "There is nothing further." "Just leave the statement," said Senator Walsh, "and we will consider it." Schaper said he had some other documents, and Walsh told him that he might leave them too.* "Is that all?" asked

* One of the documents Schaper left with the subcommittee was a letter written by Albert W. Rankin, a retired professor of education at the University of Minnesota. Rankin stated that as a member of the Committee on Academic Freedom at the University he had learned, "from reliable sources, that it was the habit of Pierce Butler to issue orders to the University president directing him to dismiss, or fail to recommend, such persons as had fallen under Mr. Butler's displeasure because of their political or economic views." The retired professor also asserted that Butler was "an aggressive and overbearing bully," a man not fit for the Supreme Court. Rankin to Shipstead, Dec. 10, 1922, Butler Confirmation Papers.

Walsh. "That is all, Senator," answered Schaper. "You will be excused then, Professor," said Senator Nelson.[34]

Schaper was crushed. He had been before the subcommittee less than ten minutes, and he did not get to read his statement. He came out of the committeeroom "with face flushed, and left the Capitol immediately." [35]

After Schaper left the committeeroom, Senator Nelson began reading aloud some of the documents he had collected in the Schaper case since the subcommittee had last met. He read the resolution of the Board of Regents dismissing Schaper and a letter from President Coffman's secretary concerning the matter. Walsh thought that the letter from the University of Minnesota, as read by Nelson, did not show that Schaper was named by the Public Safety Commission as a pro-German. Nelson then read from McGee's affidavit, which dealt with that point. Cummins was still unsatisfied. "[T]he only point that I regarded as of value the other day," he told his colleagues, "was that the Board of Regents, or the president of the University, in dismissing the man, referred to a document which the professor claims was not in existence. That was the only point that I felt in the least interested in." The following exchange then occurred:

THE CHAIRMAN: We are not going to retry that matter.

SENATOR WALSH: No, as to whether he was loyal or was not loyal.

SENATOR CUMMINS: Or to review the action of the Board of Regents. That is perfectly ridiculous to me.

THE CHAIRMAN: Yes.

SENATOR CUMMINS: But if Mr. Butler was a party to a statement that recited a thing that did not exist, and that had been created for the purpose of putting him [Schaper] out—[36]

Senator Walsh saw Cummins' point and set out to determine from the documents gathered by Nelson whether there was any basis for it. He compared the resolution dismissing Schaper and McGee's affidavit, and pointed out that McGee said such a communication had been sent by the Commission of Public Safety to the regents. Senator Cummins was still not convinced, for he had before him McGee's letter to the regents, dated July 13, 1917, which referred to disloyal professors at the university without specifically mentioning Schaper. Walsh then read a statement that had been attached to McGee's letter of July 13, 1917. The statement had been made to the commission by an undisclosed informant and charged there were disloyal professors in the University's German department. Carefully, Senator Walsh read the last sentence of the statement to his colleagues: "There are two other rabid pro-Germans in official positions in the University —Dean Owre* and W. A. Schaper." Other documents in the subcommittee's files corroborated the fact that the Board of Regents had acted on a report from the Commission of Public Safety that Schaper was pro-German. Thus it was clear that both Schaper and Lind had been mistaken; the senators were convinced that Butler and the other regents had acted honorably in the matter.[37] †

Walsh then read Schaper's press statement to the subcommittee. Cummins reiterated that the wisdom of the regents' decision was beyond the scope of their inquiry. Walsh agreed. "It is sufficient to say that they had grounds upon which to proceed," Cummins added, "and it would be absurd to claim that Butler would not be a decent Associate Justice of the Supreme Court because he joined in turning him out; and you will find that they will not make any use of that. In any argument they make before the Senate on this matter, they will carefully avoid any of that sort of stuff." [38]

The subcommittee then took up the charges concerning Professor Gray. Senator Nelson read a long telegram from Butler that stated he was not a member of the committee of

* Professor Alfred Owre, poet, pacifist, and collector of cloisonné, was dean of the dental school at the University of Minnesota. When the University supplied Nelson with a copy of the statement from the Commission of Public Safety, it deleted Owre's name at Pierce, Jr.'s suggestion because the Board of Regents had cleared him of the disloyalty charge.

† Schaper never saw the document in question and apparently went to his grave believing it never existed.

the Board of Regents that decided Gray was unsuitable for the deanship of Minnesota's new business school and had no more to do with the matter than any other member of the board, that he never appeared before Gray when he was an examiner for the Interstate Commerce Commission, that he never lodged any complaints with members of the commission against Gray, and that the statements that he injured or was hostile to Gray at the university because of his work with the commission were false and unjustified. Nelson then read a letter from I.C.C. Commissioner B. H. Meyer that corroborated most of the statements made by Butler. When Nelson finished, he said, "I think that disposes of the matter." Senator Walsh agreed. The subcommittee heard one more witness, C. F. Staples, of the Bureau of Valuation, whose testimony also corroborated the information given by Butler.[39]

Senator Walsh reverted to the Schaper matter, pointing out that Schaper charged that Butler was individually responsible for his dismissal. "There were eleven out of twelve members of the Board of Regents present when Schaper was dismissed," answered Nelson, "and it was unanimous." Senator Cummins felt that the only matter left was the Twin City Rapid Transit Company charge. "He was attorney for the company, that is all," said Nelson. "There was a suggestion," Walsh said, "that if some of these witnesses had time to get here, they might make a showing." "There was no suggestion of that," answered Nelson. Walsh was not so sure, but he conceded that all the witnesses could testify to was that Butler did no more than represent the company in court.[40]

Nelson then produced a telegram from Pierce Butler, Jr. that quoted Felix Frankfurter as stating he had no information of any kind concerning Butler's confirmation and that he was not involved directly or indirectly in opposing Butler. Nelson also produced a wire from someone at the University of Illinois, saying a member of his staff had important evidence and asking that the subcommittee's recommendation be delayed. The Senator supposed it concerned Dietrichson, and there was no occasion to delay on his account. Senator

Walsh said that the man from Butte, who had charged that Butler was "a criminal conspirator," had been located and there was no substance in his charge.[41]

The final exchange of the hearings occurred between Senators Cummins and Walsh:

SENATOR CUMMINS: There is but one thing in it all, and that is, that Butler has made up his mind in regard to railroad valuations, and that he is not a good man to put on the Supreme Court bench, on that account. . . . I have been thoroughly familiar with that work all the way through. They had to settle certain general principles with regard to valuation. Butler was the railroad lawyer. I have four briefs that he filed, and in those briefs he set forth his views about valuation of public utility properties very clearly, and very forcibly, and it of course could not be contended that he had not reached a conclusion with regard to these matters. But I, at least, would not feel that there ought to be any reluctance about admitting that if that disqualifies a lawyer from taking a place on the Supreme Court bench, then he is disqualified. But I do not think it does, and I am perfectly willing to make the report.

SENATOR WALSH: I feel that he is disqualified to act in those cases, and I am sure that he thinks so, himself.

SENATOR CUMMINS: I did not use the word "disqualified" in that sense. I am speaking about its disqualifying him for a place on the Supreme Court bench.

SENATOR WALSH: I do not think anything like that. Of course we all have some very definite opinions in these matters.

SENATOR CUMMINS: Yes; there would be very few lawyers of any prominence who would not be disqualified. It is very hard to draw a line as to just where the intimacy of a lawyer with his client disqualifies him, generally speaking.[42]

The subcommittee adjourned, its decision unanimous that the nomination of Pierce Butler should be confirmed.

VII

Senator Nelson had not said much during the hearings, but he was well prepared to answer any of the charges against Butler. He had elaborate files on the man from Butte, Rypins, Butler's participation in the John Meints and Minneapolis

Steel Machinery cases, and other matters not raised in the hearings. Findings concerning the major charges against Butler were made by the subcommittee and reported to the parent committee with its recommendation to confirm the nomination of Butler.[43]

Senator Sterling discussed the Butler matter with one of the members of the subcommittee and learned that Butler's conduct as a regent of the University of Minnesota was considered and that he was no more responsible for the dismissal of the professors than any other member of the Board of Regents. This Sterling reported to Professor Berdahl at the University of Illinois. "The subcommittee," he added, "will report favorably to the full Judiciary Committee on Monday and I expect that the full committee will adopt the report of the subcommittee and in turn report in favor of confirmation by the Senate." [44]

Taft had the same expectation. Discussing the matter over breakfast with Butler's partner Mitchell a few days after the second hearing, the Chief Justice was optimistic. He said he had arranged to have a full meeting of the committee on December 18—"at least a full meeting of Republicans." On the 18th the Senate Judiciary Committee, with Borah, Norris, Shields, and Reed of Missouri absent, met and voted unanimously to recommend the confirmation of Pierce Butler.[45]

Chapter 8

CONFIRMATION

Now all that stood between Pierce Butler and the High Court were Robert M. LaFollette, George Norris, and other senators who would join them. LaFollette said he would fight Butler's confirmation to the bitter end, which meant there would be a fight on the floor of the Senate.

I

That LaFollette would lead the fight in the Senate against Butler's confirmation was not surprising; the appointment of Butler symbolized what LaFollette had spent his entire political career fighting. Ten years before, in his *Autobiography,* he said that the supreme issue in politics was *"the encroachment of the powerful few upon the rights of the many."* Now, as he saw it, the powerful few—the economic elite of the nation—were putting one of their own men on the Supreme Court.[1]

But more than that underlay LaFollette's opposition to Butler. Butler's friends and supporters in Minnesota had long been LaFollette's enemies. In 1917 the Minnesota Commission of Public Safety had charged LaFollette with being a teacher of disloyalty and sedition for a speech he made in St. Paul to the Nonpartisan League, and the commission had petitioned the Senate to expel him. Senator Kellogg personally presented the petition to the Senate, and though the charge was subsequently dismissed, LaFollette never forgave Kellogg for his part in the affair. In the summer of 1922, when LaFollette attacked the Supreme Court in a speech before the A.F. of L. convention in Cincinnati and suggested that the Court's power of judicial review be curtailed, Kellogg rose in the Senate to brand LaFollette's speech as "subversive of representative government, the liberties of the people, and the guarantees of the Bill of Rights." That fall LaFollette campaigned against Kellogg in Minnesota, attacking him more bitterly than he had any other antagonist. Referring to Kellogg's stooped shoulders, LaFollette said the Minnesota Senator had bowed obsequiously to his masters, the corporations, for so long that "God Almighty has given him a hump on his back—crouching, cringing, un-American, unmanly." This uncharitable and uncharacteristic remark showed the depth of LaFollette's feeling about Kellogg and what he represented. The irony of it all to LaFollette was that though Kellogg went to crushing defeat in the election, he was still able thereafter to help Butler—a man like himself—to the Supreme Court. Thus Butler, like Kellogg, had to be opposed.[2]

The fall of 1922 marked the return of LaFollette as a potent political force. Now that the war was over, less and less was said about his "war record." His smashing victory in Wisconsin demonstrated that he had the full confidence of his constituents, and his successful campaigning in behalf of Shipstead in Minnesota and Frazier in North Dakota demonstrated that LaFollette progressivism was popular. Soon after the election, LaFollette called for a conference of the progressives in Congress to plan legislative strategy. Thirteen senators and senators-elect and more than twenty-three members of the House attended the Progressive Conference on December 2.

It is almost certain that Butler's nomination was discussed at the conference. Both Shipstead and Schaper were present, and Samuel Gompers, who addressed the group, shortly thereafter wrote an editorial for the *American Federationist* denouncing Butler's nomination. The People's Legislative Service, which sponsored the conference, also gathered information to support the charges against Butler. If the senators at the conference agreed with LaFollette in his plan to oppose Butler, then the following progressives, in addition to LaFollette and Norris, were likely to vote against Butler's confirmation: Borah of Idaho, Brookhart of Iowa, Capper of Kansas, France of Maryland, Ladd of North Dakota, McNary of Oregon, Owen of Oklahoma, and Sheppard of Texas.[3]

Noting press reports that LaFollette and Norris intended to oppose confirming Butler, Taft wrote to Harding on December 4:

> I observe that LaFollette and Norris are about to attack Butler's nomination. This is not that they can prevent his confirmation, but it is part of the program they are deliberately setting out upon to attack you and the Court and the Constitution. The more blatant they make it, the better I think it will be to unite the conservative elements of the country to resist their plotting against our present social order, and I hope you will feel that the best way to deal with them is to hit them between the eyes by appointment of staunch friends of the Constitution who will do nothing to sap the pillars of our Government as they have weathered the storm of many assaults and vindicated the wisdom of our ancestors.[4]

Even LaFollette did not seriously believe that he could prevent Butler's confirmation; yet, win or lose, he felt the fight had to be made if for no other reason than to educate the public and show the people that again the powerful few were encroaching upon the rights of the many.[5]

Just before the Nelson subcommittee recommended Butler's confirmation, LaFollette received a telegram from Shipstead stating Gray was physically unable to travel and was reluctant to testify against Butler, but, if summoned by the subcommittee, he would come to Washington the following week. On December 13 LaFollette wrote to Nelson formally requesting that Gray be subpoenaed by the subcommittee, but it appears that Nelson received the letter after the subcommittee made its recommendation.[6]

On the same day, DeFord's editorial, which had been sent to LaFollette earlier, appeared in the *Washington Herald,* and LaFollette had it read into the record of the Senate, serving notice to his colleagues that he would fight Butler's confirmation when it came up for a vote. The editorial began with a series of questions: "What public service has Pierce Butler rendered? What is his real character? Whom has he served? Whom will he serve? Why was Pierce Butler selected to be a justice of that court which has become the most autocratic power in the world—a power that can nullify an act of Congress; a power whose decisions no other authority can overthrow?" It ended by saying that all the public knew about Butler was that he represented railroads before the I.C.C. "It is entirely honorable for a lawyer to have a railroad among his clients," it added, "but no lawyer selected and recommended by the railroads or by the public-service corporations should ever be made Justice of the United States Supreme Court." For that reason, it was important "to know who are Mr. Pierce Butler's real sponsors and what are his real character and his fitness for the place." [7]

The subcommittee's unanimous recommendation on December 13 to confirm Butler's nomination had been a setback for LaFollette. After that, there was practically no chance of stopping the confirmation except on the floor of the Senate. And things were moving quickly—too quickly for LaFollette; he needed more time to investigate the charges against Butler. On December 16 Shipstead wired Nelson, urging him to summon Professor Gray to testify before the Judiciary Committee in regard to the Texas Midland case, but that communication did not alter Nelson's decision to have the full committee vote on Butler's nomination on December 18. On the 18th, Professor Dietrichson sent LaFollette copies of Berdahl's correspondence with Senator Sterling and expressed the hope that a little more of the truth be brought out in regard to Butler's activities as regent at the

University of Minnesota. On the 20th Professor Gray wired LaFollette collect, explaining in detail his grievances against Butler. The same day, Professor Schaper sent the following telegram to the Wisconsin senator: "DO ALL YOU CAN TO DELAY CONFIRMATION UNTIL AFTER THE HOLIDAYS. HAVE ASSURANCE TODAY THAT A RESOLUTION WILL BE ADOPTED BY THE LEGISLATURE OPPOSING THE APPOINTMENT OF BUTLER. STORM OF OPPOSITION ALSO COMING FROM THE PEOPLE IN LETTERS AND TELEGRAMS IF THE DELAY IS SECURED. LETTER FOLLOWS." Schaper's hopes were up. "The fight on Butler is not over yet," he wrote to a friend the same day. "We laid the foundation for a real scrap. The case may yet become historic." And to LaFollette, the former professor wrote on the 21st: "We know that you and other progressive Senators will put up a good fight in the executive session." [8]

II

Senator Nelson pressed for an early vote on the confirmation. On December 20, when the Senate met in executive session, Nelson asked his colleagues to act on the Butler nomination. To his surprise, it was not LaFollette who rose to object, but Senator Robinson of Arkansas. Robinson said several senators who had expressed an intention to speak on the nomination were absent and asked that the matter be postponed so that they might have an opportunity to speak. Nelson discussed the matter with Robinson, and an informal agreement was reached to take up the matter the next day.[9]

When the Senate's action was reported to Taft, he was puzzled by Robinson's request to delay confirmation. Did that mean that Robinson was going to vote against it? That seemed improbable to Taft; his contacts with the Arkansas senator indicated that he was "a pretty good man," but the Ku Klux Klan was supposedly strong in Arkansas, and its attacks against Butler had been bitter. The real opposition, Taft still thought, would come from LaFollette. The Chief Justice felt LaFollette might want to make a long speech to delay confirmation without attempting to filibuster, "but the failure to show any facts justifying the complaints before the

Judiciary Committee, and the complete refutation of the charges which were presented, will leave him without much ammunition."[10]

At three o'clock on the afternoon of December 21 Senator Jones of Washington moved that the Senate consider executive business. The doors of the Senate were then closed for three hours and forty minutes. Although what occurred during that time was not officially reported, there is enough available evidence to reconstruct the action.

Senator Nelson spoke for almost an hour. Before him were the charges made by Shipstead, a biography of Butler, two telegrams from Butler, the letter from H. R. Leonard of the Twin Cities Producers Association endorsing Butler, letters from I.C.C. officials, and several documents relating the Schaper and Gray charges, including the report made by the Bureau of Investigation. After outlining the charges against Butler, Nelson discussed the Minnesota lawyer's qualifications for the Court. He said that Butler's practice was quite general and that neither he nor his firm was "exclusively bound to any client or group and they have always been able freely to accept or decline business offered." Nelson read the two telegrams from Butler dealing with his alleged corporate connections. Butler admitted representing railroads in valuation matters as a member of the Presidents' Conference Committee from 1913 to 1918, but pointed out that during all that time he remained in general practice with his firm and was always free to take or refuse any case. Indeed, said Nelson, Butler represented cooperative associations of farmers and producers, showing that he represented all kinds and classes of people, not just corporations.

Nelson then discussed the Schaper case, explaining that Schaper's charge was based, at least in part, on the mistaken notion that the University of Minnesota regents dismissed him on the basis of a nonexistent charge allegedly made by the Minnesota Commission of Public Safety. Nelson explained that the regents had in fact received from the commission a charge that Schaper was a pro-German. In regard to the Gray charge, Nelson pointed out that it was, according to undisputed evidence, based on misinformation. And in all of the cases involving professors at the University of Minnesota, Butler was just one member of the Board of Regents acting unanimously. In short, none of the charges against Butler stood up; the subcommittee, after careful consideration, reached that conclusion; the Judiciary Committee's recommendation for confirmation was unanimous; Butler was a high-type lawyer worthy of the Supreme Court; therefore his nomination should be confirmed.[11]

As Nelson spoke, Senator Walsh of Montana listened attentively. There was no doubt as to his vote: he would vote as he had in committee—for confirmation. But he was not happy with Butler's appointment; like LaFollette, he disagreed with Butler's economic philosophy. Yet as he listened to Nelson, Walsh could not help seeing similarities between himself and Butler. Both had been born in the Midwest; both were Irish Catholics; both had come from humble backgrounds; both had taught school before becoming lawyers; both had been successful trial lawyers; both were Democrats. Their personalities were also similar, and during the war Walsh had felt the same intense patriotism Butler manifested in the Schaper case. Indeed, though he was in sympathy with many of LaFollette's ideas, Walsh felt the Wisconsin senator should have been expelled from the Senate for his St. Paul speech in 1917. And there was something else—Robinson's request to delay the confirmation. Did the recent rise of the Ku Klux Klan have anything to do with it? Walsh genuinely feared the Klan and what it might do to the Democratic Party. When Nelson finished, Walsh rose and spoke in favor of confirming Butler.[12]

LaFollette was the last to speak. As Taft had suspected, the Wisconsin senator planned no filibuster. His strategy was to speak against Butler in the hope of convincing enough senators to refer the nomination back to the Judiciary Committee, where Gray, Dietrichson, and the others might still get their hearing. The senators had a pretty good idea of what LaFollette was going to say concerning the Supreme Court. Three months before, when Senators Kellogg and

Edge attacked his A.F. of L. speech on the Court, he read the speech word for word to his colleagues, saying: "The actual ruler of the American people is the Supreme Court of the United States." The law, he added, and even the Constitution are what those "nine men" say it is, and a bare majority of them have overridden the will of the people to suit "their peculiar economic and political views." But if LaFollette was to convince his colleagues, he would have to say more than this; he would have to present evidence that raised at least substantial doubt about Butler's fitness.[13]

LaFollette spoke more than an hour. Though his precise words were not recorded, his position on Butler was. In substance, he said:

> The appointment of Pierce Butler has done much to shake further the faith of the American people in the Supreme Court of the United States. A study of his record leaves one with a conviction that the highest court in the land is being builded into a final citadel for special privilege in general, and special railroad privilege in particular.
>
> During the past few years there have been very few cases of importance affecting the valuation of railroad property in which Mr. Butler has not appeared before the Interstate Commerce Commission for the great railroad systems. The stake involved in the railroad cases is enormous. The railroads are contending for a valuation upon a basis, which, if allowed, will absorb the water in their book valuation amounting to upwards of eight billion dollars.
>
> The railroad companies are entitled to be represented by counsel in these cases. It is to be expected that they will employ trained railroad lawyers in that service. But I believe that it is shocking to have the President select such an attorney for appointment to the Supreme Court. Especially so when it is remembered that these valuation cases will finally be reviewed by that court. Even though Mr. Butler shall not take part when these cases are heard and determined by the Supreme Court, his intimate and daily association with the sitting judges, cannot fail—all unconsciously upon the part of either—to exert an unwholesome influence in the public mind regarding the decisions of that court in those cases.

LaFollette argued that Butler's entire record stamped him as a man lacking a judicial temperament. In support of the assertion, LaFollette cited only Professor Gray's case. Armed with the research of Basil Manley, of the People's Legislative Service, and the telegram from Gray, LaFollette's facts, as usual, were accurate, but all the charge amounted to was that after Gray acted as examiner in a case in which Butler was counsel of record, Gray was asked to resign as head of his department at the University of Minnesota; and, to maintain his self-respect, Gray resigned, "as it was clearly anticipated he would do by Pierce Butler and his associate regents." [14]

Among the senators carefully listening to LaFollette was Thomas Sterling, who was unimpressed. He later said that most of the senators thought LaFollette's case was unusually weak in that nothing was said that affected the qualifications of Butler for the Supreme Court.[15] When LaFollette finished, no other senator spoke in behalf of or against confirmation. LaFollette then moved that the nomination of Butler be recommitted to the Judiciary Committee. The motion was defeated 63 to 7, with twenty-six senators not voting. The vote on confirmation followed, resulting in 61 yeas, 8 nays, and 27 abstentions. In addition to LaFollette and Norris, Senators George and Harris of Georgia, Heflin of Alabama, Norbeck of South Dakota, Sheppard of Texas, and Trammell of Florida voted against confirmation. Brookhart of Iowa announced that if he had not been paired with Calder of New York, he would have voted against confirmation. Senator Norris moved that the votes taken be made public. By unanimous consent the rules were suspended and the votes were reported.[16]

As the senators left the chamber, the Clerk of the Senate recorded: "So, the nomination of Pierce Butler as Associate Justice of the Supreme Court of the United States was confirmed." Reporters asked LaFollette what he thought of the Senate's action. "It speaks for itself," he said, and walked off. Asked the same question, Nelson smiled and told the newsmen: "In the words of Napoleon, the Lord was on the side of the strongest battalions." [17]

III

By and large the press was gratified with Butler's confirmation. The *New York Times* said it was tired of hearing "continual bleating" about corporation lawyers. "Mr. LaFollette and the others, along with our omniscient 'intellectuals' don't want Judges with a judicial mind. They want Judges committed by belief and habit to seeing only the side of labor cases and cases against corporations." [18]

The *St. Paul Dispatch* was happy to see that the attacks against Butler received little support in the Senate. "Why," the *Dispatch* asked, "should an attorney be selected for the Supreme Bench who has never risen above mediocrity? . . . Why should any but a 100 per cent American sit on the bench of the highest court?" And the newspaper concluded: "Right-mindedness, intelligence and patriotism in the Senate voted solidly for the confirmation. This should be wholly satisfactory to Mr. Butler and we are sure it is to the country at large." [19]

The *Philadelphia Evening Bulletin* saw Butler's confirmation as the happy ending of the American success story. "The Supreme Court of the United States," it said, "knows no class, no creed, and in the accession to its high honor, of the boy who went from the immigrant's farm in the opening Northwest to the meagre offerings of a country school-house, and continued to work his way through college, fitted himself for the bar and step by step made his way to distinction, there is a story typical of the land and its opportunity, worthy to be written in the copy books of the boys and girls coming up into future citizenship." [20]

The *St. Louis Post-Dispatch,* on the other hand, was bitterly critical. It regarded Butler's appointment as "a calamity." Butler's representation of corporations, it said, prejudiced his "eligibility as a guardian of the public interest," but that, in itself, did not disqualify him for the Court. His qualities of mind, however, did; and these the *Post-Dispatch* saw as "bigotry, intolerance, narrowness, and partisanism." The editorial concluded with the statement that the appointment, at the beginning of Butler's service on the Court, "looks . . . like one of the most damaging acts of stupidity achieved by the Harding administration." [21]

IV

During the holidays, the St. Paul bar honored Pierce Butler, the only Minnesota lawyer to go to the Supreme Court, with a dinner. Even James Manahan, Butler's former friend and antagonist, could not resist the temptation to make a speech in honor of the new Justice.[22] The highlight of the occasion, however, was a tribute to Butler written by Chief Justice Taft, in which he said:

> The duty imposed on the President of selecting members of the Supreme Court of the United States is a difficult one, far more difficult than that of the Premier and Lord Chancellor of England in selecting the Judges of their Supreme Court of the Judicature. There that part of the Bar from which the selections must be made is a comparatively small body, the members of which are constantly engaged in the courts at London and at Westminster, so that their comparative excellence and qualifications for promotion are clearly seen and known of all men. In this country there is no such division of the Bar, and no such centralization of talent, enabling an appointing authority easily to select. Mr. Butler fulfills every definition and requirement of a barrister. His work has been in the trial of cases, not for one class of clients, and not for another, but for any who solicited his service in reputable advocacy. He has won a position for himself in the Northwest that entitles him to be called one of the great leaders of the Bar of that section, especially familiar with the principles of those fields of law in which the Supreme Court of the United States has to administer justice. He has come from the lowest rung of the ladder and has steadily climbed to the top. He has that sympathy, therefore, with all sorts and conditions of men, and that sense of proportion, that common sense, which is so indispensable to

the proper working of the judicial mind in dealing with the affairs of the people. It was a most fortunate circumstance for all of us that the President had the opportunity and exercised the judgment to choose Mr. Butler for the Supreme Court.[23]

A few days later Butler was standing before the Supreme Court. The Chief Justice had just announced that Mr. Butler was ready to take his oath of office. As the Clerk read the commission, Butler looked at the bench. On the far left he saw an empty chair, then the men who would be his colleagues—Brandeis, Van Devanter, McKenna, Taft, Holmes, McReynolds, Sutherland—and finally another empty chair. When the Clerk finished, the Chief Justice administered the oath; then Mr. Justice Butler was escorted to the chair on Brandeis' right.

Part Three: Why

Chapter 9

TRANSACTIONS

How can Pierce Butler's appointment to the Supreme Court be explained? This chapter explores the question generally; the following two chapters take it up specifically. Although such questions are extremely complex, it is surprising to find that they are often answered with deceptive simplicity.

I

Self-action is a typical answer. In self-actional explanations, persons and things are viewed as acting under their own power; that is, A causes B.[1] Early in man's history, physical phenomena were explained in this way; thunder, lightning, and rain were attributed to gods who caused them. Today, such explanations are untenable. "It took Jupiter Pluvius to produce a rainstorm for the early Romans, whereas modern science takes its *pluvius* free from Jupiter." [2] But explanation of political phenomena is not yet free of Jupiter. Consider, for example, the following so-called "ready explanation" of Butler's appointment:

> Harding's choice of Butler points to three motives. First, the President liked his record of almost four decades of service in the law and in public life; second, and probably

> most important, Harding found Butler's ideological ultra-conservatism to be entirely sympathetic . . . ; and third, the President deemed it politically advantageous to appoint a man who combined the here seemingly desirable factor of being a "safe" Democrat . . . with that of being a member of a then "unrepresented" minority religion (Roman Catholic) and a native Minnesotan. . . .[3]

Here motive appears to reign as Jupiter; Butler's appointment is viewed as the result of Harding's self-action. In light of the data presented in this study, such an explanation seems untenable.

Interaction is another typical answer. In interactional explanations, persons or things are viewed as coming into contact with each other, thereby causing events; that is, A interacts with B, causing C.[4] Justice Robert H. Jackson provides a good example of an interactional explanation: "Manton had come within an ace of being appointed to the Supreme Court at the time of the appointment of Pierce Butler. I understand that it was only due to the intervention of Chief Justice Taft that this appointment was prevented."[5] The statement has a certain plausibility because Taft's interactions with Harding clearly appear to be connected with the demise of Manton's candidacy and Butler's appointment; yet it omits a great deal and is, at best, an inadequate explanation.

Transaction, though an atypical answer, seems more tenable than either self-action or interaction.[6] In transactional explanations, events are understood within the situation in which they arise, and are explained in terms of postulated relationships among activities. The phenomena of man perceiving, describing, and otherwise acting in process with his environment are observed in fields of connected activity called *transactions*. The prefix *trans* means that the fields of activity are seen in overview just as they appear in time and space. They are not broken up into their so-called component parts, such as perceiver and thing perceived, for it seems meaningless to speak of a thing perceived without taking into account the perceiver. In other words, perception can be understood only within the situation—that is, the transaction—in which it arises. And just as perceivers and things perceived cannot be separated in perception, neither can perceiving, describing, nor acting be separated from each other, for all are facets of a single, common process, and ultimately must be understood together in that process. Thus the first step toward a tenable explanation of Butler's appointment is to view the activity comprising it as a transaction.[7]

II

Perception is an important activity in all human transactions and must itself be understood in transactional terms because:

1. The facts of perception always present themselves through concrete persons acting within transactions.
2. Within transactions, perceiving is always done by a particular person from his own unique position in space and time and with his own combination of experiences and values.
3. Within transactions, the perceiving person, through perceiving, creates for himself his own psychological environment that he tends to believe has "existence" independent of his experience.[8]

Each man, then, lives in his own perceptual world, and for him that is the "real" world. The recognition of that fact is important in political analysis, for then apparently divergent perceptions of the same phenomena are intelligible. Butler, for example, was perceived as a great man by Judge Sanborn, whereas he was perceived as an unfair bully by Professor Schaper. Both perceptions were true perceptions and can be understood in terms of the values and experiences of Sanborn and Schaper, especially of their experiences with Butler.

Because of the creative aspect of perception, facts and values cannot be separated completely in political analysis. A person's values and experiences are lenses through which he perceives phenomena. Taft and Van Devanter saw their activity in behalf of Butler as clearly in the public interest. To them, the appointment of Judge Manton to the Supreme Court would have been a national tragedy, and even if someone else were appointed, they still would have preferred Butler because they knew he shared their values, especially on matters touching the Constitution; hence his appointment was good for the country. Just as clearly LaFollette, Norris, Schaper, and Shipstead saw Butler's appointment as contrary to the public interest. To them, a man who had spent a lifetime serving the interests of corporations, and who acted as Butler did when he was a regent of the University of Minnesota, held values contrary to theirs and for that reason could not be trusted to interpret the Constitution; hence his appointment was bad for the country. Thus perceptions of Butler and the public interest by both groups were strongly colored by their values.

Perception and description, though conceptually distinct, are so intimately linked in transactions that at times they appear identical. This is particularly true in situations in which one considers events in which he has not participated, for then description is usually the only evidence of perception. Sanborn, therefore, is said to have perceived Butler as a great man because he used those words in describing him.

Yet there may be discrepancies between perceiving and describing, even when both activities are performed by the same person. When that occurs, perception, it appears, tends to conform with description. In October, 1922 Taft's perception of Butler was changing. Undoubtedly Sanborn's strong letter in behalf of Butler raised Taft's estimate of the St. Paul lawyer. Nevertheless, even after the letter, Taft still ranked Davis and Butler as his first and second choices, respectively. Yet when Taft went on record for Butler in his letter to Harding, he described Butler as an equal of Davis. When one views Taft's letter within the situation, it appears that Taft, having given up on Davis, was seeking to persuade Harding that Butler was the best possible appointee; hence the words Taft used to describe Butler were probably an exaggeration of his perception of Butler at the time. But thereafter Taft apparently believed the man he had described to Harding was in fact Butler. In other words, perception tended to conform to description.

Taft had more than a fair idea of Harding's perceptual

world. He knew in a general way Harding's experiences and values, and he also knew Harding's perception of a suitable nominee to take Justice Day's place. Thus, when Taft went on record for Butler, he skillfully described his candidate to fit Harding's perception.* As a lawyer, said Taft, Butler ranked with John W. Davis, whom Harding had said he was willing to appoint. Butler was not only a Democrat, but a "Democrat of the Cleveland type," that is, a good Democrat, not a Wilson-Tammany Democrat like Manton.† Butler was not only a Catholic, but "was a great friend of Archbishop Ireland," who had been known as a good Republican. Butler was of the proper age, "about fifty-four, certainly under sixty"—more than ten years older than Manton but still young enough. Butler "would make a great Justice of our court," for he possessed "the rugged character and force of Justice Miller"—a man of humble origin like Butler who, in his day, was a giant in the Court. And Butler was a self-made man who "builded himself up from the bottom" and a solid citizen —"one of the regents of the Minnesota University." This description of Butler was only the first part of Taft's presentation of his candidate. The second part consisted of the support stimulated directly or indirectly by Taft. That support corroborated and reinforced Taft's description of Butler. Since there were virtually no contrary perceptions of Butler conveyed to Harding prior to the nomination, he undoubtedly believed that Butler was the man described by his supporters.

* Taft's description of Butler varied somewhat depending on the person to whom he was writing. To the practicing lawyer J. M. Dickinson, Taft gave this description of Butler: 'He is an all-around, hard-fighting, thorough lawyer, and is a Cleveland Democrat." Nov. 2, 1922, Taft Papers. To the elder statesman Elihu Root, Taft described Butler in these terms: "Pierce Butler is the leader of the bar of the Northwest, in my judgment. He's a Democrat and a Catholic. He is a great broadminded, hard-working, big man, with a very wide experience in the conduct of cases. He has been on all sides. . . . His practice brings him into the class of English barristers." Nov. 16, 1922, *ibid.*

† In 1911, when President Taft was considering William T. Pigott, a Democrat, for the federal bench in Montana, he described him to the editor of the *Anaconda Standard* as follows: "He is a Democrat of the Cleveland type." Taft to J. H. Durston, Nov. 22, 1911, *ibid.*

That, however, is not to explain the nomination of Pierce Butler to the Supreme Court simply in terms of Taft's structuring Harding's perception of him. To be sure, that appears to be a part of the explanation, but far more must be taken into account. Indeed, the entire transaction—the manifold connected perceptions, descriptions, and other activity of Harding, Daugherty, Taft, Van Devanter, Butler, LaFollette, and scores of others—must be mapped and specified. Only when that is done can an adequate explanation be ventured.

III

Although the subject of this study is a transaction that occurred during the latter part of 1922, the study itself is the result of another transaction—the research transaction—that occurred in the early 1960's. In that transaction the researcher's perceptions were of the utmost importance, and underlying those perceptions were his own values and experiences. What was presented as the Butler appointment transaction was what the researcher perceived it to be, and that is something conceptually distinct from what happened in 1922. That should surprise no one; it is true of all attempts to report past activity. The psychoanalyst Ranyard West put it this way: "We do not see things and people as they are—first of all because of our common prejudices, and secondly because of the special prejudices of each one of us. This mechanism is constantly at work in society, falsifying all situations of life where our emotions are strongly engaged, giving us our predilections in government and our prejudices of class and creed and race and colour. So that in the very fact of labelling an experience we must needs go on and identify it with some fantasy or other, and docket it accordingly." [9] The Jesuit Teilhard de Chardin also recognized the problem. "During the last fifty years or so," he wrote in 1947, "the investigations of science have proved beyond all doubt that there is no fact which exists in pure isolation, but that every experience, however objective it may seem, inevitably becomes enveloped in a complex of assumptions as soon as the scientist attempts to explain it." [10]

Therefore, in reporting past experience, the researcher is necessarily involved in a creative process. To seemingly chaotic activity, he seeks to give order—but it is his order, based on his assumptions. He probes another's experience and, at times, finds he is probing the wellsprings of his own experience as well. To be sure, he seeks to be objective, but that is more difficult than simply resolving to keep an open mind. He must refrain from attempting to enter the transaction he is studying; that is, he must refrain from reperceiving the phenomena in the transaction under inquiry as though he were one of the transactors, for his own reperceptions are irrelevant. The values and experiences of the transactors, however, are relevant, and if the researcher studies them, he has some basis for understanding the world as they perceived it. After he has done that, he is equipped to study the activity in which he is interested and to seek the connecting thread that makes it a transaction. Yet no matter how objective he tries to be, or how diligently he seeks to report relevant details, he can never fully recapture the original transaction; he must settle, as must his readers, for a counterfeit of his own making, the product of the research transaction—in this case, the present study.

IV

Beyond the original and research transactions, there is yet another transaction—the reading transaction. In that transaction the reader views the preceding transactions in terms of his values and experiences. The reader, like the researcher, is involved in a creative process. Different readers will perceive this study differently. Past perceptions of Taft, Harding, Daugherty, Butler, and others mentioned in the study will, to some extent, color present perceptions arising out of it, as will attitudes towards the Supreme Court, the Roman Catholic Church, corporations, conservatives, liberals, and so forth. The time when the study is read will also be significant. Today, for example, when the Supreme Court is an instrument of the government and its decisions often turn upon the vote of a single Justice, a study such as this will not have the same meaning it would have in an era when the Supreme Court is less important in American government.

The preceding discussion is applicable to virtually all scholarship in the field of politics and not just to this study. The superiority of transactional explanation and the distinction between original, research, and reading transactions may be obvious to many readers; yet seldom is the subject mentioned, even obliquely. Hence laboring the obvious is perhaps pardonable. At any rate, it appears necessary for what follows.

Chapter 10

INFLUENCE

Lasswell's dictum, "The study of politics is the study of influence and the influential," [1] is now a commonplace in political science. That there is more to the study of politics than the study of influence is conceded, yet influence remains one of the most fruitful concepts in the explanation of political phenomena—at least to the extent that it is adequately understood. Although in recent years a substantial literature has developed concerning the meaning and measurement of influence, seldom has the concept been viewed in transactional terms.[2]

I

The term influence denotes a specific relationship among activities in a transaction. Activity *x* occurs (Taft asks Butler to seek the support of the Archbishop of St. Paul); thereafter activity *y* occurs (Butler seeks the support of the Archbishop). For purposes of analysis, activities *x* and *y* may be postulated in an influence relationship:

→Taft—*x*→Butler—*y*→

Whether or not there was such a relationship depends upon whether *x* was connected with *y* in the sense that it contributed to the occurrence of *y*.[3] In order to demonstrate such a connection, it is necessary to show:

1. That *x* occurred prior to *y*.
2. That, *ceteris paribus,* if *x* had not occurred, *y* would not have occurred.

The first requirement can be easily shown; the second requirement can be shown only with difficulty and sometimes not at all. Often when one is dealing with a postulated influence relationship arising out of a historical situation, as distinguished from an experimental situation, the best that can be done is to make an informed guess in terms of probability.[4]

Assuming both requirements are met, an influence relationship is said to be present, but that is not to say that *x* caused *y*. There are two reasons for this:

1. *x* is part of a complex of activities and has no independent status. The same is true of *y*. Both can be understood only in terms of the transaction of which they are a part, and not simply in terms of each other.
2. Though *x* may be said to be connected with *y* in the sense that it contributes to *y*'s occurrence, other activities are similarly connected with *y*.

To illustrate the second reason, it will be recalled that even before Taft asked Butler to seek the aid of the Archbishop, Van Devanter (with Taft's knowledge and approval) wrote Judge Sanborn and suggested that the Archbishop be approached in Butler's behalf. Thereafter Sanborn impressed upon Mitchell the importance of the Archbishop's support; undoubtedly Sanborn's advice was reported to Butler by Mitchell. Also it is likely that Butler discussed the matter with Mitchell and Pierce, Jr. before acting. Thus, although Taft's activity *x* appears to have contributed to the occurrence of *y*, the activities of Sanborn and others may also have been necessary for *y*'s occurrence; if they were, then they, too, were connected with *y* as an integral part of the influence relationship, which must now be postulated as follows:

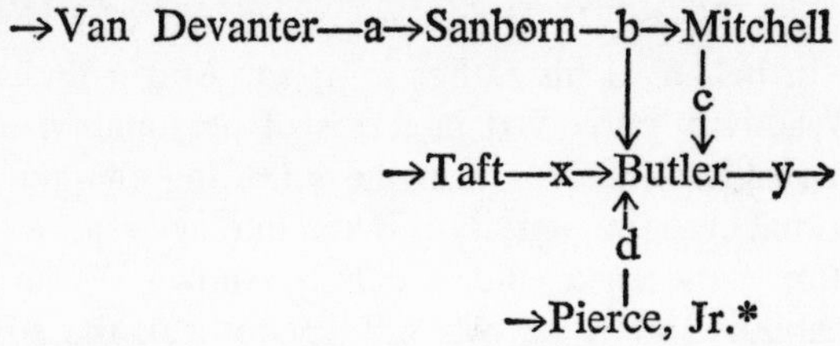

```
→Van Devanter—a→Sanborn—b→Mitchell
                              |       |
                              |       c
                              ↓       ↓
                     →Taft—x→Butler—y→
                              ↑
                              d
                              |
                        →Pierce, Jr.*
```

In addition to the activity on the surface of influence relationships—the *x*'s and *y*'s—there is other activity that must also be taken into account if the requisite connections between *x*'s and *y*'s are to be shown. That activity is designated *background activity* to differentiate it from *surface activity,* which occurs only within the time-space boundaries of the transaction. In a given transaction, most background activity occurs prior in time to any surface activity in the transaction.

Nevertheless background activity is a part of the transaction, at least for explanatory purposes, for it is connected with surface activity in that it has structured the assumptions, expectancies, and intrapersonal relationships of the transactors. It includes social and cultural experience that makes for a man's values and his perception of the world; for example, Van Devanter, a product of the late nineteenth century American frontier, perceiving Butler, a similar product, as an ideal appointment to the Supreme Court. It includes past perceptions impinging on present perceptions; for example, Butler's perceptions of Taft through the years as circuit judge, Secretary of War, President, and Chief Justice blending with his perception of the man who asked him to seek the support of his archbishop. It includes myriad activities that constitute friendship relationships; for example, the conversations, the dinners, and other activities in which Taft and Butler participated together during the Grand Trunk Arbitration in 1921. It includes the activities that make up filial relationships; for example, the activities of a lifetime involving Butler

* The perceptions of the transactors are an integral part of the postulated influence relationship shown above. Hence the discussion in Chapter 9, II, is directly applicable here.

and his son Pierce, Jr. that were connected with the latter's activity in behalf of his father in 1922. And it includes patterns of activity perceived in terms of personality, a subject that is considered at length in the following chapter.

When background activity is taken into account, a plausible connection between *x* and *y* can be shown. From what is known about Butler, he was not apt to seek the support of his church to attain political office—at least not under ordinary circumstances. But the request to do so from Chief Justice Taft, whose friendship Butler highly valued, together with the same advice from Judge Sanborn, whom he also highly esteemed, constituted something out of the ordinary, and Butler acted as requested. If Butler's action was closely connected with Taft's and Sanborn's activity, it is not surprising; men often do things for friends they would not do otherwise. In seeking to explain the occurrence of *y*, it seems that the friendship between Taft and Butler and Sanborn and Butler was important, and without evidence of activity from which those relationships could be inferred, it would be difficult, if not impossible, to demonstrate that there were connections between the activities of Taft and Sanborn and Butler's subsequent seeking of support from his archbishop.

If background activities are shown as $(a^{1,2,3 \cdots j})$, a more accurate depiction of the postulated influence relationship being considered is:

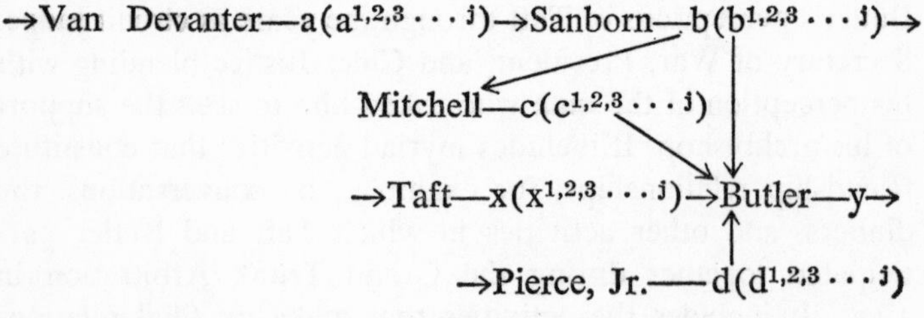

→Van Devanter—$a(a^{1,2,3 \cdots j})$→Sanborn—$b(b^{1,2,3 \cdots j})$→

Mitchell—$c(c^{1,2,3 \cdots j})$

→Taft—$x(x^{1,2,3 \cdots j})$→Butler—y→

→Pierce, Jr.—$d(d^{1,2,3 \cdots j})$

II

With the foregoing as an introduction, a diagram of the activity of a portion of the transaction under inquiry is now useful in attempting to explain the Butler appointment. Diagram 1 maps the known surface activity in Butler's behalf

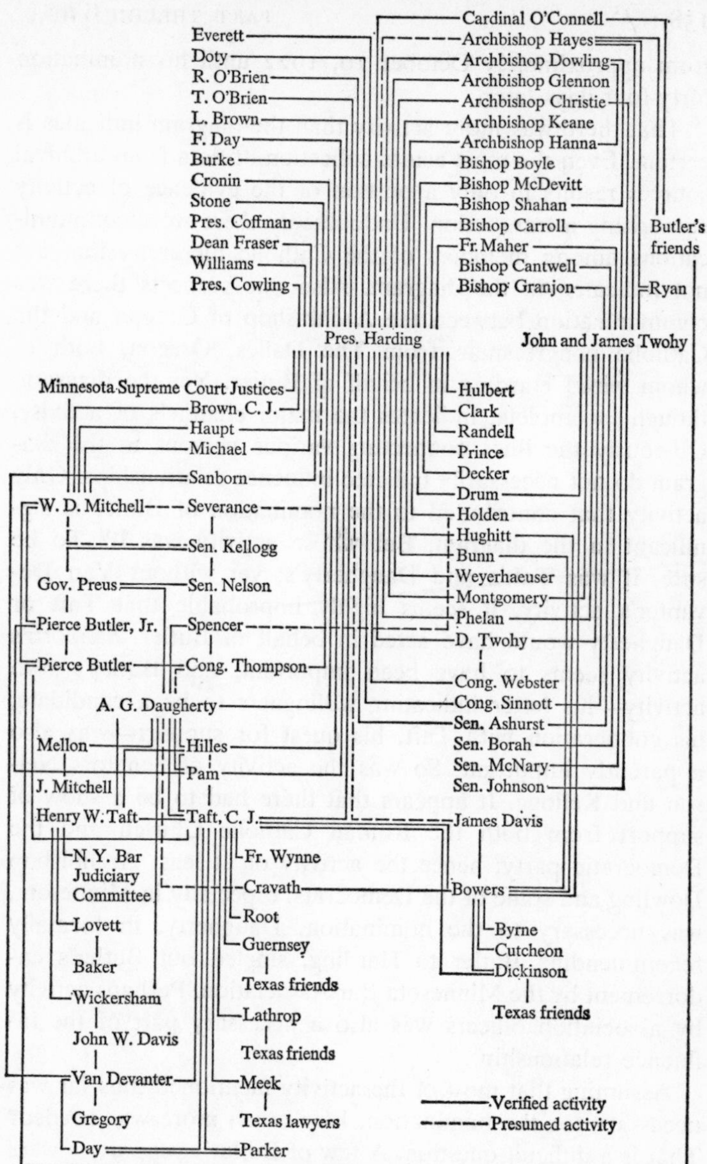

Diagram 1.

Surface Activity of a Sector of the Butler Appointment Transaction (October 10, 1922—November 23, 1922)

from approximately October 10, 1922 until his nomination forty-four days later.

That there was more activity than the diagram indicates is certain. Even the most astute collection of data from archival sources results in only a portion of the evidence of activity comprising a transaction. Undoubtedly there were communications among members of the Catholic hierarchy that are not indicated in the diagram. Also one suspects there was communication between the Archbishop of Oregon and the Catholic congressman from The Dalles, Oregon, both of whom wired Harding in behalf of Butler. Yet the diagram, though incomplete, indicates the major channels of activity. Obviously the lines connecting various persons in the diagram do not necessarily indicate influence relationships. Only activity that contributed to the nomination of Butler is significant in the diagram. But whose activity was it? To be sure, it was Taft's and Daugherty's; yet without Van Devanter's activity, it seems highly improbable that Taft or Daugherty would have acted in behalf of Butler. Sanborn's activity seems to have been important, and Butler's own activity—his letter indicating willingness to be a candidate, his cooperation with Taft, his quest for support—was also apparently important. So was the activity of Senators Nelson and Kellogg. It appears that there had to be a show of support from both the Roman Catholic Church and the Democratic party; hence the activity of at least Archbishop Dowling and some of the Democrats, especially in Minnesota, was necessary to the nomination. Daugherty, in formally recommending Butler to Harding, singled out Butler's endorsement by the Minnesota Bar Association. Perhaps activity by association officers was also a necessary part of the influence relationship.

Assuming that most of the activity mentioned thus far was necessary for the nomination, how much more was needed? That is a difficult question. A few of Butler's supporters were unimportant, and even among the important ones, after a certain point in the transaction, more support was only cumulative. Yet support of the eight additional archbishops and bishops, the chief justice and justices of the Supreme Court of Minnesota, President Coffman, Dean Fraser, Senator Ashurst, former Senator Phelan, Hale Holden, F. E. Weyerhaeuser, John R. Mitchell, John S. Drum, Paul Cravath, Homer P. Clark, Cordenio Severance, Carmi Thompson, and James Davis cannot be discounted. Nor can the behind-the-scenes activities of Bowers, Mitchell, and Pierce, Jr., and the Twohys. Although it cannot be proven that if the activity of one of those men had been lacking Butler would not have been nominated, it seems safe to say that the activities of some of the men named contributed to his nomination. Thus the totality of the connected activity in behalf of Butler, understood in the context of the situation, is a tenable explanation of Butler's nomination and hence his appointment.

III

Though the explanation of Butler's appointment given above largely in terms of surface activity is a tenable one, it does not go far enough. The question remains: Why did the transactors perform the activity in the transaction? To some extent that question was raised in the discussion of background activity. Mitchell's and Pierce, Jr.'s activity, given their close personal relationship with Butler, is not difficult to explain. Although the explanation of Tom Bowers' activity is not so obvious, it too can be explained in terms of background activity.

Two days after Butler was nominated, Taft wrote to his brother that Butler "was a great admirer of Judge Wilson, who was the father-in-law of Lloyd Bowers, and knew Lloyd when he was in Minnesota quite well. He was Judge Wilson's assistant as counsel for one of the railroad companies for several years in Minnesota when he gave up that employment to go into general practice. Tom Bowers has been very active in securing letters in his behalf." [5]

Tom was Lloyd Bowers' son, and Lloyd was one of Taft's close friends from the time they were students together at Yale. When Taft became President, he made Lloyd Bowers his Solicitor General, intending to put him on the Supreme

Court when the opportunity arose. Bowers died, however, in 1910, before Taft could make the appointment. Nevertheless, the Bowers and Taft families continued their close relationship; Tom and Taft's son Robert became close friends, and Tom's sister Martha married Robert. Given these ties of blood and friendship, it is not difficult to understand why Bowers was willing to solicit support for Butler at Taft's request.

The explanation of the Taft-Bowers influence relationship suggests that perhaps ties of blood, friendship, and professional association pervade the transaction under inquiry. Diagram 2 appears to confirm this.

Like the ties of friendship and professional association, the tie of religion is strongly in evidence in the transaction. Butler's activity as a Catholic linked him to a number of Catholics who otherwise most likely would not have come to his aid in the campaign for the nomination. And they were not only members of the hierarchy but men like John S. Drum, James D. Phelan, John D. Ryan, Congressman Sinnott, and Senator Ashurst, men who had positions of power in the secular society.

IV

Even a cursory examination of Diagrams 1 and 2 raises the question whether they depict a portion of the power elite of the United States in 1922. If such an elite is defined as "those who are able to realize their will, even if others resist it" and have "access to the command of major institutions," [6] the answer appears to be yes.

The diagrams, however, show several overlapping elites rather than a single elite. First and foremost was an elite in which Taft was central, consisting mostly of his friends, relatives, and former associates from the days when he was President—men like Pam, Guernsey, Henry Taft, Van Devanter, Sanborn, Hilles, Wickersham, Dickinson, Root, and Butler. Then there was a Minnesota elite consisting of men like Senators Kellogg and Nelson, Governor Preus, Severance, Archbishop Dowling, Judge Sanborn, Clark and Randall of

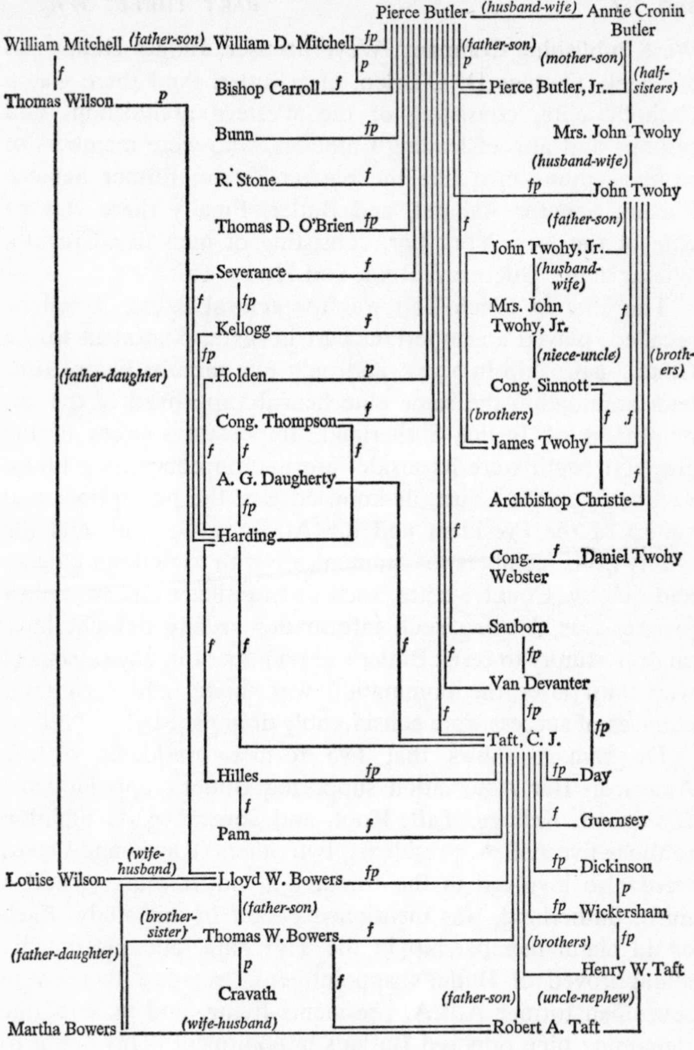

Diagram 2.

Some Ties of Blood, Friendship, and Professional Association in the Butler Appointment Transaction

West Publishing Company, Weyerhaeuser, Judges Haupt and Michael, Thomas D. O'Brien, and Butler. And there was a Catholic elite, consisting of the Western archbishops and bishops and also of leading Catholics, who were members of secular elites—men like the banker Drum, former Senator Phelan, Senator Ashurst, and Butler. Finally there was an elite of the New York bar, consisting of men like Cravath, Wickersham, Guernsey, Root, and Henry Taft.

The elite in which Taft was the central figure, it will be recalled, played an important part in his appointment to the Chief Justiceship in 1921, and only two months before Butler's nomination the same elite heartily approved of the appointment of Justice Sutherland. Important sources of the elite's strength were its inside information concerning future vacancies on the Court, its knowledge of the perceptions and values of the President and the Attorney General, and the ability of its members to communicate with each other quickly and quietly. Counter-elites, such as LaFollette and his fellow progressives, lacking such information, really did not have an opportunity to resist Butler's appointment in any organized way until after the nomination was made, and then their chances of success were considerably diminished.

Diagram I shows that five former presidents of the American Bar Association supported Butler's appointment: Dickinson, Kellogg, Taft, Root, and Severance. In addition to those five A.B.A. presidents, two others, Rawle and Davis, were also involved in the transaction under inquiry, and a third, Sutherland, was mentioned earlier in this study. Each could claim membership in the Taft elite, and presumably all approved of Butler's appointment. In 1922 there were seventeen former A.B.A. presidents living, and none of the remaining nine opposed Butler's appointment. This is not to argue, however, that former A.B.A. presidents constituted a separate elite, but rather to show the strength and overlapping character of the elite in which Taft was a central figure.

V

The activity of the confirmation phase of the transaction can also be viewed in terms of postulated influence relationships. Before the roll was called, several things had occurred that would have led to a prediction that the Senate would vote as it did. To begin with, though there had been a vigorous fight over Brandeis' confirmation in 1916, the Senate had not rejected a Supreme Court nomination in more than twenty-five years. Also, Butler's nomination came to the floor of the Senate with practically every institutional blessing of that body: a bipartisan subcommittee led by the chairman of the Judiciary Committee had investigated the charges against Butler and had unanimously recommended confirmation, and the committee unanimously made the same recommendation. Finally, on the floor of the Senate, the chairman of the Judiciary Committee, a Republican from the same state as the nominee, urged confirmation, and the Democratic member of the subcommittee also spoke in the nominee's behalf. A maverick Republican spoke against confirmation, it is true, but no other senator joined him and he said little that the senators did not already know. With that kind of activity before the roll call, it was practically a foregone conclusion that the nomination would be confirmed.

The stalwarts of the Republican party could, of course, be counted on to go along with Harding, the man they believed they put in the White House. No senator who had been in the "smoke-filled room" during the Republican convention in 1920 voted against Butler's confirmation. Of those thirteen senators, eleven voted for confirmation, and two—Borah and McCormick—were recorded as not voting.

Since the vote was taken during a lame-duck session of Congress, someone like Senator Norris would have expected the lame ducks, in hope of "fat executive appointments," to do the bidding of Harding by confirming Butler's nomination. As it turned out, no lame-duck senator voted against confirmation; twelve of fourteen lame ducks voted for confirmation, and two, France and Culberson, were recorded as not voting. Yet it would probably be a mistake to stress the connection betweween the lame-duck status of these senators and their vote on confirmation; most of them—particularly senators like New, Kellogg, Poindexter and Pomerene—would most likely have voted for confirmation anyway.[7] *

In view of the earlier discussion of religious ties as significant background activity, one might have thought that the five Catholics in the Senate—Henry F. Ashurst of Arizona, Edwin S. Broussard and Joseph E. Ransdell of Louisiana, David I. Walsh of Massachusetts, and Thomas J. Walsh of Montana—would have voted for Butler's confirmation in part because he was a co-religionist. In fact, four of them—Ashurst, Broussard, and the two Walshes—did vote for Butler's confirmation; the fifth Catholic, Ransdell, was recorded as not voting. All were Democrats, and the four who voted for confirmation were known to be progressive; hence, in view of LaFollette's argument against Butler's confirmation, perhaps the religious tie explains their votes. This might have been true in the case of Walsh of Montana, for a Senate secretary who knew Walsh in 1922 said some years after the confirmation that only Walsh's desire to see a fellow Catholic on the Supreme Court overcame his repugnancy to the Butler nomination.[8] Although such evidence is of questionable reliability, it is known that Walsh was very much concerned about the rise of the Ku Klux Klan about the time Butler was nominated, and on December 13, 1922, the same day the Senate subcommittee recommended Butler's confirmation, Walsh was the Catholic speaker at a tolerance meeting at the First Congregational Church in Washington, D.C. that protested the Klan's activity.[9]

If the religious tie partially explains Walsh's vote, it does not necessarily explain the votes of the other three Catholics,

---

* It must be pointed out, however, that New was soon thereafter appointed Postmaster General by Harding, and Kellogg, Poindexter, and Pomerene were given diplomatic assignments. During the lame-duck session of Congress in which Butler was nominated, Senator Norris wrote his initial report on the Lame Duck Amendment, which was filed with the Senate on December 5, 1922. That was the first important step toward the abolition of lame-duck sessions of Congress. In January, 1933 a sufficient number of state legislatures had ratified the Lame Duck Amendment to make it the Twentieth Amendment to the Constitution of the United States.

for it appears they would have voted for Butler regardless of his religion. Three years later, when Coolidge nominated Harlan Fiske Stone to the Supreme Court, Senator Norris made an argument against his confirmation similar to LaFollette's argument against Butler's confirmation. For Norris and some other senators it was the Butler case all over again, except that Stone was a Protestant and a Republican. If the religious tie were necessary for the Catholic senators' votes for Butler, then it was highly probable that they would vote against Stone. But they did not; Ashurst, Broussard, Ransdell, and David Walsh voted for Stone's confirmation, and Thomas Walsh was recorded as not voting.[10] Thus, except perhaps in the case of Thomas Walsh, no clear connection between Butler's activity as a Catholic and the votes of the Catholic senators can be demonstrated.

It has been said that the opposition of the Ku Klux Klan "is the only possible explanation for the opposition to Butler of several conservative southern Democrats." [11] The Klan hypothesis has some plausibility, because every Democrat who voted against confirmation was from the South, where the Klan had its greatest strength. The Democratic nay-sayers were Walter F. George and William J. Harris of Georgia, J. Thomas Heflin of Alabama, Morris Sheppard of Texas, and Park Trammell of Florida. Sheppard had attended the Progressive Conference the same month as the confirmation vote; hence it is difficult in his case to determine whether he was influenced by his past progressive activity and LaFollette's speech in the Senate, Klan activity, Harding's rejection of his candidate, Phillips, or something else. In regard to George, Harris, Heflin, and Trammell, the vote on Stone's confirmation three years later offers some insights. If they voted for the confirmation of Stone, the Protestant Republican, after having voted against the confirmation of Butler, the Catholic Democrat, then there may be something to the Klan hypothesis. But most of them did not vote for Stone's confirmation: Heflin and Trammell voted against it, and Harris was recorded as not voting. Only George voted to confirm Stone.[12] This does not rule out the Klan hypothesis in explaining the southern Democrats' votes on Butler's confirmation, but it does weaken it.

LaFollette's appeal to his colleagues to reject Butler's nomination was apparently successful in regard to a few fellow progressives. Of the ten senators who attended the Progressive Conference, none voted to confirm Butler: in addition to LaFollette, Norris, and Sheppard, who voted against confirmation, Smith W. Brookhart of Iowa indicated he would have voted with them if he had not been paired with Senator Calder. Besides the Progressive Conference senators, LaFollette may have convinced one other Republican—Peter Norbeck. Early in his political career Norbeck had been a LaFollette man; he had been one of the first subscribers to *LaFollette's Magazine,* and LaFollette had been his choice for the Presidency in 1912. Like LaFollette, he mistrusted big business—the powerful few who controlled the lives of the many—and he too was for the little man, especially the small farmer. Hence he may have responded to LaFollette's appeal.[13] In addition to Norbeck, LaFollette may have convinced some of the southern senators who voted against confirmation, especially Heflin and Trammell. His activity may also have been significant to the twenty-five senators who were recorded as not voting. That his activity was related to some of the votes cannot be denied. His argument, though premature, contained the seeds of success. Later Senator Norris would see it bear fruit.[14]

Chapter 11

PERSONALITY

Personality is an important dimension of political transactions because, among other things, it provides a means for establishing and understanding connections among activities in influence relationships.[1] But personality is not an empirical entity or any other kind of entity; it is only a concept having explanatory value, a symbol referring to perceived regularities of activity that differentiate one individual from another.[2] To illustrate the usefulness of the concept in political analysis, and at the same time extend the explanation of Pierce Butler's appointment to the Supreme Court, the personalities of Warren G. Harding and Harry M. Daugherty are considered in this chapter.

Karen Horney's theory of personality was chosen as the basis of the analysis that is to follow primarily for two reasons:

1. It is compatible with a transactional approach to human phenomena.
2. It appears to have explanatory value in regard to the activity of Harding and Daugherty in the appointment of Butler.[3]

Horney viewed personality at the first level of abstraction in terms of behavior patterns. When she referred to personality types, the term "types" was merely "a simplification for persons with distinct characteristics." [4] She was well aware that multifarious human phenomena often defy classification, and conceded that to speak of "human types" was only "a means of looking at personalities from certain vantage points." [5]

I

Harding's behavior pattern bears a remarkable resemblance to the personality type Horney described as "compliant" or "self-effacing." [6] This type, in an effort to resolve his inner conflicts, is compulsively driven "to move toward people." [7] His primary needs are affection and approval. He tries to strike this bargain with the world: "I'll be kind and loving and good to you if you will be the same to me." Hence he is sensitive to the needs of others and tries to live up to their expectations of him. He sees himself as unselfish, humble, self-sacrificing, kind, loving, generous, trusting; and he is usually perceived by others in the same way because he manifests such behavior. His behavior pattern in that regard, however, is extreme and rigid. He overrates his congeniality and what he has in common with others; he is overconsiderate and overgenerous. Desiring affection from all, he believes that he likes everyone, "that they are all 'nice' and trustworthy, a fallacy which not only makes for heartbreaking disappointments but adds to his general insecurity." [8] He avoids intrapersonal conflict, is conciliatory, and is hesitant to assert himself or give orders. He is essentially submissive and compliant. His underlying principle of action is: "If I give in, I shall not be hurt." [9]

The compliant type has need of a special partner—usually a friend or spouse—someone with an opposite personality who will aggressively protect him and his interests, who will give him approval and affection, who will "fulfill all expectations of life and take responsibility for good and evil. . . ." [10]

Other characteristics of the compliant type are self-subordination, helplessness, and a tendency to rate himself in terms of what others think of him. He readily assumes that others are superior to him—more intelligent, more able, more worthy. He often feels that they could do his job better. He is quick to admit his feeling of helplessness to himself and others. His frequent plea is: "You must love me, protect me, forgive me, *because* I am so weak and helpless." Since others tend to structure the compliant type's image of himself, criticism, rejection, or desertion are catastrophic, and anticipation of the possibility of these untoward events is depressing.[11]

Practically all that has been written about Harding is consistent with the hypothesis that he was a compliant type. Here are a few examples:

H. F. Alderfer's dissertation:

> The desire for approval was his [Harding's] chief motivation.[12] Above all, Harding desired approval of the powers.[13]

Allan Nevins in the *Dictionary of American Biography:*

> [Harding] was genial, . . . easy-going, and frank in admitting his lack of unusual abilities or intellectual tastes.[14]

John Hays Hammond's autobiography:

> Harding was generous to his friends, but much too easy-going and trustful.[15]

Newton H. Fairbanks' memoir:

> [Harding] was a kind-hearted man and was the last person to believe it possible for a person he thought to be his friend not to be a true and dependable one. This trait caused him to be imposed upon by persons appointed to subordinate official positions who turned out to be rascals.[16]

In an effort to verify the hypothesis more precisely, the content of Daugherty's book, *The Inside Story of the Harding Tragedy,* was systematically analyzed for the present study to determine how Daugherty perceived Harding. Daugherty saw Harding primarily as dependent, trusting, generous, friendly, conciliatory, compliant, humble, anxious, popular, gentle, and naive.[17]

There is other evidence supporting the hypothesis. Harding's unwillingness to seek high office except when prodded to do so, his depression when he anticipated rejection by his party or the electorate, his habitual deference to power, his inability to say no to "deserving" friends, his feeling of helplessness, his fond hope that he would be remembered as the nation's best-loved President, and his low estimate of his own ability would all seem to point to a compliant type.[18]

So do many of Harding's comments about himself. "You know my personal attitude as well as anybody in Ohio," he wrote to Daugherty in 1918. "I am always seeking to harmonize. . . ." At times Harding thought that because of his conciliatory attitude, politicians tried to take advantage of him. "Because I am inclined to be courteous and considerate and do not tell every political crook what is in my heart," he wrote to a friend in 1920, "they look upon me as one unwilling to indulge in a scrap. Really, when it comes down to brass tacks I would just as soon have a row as anybody would, and I am always perfectly philosophical about the outcome." Despite these brave words, which he may have thought his correspondent expected, Harding had no taste for political battle. In fact, in the same letter he said he found the endless jealousies and petty conspiracies of politics "all very nauseating and disgusting." "Sometimes," he added, "I wish I had told all of them to go jump in the Ohio River and become my self-respecting self again without the annoyance which comes with the political candidacy." [19]

And it seems clear that Daugherty was one of Harding's "special partners." It was Daugherty who performed many of the aggressive acts necessary for Harding's political rise; it was Daugherty who acted as Harding's protector, adviser, and manager; and it was Daugherty who attended to Harding's emotional needs. Harding's statement to Daugherty after he offered the latter the attorney generalship—"Are you going to continue to stand by me, or desert me after all these years? I have never needed you in my life as I need you today"—is as good as any illustration given by Horney of the compliant type's dependence on his partner.[20]

Harding's statement when he was President—"My God, but this is a hell of a place for a man like me to be!"—provides an apt illustration of the compliant type's feeling of helplessness.[21] Indeed the Presidency could not be any other kind of place for a compliant type.

II

Daugherty's behavior pattern bears a remarkable resemblance to the personality type Horney described as "aggressive" or "arrogant-vindictive." [22] This type is the polar opposite of the compliant personality. He too is insecure, but, in his effort to resolve inner conflicts, he is compulsively driven "to move against people." [23] His primary need is vindictive triumph. His perception of the world is Hobbesian; he believes that, at bottom, men are wolves to each other. He accepts that world on its own terms, girds himself for battle, and eagerly enters the fray. He sees himself as tough and would like others to see him that way too; toughness is highly valued because, in his way of thinking, only the tough can survive. Those who make friendly gestures, who claim they value love over power, who appear altruistic, are to him either hypocritical or naive. For that reason he is suspicious of everyone until his honesty is proven. He asserts that at least he is honest in that he admits he wants power, prestige, and recognition and will fight for them. In his quest for power, he seeks to exploit others, to outsmart them, to bring them to their knees. Often he operates openly, but "he may prefer to be the power behind the throne." [24]

The aggressive type lives by his wits and is proud of his self-sufficiency in doing so. He is vigilant, plans ahead, calculates the strength of his enemy, estimates his chances of success, and plots the moves he will make in battle. Ordinarily the battle must be his show, and he is so proud of going it alone that it is difficult for him to ask for help. To do so seems humiliating to him because it raises questions about his self-sufficiency.[25]

In the interest of expediency, he may curb vindictive expression. For the same reason he may present a façade of politeness and good fellowship. And he may stoically suffer the barbs of others' aggression, but he neither forgives nor forgets. Some day, he tells himself, "they" will pay; some day he will be on top, and then he will show "them." These are not idle fantasies. "They determine the course of his life," wrote Horney. "Driving himself from victory to victory, in large and small matters, he lives for the 'day of reckoning.' "[26]

The aggressive type is drawn toward his compliant counterpart, who is often most useful. Twentieth-century American society, though fairly tolerant of aggression, does not accept the aggressive type pure and simple, especially if he is blatant in his quest for power. Thus it would appear that by suppressing the more tender, lovable aspects of his personality to attain his goals, the aggressive type is involved in a self-defeating process. Not necessarily, for he can simulate the requisite modesty and good fellowship, or he can form a partnership with someone whose personality complements his own, someone who is lovable, modest, trusting, conciliatory—in short, the compliant type. In a sense, when the two types come together in partnership, they acquire a wholeness neither had individually, and, with that wholeness, a strength neither had before. The aggressive type is, of course, exploiting his counterpart, using him as a means to his end of vindictive triumph, but then the compliant type is also using his aggressive partner.

Contemporary perceptions of Daugherty are consistent with the hypothesis that he was an aggressive type. Here are a few examples:

Chief Justice Taft in his correspondence:

> Daugherty is a fighter . . . a very bitter hater and a very warm friend, but he is suspicious of a good many people.[27]
>
> [Daugherty] was constantly in politics, and had a facility for creating and fighting enemies, and, I may say, a courage in doing so. . . .[28]

H. F. Alderfer's dissertation:

> Daugherty was an Ohio politician of the first water. . . . He gained the reputation of a fighter, a shrewd manipulator and a slippery customer.[29]

S. T. Williamson in the *New York Times:*

> The kind of fighting in which he [Daugherty] has often been engaged is the safest observed from afar; yet unprejudiced witnesses of his combats with his enemies never can swear that they actually saw gouging and biting in the clinches.[30]

Mark Sullivan in *Our Times:*

> [Daugherty] cared more for the game than the fee; he liked the clash of personalities; he liked the thrill of climactic success, of putting something over.[31]

The content analysis of *The Inside Story of the Harding Tragedy* revealed that Daugherty perceived himself primarily as influential, dutiful, clever, self-assured, persecuted, suspicious, friendly, honest, generous, aggressive, unpopular, righteous, and courageous.

Daugherty said he lived in "a hard-boiled age"; he referred to himself as "a practical politician," not one who tied himself to the "fizzling pinwheels of so-called reform and progress"; he loved the excitement of political battle so much, he said, that he twice turned down opportunities to go on the federal bench; with pride he told of fighting his rivals with "ferocity," and "naturally, [he] made enemies." [32] All of this points to an aggressive type. So do other things about Daugherty—his suspiciousness, his vindictiveness, his emphasis on strategy, his willingness to stand alone against the whole world if necessary, his inability to accept graciously a post he wanted, his patient waiting and working toward his supreme moment of vindictive triumph—the nomination of Harding for the Presidency.[33] And there seems to be no question that Daugherty saw himself as "hard-boiled" as the age in which he lived. In 1939, far removed from the centers of political conflict and close to his death, Daugherty said: "I live a quiet life [now], but I liked the tough life I used to lead." [34] *

* When Daugherty was forced out of the attorney generalship during the Coolidge administration, he rolled with the blow. Mixing sacred and profane allusions, he wrote to a friend: "[O]n the principle that the Lord tempers the wind etc., and the devil takes care of his own, I will get along somehow. . . . If anybody does not like my position

Although Harding and Daugherty were partners in Horney's sense, they sometimes disagreed. Harding, characteristically bent on harmonizing the diverse Republican factions in Ohio, at times had to ask Daugherty to desist in taking reprisals for past grievances. He said he could not join in drumming Republicans out of the party simply because they were not in complete accord with Daugherty. Daugherty, characteristically, would refuse to back down. With complete candor—"I never play any cards under the table in politics or anything else"—he would explain why his action was necessary, suggesting that Harding was getting advice and information from unsafe sources—that is, from persons who were not under obligation to Daugherty. Despite such disagreements the bond between Harding and Daugherty remained firm.[35]

Daugherty's partnership with Harding was crucial to his political rise. Daugherty wanted power. Though in his book he said that he became "a political leader" instead of an officeholder by choice, he later admitted that his ambition was to become a United States Senator.[36] He made an attempt to secure the Republican nomination for that office in Ohio once, but, as usual, his many enemies united against him, and he was defeated. But with Harding as front-man, Daugherty was a success. In a real sense, each Harding victory was also a victory for Daugherty. Daugherty was for many years "a power behind the throne"; his challenge in life was to increase the power of the throne, which, some would say, he succeeded in doing on a grand scale in 1920. The relationship between these two men was important in a number of events in American history from 1920 to 1923, among them the appointment of Pierce Butler to the Supreme Court.

III

Viewing Harding's and Daugherty's activity in terms of Horney's personality theory provides some insights into an

---

you can tell them to go to hell." Daugherty to Fairbanks, April 3, 1924, Fairbanks Papers.

important sector of the transaction under inquiry. The filling of the vacancy created by Justice Day's retirement was one of the many events that made the Presidency "hell" for Harding. The appointments of Taft and Sutherland really presented no problems for him other than to determine which of the men was to receive the first appointment. Indeed, in terms of his personality, both were ideal appointments. He regarded both men as friends and valued their friendship. In view of what amounted to promises of appointment to them, he would have been greatly disturbed if he had reneged. Also, Harding wanted approval of both Congress and the nation in making such important appointments. Hence he was greatly pleased with the enthusiasm with which both nominations were received in the Senate and across the nation. Finally, Daugherty highly approved of both men; in fact, he regarded Taft as his candidate. Thus everything fit: the partner approved; approval in Congress and the nation seemed likely; and on top of that, Harding could do a good turn for "deserving" friends.

But that was not the case with the Day vacancy. There was no Taft or Sutherland to be nominated. John W. Davis was as close as Harding could come to another Taft, but Davis refused to be a candidate. This left a political vacuum that was soon filled with the claims of Southerners, Democrats, Republicans, New Yorkers, Pennsylvanians, Catholics, former Senate colleagues, and others. And in the center of this web of would-be influence relationships sat Harding, not knowing which way to turn or what to do.

He knew what he did not want to do: he did not want to hurt anybody. It will be recalled that when Taft requested him to ask Justice Day to specify a definite retirement date, he refused to do so for fear of "wounding" Day's feelings. What about the feelings of his other "friends"? There was, for example, R. B. Creager, who used to come from Texas to Washington to play poker with Harding, and Jesse Jones, Harding's old golf partner: both were supporting Nelson Phillips. There was also Charles M. Schwab, another poker-playing friend, and Judge Gary, who apparently did not play poker with Harding but who was nonetheless counted as a friend: both were for Martin T. Manton. Then there were Chief Justice Taft and Senator Kellogg, who were for Pierce Butler. Kellogg was known to be an especially close friend of Harding. And there were Senators McKinley, Underwood, Pepper, and other former Senate colleagues pressing their candidates. No matter whose candidate Harding chose, some friends were bound to be disappointed and feelings might be wounded.[37]

And Harding could not resolve the matter by deferring to power. Creager was head of the Republican organization in Texas; Schwab, Gary, and Jones were at the top of the business-industrial elite; Taft and Kellogg were big men in the Republican party. Power had spoken with many tongues, uttering names of men unknown to Harding.

If the candidates being pressed were unknown to Harding, how could he be sure that the Senate and the nation would approve of the one he chose? There was no way that he could know; he would have to trust his friends, which he was willing to do. Yet he probably wished the candidates were better known. Perhaps that is why he made the peculiar offer to Senator Underwood. It was quite unlikely that the Senator would accept, but if he did, there was no doubt that the nomination of the Democratic floor leader would be enthusiastically received in the Senate, and, given the swing toward the Democrats in the recent election, it was likely to be popular nationally. Although Underwood declined as expected, Harding had the satisfaction of making a friendly gesture to a former Senate colleague and a southern Democrat.

The importance of Chief Justice Taft in Harding's attempt to come to grips with the Day vacancy cannot be overestimated. Having been an Ohio judge, United States Solicitor General, federal circuit judge, and only the third President to have appointed more than five Supreme Court Justices, Taft could justifiably claim expertise in the area of judicial appointments; and if Harding felt that Taft could have handled this aspect of the Presidency better, that conclusion did not stem simply from his feelings of insecurity. After all, as Taft pointed out to several persons at the time, Harding was not even a lawyer. Harding was painfully aware of all this and knew that, in regard to judicial appointments, Taft was sitting in judgment on him. He of course wanted Taft's approval in filling the Day vacancy, just as he was happy to have had it in making other judicial appointments during his administration. Although that did not mean that Taft controlled the appointing process, it did mean that if he objected to a particular candidate, that candidate had practically no chance of nomination. Besides, Taft's advice on prior appointments had been good. If Taft said Butler's reputation was national and his nomination would be well received, there was every reason to believe it, especially when top people in the Midwest—archbishops and bishops, lawyers, judges, educators, corporate executives, and politicians like Senators Nelson and Kellogg—went on record for Butler.

Important as Taft's approval of Day's successor was to Harding, Daugherty's approval was probably even more important. As Attorney General, it was his job to recommend the nominee, and when that is considered together with his special relationship with Harding, it was extremely unlikely that Harding would have nominated anyone his partner did not approve. For to do so would have meant to risk losing the support of the man upon whom Harding had leaned for some twenty years, and to Harding, that would have been unthinkable. In view of the relationship between them, it is easy to picture Harding saying to Daugherty: "Harry, this Day vacancy has been giving us a lot of trouble. Which one of the candidates should we name?" And Daugherty answering: "I think Pierce Butler is the best man." In fact, Daugherty maintained that it happened much that way. Some years later he claimed that he "made over the Supreme Court" in the early 1920's and that Harding followed every one of his recommendations. "I even recommended a Democrat, Pierce Butler," he said, "but he was all right." [38]

To some extent, the early strength of Phillips' candidacy can be explained in terms of Daugherty's tentative approval of the Texan when Harding sent him Creager's letter in behalf of Phillips.[39] And the rejection of Manton can be partially explained in terms of Daugherty's opposition to him. In fact, Taft and his brother Harry were counting on Daugherty's opposition to stop Manton's drive for the Court, yet they were not sure that the pressures on the compliant Harding were not so great that he might act contrary even to Daugherty's recommendation. Daugherty, on the other hand, knowing Harding better, was certain that Manton would not be nominated.

Daugherty found Taft useful and exploited him. The Chief Justice screened a great number of candidates for the federal judiciary during the Harding administration. Daugherty was not only happy to have Taft do this painstaking work for him; he was pleased with the additional legitimacy a Taft candidate had. If a senator or someone else questioned a particular nomination, Daugherty could have countered: "Do you know that the Chief Justice thinks highly of this man and approves of him for this post?" Hilles, who knew Daugherty well, suspected that he was taking advantage of the Chief Justice in this way and wrote Taft that, on top of the Chief Justiceship, he thought it was too much of a burden to carry. Taft's answer was that it was "labor of love." Though undoubtedly it was, Hilles' suspicions about Daugherty exploiting Taft were correct. Yet it was because Taft was being used in this way that he was in a position to be influential in the nomination of Butler.

Taft was important to Daugherty for another reason. Daugherty had grandiose notions about his ability, not only as a politician but as a lawyer. Almost everyone conceded that he had to be an extraordinary politician to do what he did with Harding's career, but the legal profession never regarded Daugherty as a top-rank lawyer, and this disturbed him. His appointment as attorney general did not change matters; thereafter it was openly said in the profession that politics, not ability, was the basis of Daugherty's selection. Taft understood Daugherty's feelings in the matter, and though privately he agreed that Daugherty was not a first-rate lawyer, outwardly he treated him as a man worthy of being attorney general.[40] This confirmed Daugherty's own sense of worth and provided support for his notion that he was in the top ranks of the legal profession.

The deference Taft showed Daugherty was especially important to the latter in the fall of 1922. In September Daugherty went to Chicago and personally secured an injunction against the railroad strike, which was then in progress, and thereby incurred criticism not only from labor groups, but from persons within the Harding administration. In the Cabinet meeting following the injunction, Secretary of Interior Fall claimed he said to Daugherty: "You don't know any law, and you can't learn any." [41] Soon thereafter, Congressman Oscar E. Keller of Minnesota, an ally of Samuel Gompers, rose in the House of Representatives and said: "Mr. Speaker, I impeach Harry M. Daugherty, Attorney General of the United States, for high crimes and misdemeanors in office." [42] While he fought the impeachment in the months that followed, Daugherty found solace in his relationship with Taft. Though he perceived the world as essentially dishonest, Daugherty could feel that at least Taft, like Harding, was an honest man. Hence he trusted the Chief Justice, and that trust had bearing on Butler's appointment.

Viewing Harding's and Daugherty's activity in terms of Horney's personality theory makes for a deeper understanding of the transaction under inquiry and extends the explanation of the appointment of Pierce Butler to the Supreme Court. Although there is no way of proving the matter either way, it seems highly probable that if Harding and Daugherty had different personalities, Butler would not have been appointed. Hence personality is a valuable concept for organizing background activity so that connections among activities in postulated influence relationships can be established and understood. But it must be remembered that personality is only a concept, a way of viewing "perceived regularities of activity that differentiate one individual from another."

Chapter 12

CONSEQUENCES

The future is always to some extent a dimension of man's perception of the present. It was Butler's expected activity on the Court—his arguments in conference, his votes, his opinions—that, for friends and enemies alike, gave meaning to his appointment. That activity of Butler's was indeed an important consequence, perhaps the most important consequence, of his appointment, but there were other consequences. In the Senate, the experience of the Butler controversy would live and be drawn upon by Senator Norris and others. For Nelson Phillips and Martin T. Manton, the consequences of Butler's appointment seemed clear: history had passed them by, perhaps for good. For William A. Schaper, the consequences were less clear: true, he did not prevent Butler's confirmation and in the process obtain vindication, as he had hoped, yet his case had received considerable publicity; perhaps he would yet be vindicated, or at least be given a measure of justice.

I

In the first chapter of this study, it will be recalled, Butler's basic values were considered. An analysis of his speeches revealed that he highly valued patriotism, laissez faire, morality, law, order, justice, tradition, and freedom. The opponents of his appointment also had some idea of Butler's values, based on their knowledge of his past activity, and they expected him to reflect those values in his decisions. Schaper would have readily agreed that patriotism was one of Butler's values. But he probably would have denied that Butler valued freedom; in fact, it was Schaper's expectation that the newly appointed Justice would be insensitive to civil-liberties claims, especially claims of procedural due process, just as he appeared to be when Schaper was dismissed from the University of Minnesota in 1917. LaFollette, Norris, and the other progressives would have agreed that Butler valued laissez faire, but to them it simply meant that he was for big business. From their knowledge of his representation of railroads and corporations, they expected him to vote for the railroads and utilities in rate and valuation cases and to side generally with business in other economic cases. Members of the Ku Klux Klan and others perhaps would have agreed that Butler valued morality, but they would have called it pro-Catholicism. Knowing only that he was a Catholic was enough for them to expect his activity on the Court to benefit his church.

There is little doubt that the values articulated in Butler's speeches were related to his work on the Court.[1] Yet his opponents were not entirely correct in their expectations concerning his judicial behavior. Contrary to Schaper's expectation, Butler was not only sensitive to claims of procedural due process; his record indicates he was the Court's champion of those claims from 1923 to 1939. In the sixteen nonunanimous criminal cases involving issues of due process decided during that period,[2] Butler voted for the defendant 75 percent of the time, compared with the majority's score of 44 percent.[3] Voting in the same sixteen cases, Brandeis scored 69 percent and McReynolds 38 percent. The fact that Butler dissented in favor of due-process claims in eight of those cases is a measure of the intensity of his feeling on such issues, for he abhorred the expression of dissent and frequently acquiesced in silence to decisions he voted against in conference.* But in matters he believed important, he recorded his dissent even though no other Justice would join him. In *Palko* v. *Connecticut,*[4] for instance, he stood alone in dissent, while eight of his colleagues—including Black, Brandeis, Cardozo, and Stone—held that a state could try a man twice for the same offense and then execute him without violating the due-process clause of the Fourteenth Amendment.

At times, because of value conflicts, loyalty to the opinion of the Court, or respect for those with whom he differed, Butler found it difficult to express his dissenting views even in defense of due process. It appears that *Olmstead* v. *United States,*[5] which upheld the constitutionality of wiretapping, was such a case. Chief Justice Taft, who wrote the Court's opinion for a majority of five, saw the problem primarily in terms of his values of law and order. As he told his brother soon after the case was decided, professors in the law schools might be critical of the decision and "point the finger of scorn" at him, "but if they think we are going to be frightened in our effort to stand by the laws and give the public a chance to punish criminals, they are mistaken." [6] Although Butler also highly valued law and order, he saw the problem somewhat differently. From his early experience at the criminal bar, he knew of unfair police practices, of the zeal of prosecutors to convict, and of the great advantage the state has over the individual in criminal prosecutions. He disliked crime as much as Taft did; but, as he put it in one of his opinions as Circuit Justice, "Abhorrence, however great, of persistent and menacing crime will not excuse transgression in the courts of the legal rights of the worst offenders." [7] And Butler be-

* Butler succinctly stated his views on dissent on the back of Justice Stone's slip opinion in *The Malcolm Baxter, Jr.,* 277 U.S. 323 (1928): "I voted to reverse. While this sustains your conclusions to affirm, I still think reversal would be better. But I shall in silence acquiesce. Dissents seldom aid in the right development of the law. They often do harm. For myself I say: 'lead us not into temptation.'" Stone Papers; Butler to Taft, May 19, 1928, Taft Papers. Up to 1936 Butler recorded his dissent an average of 4.5 times a year. In his last three years on the Court, however, that average rose to 24 recorded dissents a year.

lieved it did not excuse the use of evidence obtained by wire-tapping. Thus he decided to write a dissenting opinion in *Olmstead* but apparently not without some inner struggle, for he began the opinion by saying he "sincerely regret[ted]" that he was unable to agree with Taft and the majority and concluded with the statement: "With great deference, I think [the defendants] should be given a new trial." [8]

Butler's record in cases involving substantive issues of freedom, however, was a curious reversal of his due-process record. In the fourteen nonunanimous cases that presented substantive issues of freedom,[9] such as freedom of speech or conscience, he voted for the individual only 29 percent of the time, compared with the majority's score of 50 percent. Brandeis' score was 85 percent and McReynolds' score 21 percent. A plausible, partial explanation of Butler's curious reversal is that in the ten cases in which he voted against the individual some competing value was present that was more important to him than freedom.

In one of the cases, *Schwimmer* v. *United States,*[10] which held that a forty-nine-year-old woman was not entitled to become a citizen of the United States because she could not in good conscience swear to bear arms in defense of the nation, the competing value was apparently patriotism. Butler perceived the case largely in terms of World War I experience. In his opinion for the Court, he identified Madame Schwimmer with pacifists and conscientious objectors during the war who not only refused to bear arms but who also refused to obey the laws and encouraged disobedience in others. Pacifists, he wrote, lack a "sense of nationalism"; they do not have the "ties of affection" to the government of the United States that are requisite for aliens seeking naturalization. Butler had expressed similar ideas in his patriotic speeches of 1915 and 1916; in fact, some of the language was almost identical.*

---

* Compare the following statements by Butler. The first is from a 1916 speech he made to the Minnesota Bar Association; the second is from *Schwimmer* v. *United States*:

Allegiance to government and protection by it are reciprocal ob-

An examination of the remaining nine freedom cases reveals that seven of them involved either Communists, members of International Workers of the World, or aliens who refused to swear unqualified allegiance to the United States.[11] When Butler had to choose between such persons and the government, patriotism was apparently dominant. In the remaining two cases, tradition appears to have been the competing value, for in both cases Butler argued that the majority was departing from precedent.[12]

Thus in cases raising issues of substantive freedom, Schaper's expectations concerning consequences of Butler's appointment were, for the most part, correct: where freedom and patriotism conflicted, as in Schaper's case in 1917, the latter value prevailed. Since the value of patriotism was seldom, if ever, involved in the due-process cases, Butler's value of freedom—or more precisely his value of the procedural safeguards of freedom—could compete successfully with other values such as law and order. In addition, cutting across and qualifying these values was his value of tradition, which, on the Court, meant *stare decisis*. Although that value undoubtedly often reinforced decisions based primarily on other values, it is quite likely that in some cases it was the dominant value for Butler.[13]

The expectations of LaFollette and his fellow progressives concerning Butler's activity in cases involving government and the economy were more accurate than Schaper's expectations concerning civil-liberties cases. This is demonstrated in Table I, which is a scalogram of economic cases involving government (including tax cases) decided by the Supreme Court during the historic 1935 term.[14] The scalogram also shows the importance of Butler's appointment, for he was in the majority in such important 5-to-4 decisions as *More-*

---

ligations, and stripped of all sentiment, the one is the consideration for the other; that is, allegiance for protection and protection for allegiance. [Quoted above, p. 15.]

All [citizens] owe allegiance to the Government, and the Government owes to them the duty of protection. These are reciprocal obligations and each is a consideration for the other. [279 U.S. at 649.]

TABLE I
SCALOGRAM OF CASES INVOLVING GOVERNMENT AND THE ECONOMY (1935 TERM)

Cases	McReynolds	Butler	Sutherland	Van Devanter	Roberts	Hughes	Brandeis	Stone	Cardozo	Vote
Ashwander v. *T.V.A.*	x	—	—	—	—	—	—	—	—	1–8
U.S. v. *Safety Car Heating Co.*	—	x	x	—	x	—	—	—	—	3–6
Helvering v. *City Bank Co.*	x	x	x	x	—	—	—	—	—	4–5
Borden's Co. v. *Ten Eyck*	x	x	x	x	—	—	—	—	—	4–5
Helvering v. *St. Louis Trust Co.*	x	x	x	x	x	—	—	—	—	5–4
Becker v. *St. Louis Trust Co.*	x	x	x	x	x	—	—	—	—	5–4
Morehead v. *N.Y. ex rel. Tipaldo*	x	x	x	x	x	—	—	—	—	5–4
Ashton v. *Cameron Cty. Dist.*	x	x	x	x	x	—	—	—	—	5–4
Carter v. *Carter Coal Co.*	x	x	x	x	x	—	—	—	—	5–4
McFeely v. *Commissioner*	x	x	x	x	x	x	—	—	—	6–3
Schuylkill Trust Co. v. *Penn.*	x	x	x	x	x	x	—	—	—	6–3
Colgate v. *Harvey*	x	x	x	x	x	x	—	—	—	6–3
U.S. v. *Butler*	x	x	x	x	x	x	—	—	—	6–3
Great Northern Ry. v. *Weeks*	x	x	x	x	x	x	—	—	—	6–3
Mayflower Farms v. *Ten Eyck*	x	x	x	x	x	x	—	—	—	6–3
U.S. v. *Elgin Ry.*	x	x	x	x	x	x	—	—	—	6–3
Graves v. *Texas Co.*	x	x	x	x	x	x	—	*	—	6–2
Koshland v. *Helvering*	x	x	x	x	x	x	x	—	—	7–2
Totals	17–1	17–1	17–1	16–2	15–3	9–9	1–17	0–17	0–18 / 92–69	92–69 / 161
Scale positions	18	17	17	16	14	9	1	0	0	
Scale scores	1.00	.88	.88	.77	.55	.00	−.88	−1.00	−1.00	

$$R = 1 - \frac{2}{152} = .987 \qquad S = 1 - \frac{2}{18} = .889$$

Legend: x = vote against government
— = vote for government
* = not participating in decision but on Court at time of decision

head v. *New York ex rel. Tipaldo,*[15] which invalidated New York's minimum wage law for women, and *Ashton* v. *Cameron County Water Improvement District,*[16] which declared unconstitutional the Municipality Bankruptcy Act. And if there is anything to the hypothesis that Chief Justice Hughes sometimes cast his vote with the majority in closely divided cases in order to avoid a great number of embarrassing 5-to-4 decisions, then the number of economic cases in which Butler's vote was crucial may have been as high as twelve in the 1935 term alone. One wonders how those cases would have been decided if Nelson Phillips or Martin T. Manton had been appointed to the Supreme Court in 1922 instead of Butler.*

The progressives' expectation that Butler would side with the railroads and utilities in rate and valuation cases was also correct, as the scalogram in Table II shows. In the nineteen nonunanimous rate and valuation cases decided by the Court during Butler's tenure, he voted for the railroads or utilities in eighteen of them, and his vote in the nineteenth case does not appear as an inconsistency in the scalogram.

There is also evidence supporting the hypothesis that Butler's appointment was related to the Court's adoption of the cost-of-reproduction rule for federal valuation of railroads—

---

* There is good reason for believing that Nelson Phillips' behavior on the Supreme Court would have been similar to Butler's during the New Deal. Though Phillips voted for Roosevelt in 1932, he was opposed to most New Deal legislation and voted against F.D.R. in 1936. Apparently he did not approve of Roosevelt's early appointments to the Supreme Court, for upon Phillips' death, a member of the Fort Worth bar said of him: "He believed . . . that a seat upon that tribunal . . . was one which should be illuminated and made illustrious by men trained in the trial of cases and in the application of the law to facts, and not to dreamers, and to intellectual speculators who gamble with the gossamer and iridescent ideals of Utopia. He believed that taxation should never be a secret instrument for confiscation nor the basis for the program of the socialists who would seek to level the prosperity of one by enriching another, and drag down progress to poverty." Nelson Phillips, Jr. to D. J. D., Oct. 11, 1963; *In Memoriam, Proceedings in the Supreme Court of Texas Touching the Death of Nelson Phillips* (Austin: privately printed, 1939), p. 39.

precisely what the progressives feared would happen. In the Taft Court it was common practice for the Justices to defer to the judgment of colleagues who were regarded as experts in certain fields of the Court's jurisdiction. Both Butler and Brandeis were regarded as experts in rate and valuation matters,* but their views were antagonistic: Butler supported the cost-of-reproduction rule, which favored the railroads and utilities, and Brandeis supported the prudent-investment rule, which did not. Table II shows that in the Taft Court, when the experts disagreed, a majority of the Justices deferred to Butler rather than Brandeis in eight out of nine cases. Although Butler disqualified himself in *St. Louis & O'Fallon Ry.* v. *United States,*[17] the case that required the Court to determine the proper rule to be used by the Interstate Commerce Commission in its valuation of the nation's railroads, his past activity contributed to the decision. McReynolds, who wrote the Court's opinion, cited six decisions in support of the majority's adoption of the cost-of-reproduction rule. The first three Butler had often cited in his briefs for the railroads and in one of the cases he had acted as counsel.[18] Butler had written the Court's opinion in two of the remaining three cases,[19] and had participated in the decision of the third.[20]

Butler's activity in economic cases was consistent with his value of laissez faire. In no area was that clearer than in cases involving freedom or impairment of contract.[21] Believing that contracts freely and fairly entered into were "sacred," he never voted against the assertion of a contract right when the Court divided on that issue.[22] He agreed with Amasa Walker, the author of his college political-economy textbook, that government had no right to regulate the hours and wages of workers, and when those issues were before the Court in 1923, 1935, and 1937, he voted accordingly.[23] To the very end, Butler remained faithful to Walker's dictum: "Econom-

* Taft said he disliked extremely rate and valuation cases and found himself incompetent in them. "We have some experts on our Court," he added. "One is Pierce Butler, the other is Brandeis, and I think McReynolds aspires to figure in that field of our jurisdiction." Taft to Robert A. Taft, Oct. 21, 1928, Taft Papers.

TABLE II
SCALOGRAM OF RATE AND VALUATION CASES
(1923–1939)

Cases	McKenna	Butler	Sutherland	Van Devanter	McReynolds	Taft	Sanford	Roberts	Reed	Hughes	Holmes	Stone	Brandeis	Frankfurter	Cardozo	Black	Vote
Ga. Ry. v. *R.R. Comm.* (1923)	x	—	—	—	—	—	—				—		—				1–8
L.A. Gas Co. v. *R.R. Comm.* (1933)		x	x	*	—			—		—		—	—		—		2–6
R.R. Comm. v. *Pac. Gas Co.* (1938)		x	*		x			—		—		—	—		—	—	2–6
United Gas v. *Texas* (1938)		x			x			—	*	—		—	—		*	—	2–5
Gilchrist v. *Interborough* (1929)		x	x	x	—	—	—				—	—	—				3–6
So. Pac. Co. v. *U.S.* (1939)		x			x			x	—	—		—		—		—	3–5
Texas & Pac. Ry. v. *U.S.* (1933)		x	x	x	x			x		—		—	—		—		5–4
St. L. & O'Fallon Ry. v. *U.S.* (1929)		*	x	x	x	x	x				—	—	—				5–3
R.R. Comm. v. *L.A. Ry.* (1929)		x	x	x	x	x	x				—	—	—				6–3
United Rys. v. *West* (1929)		x	x	x	x	x	x				—	—	—				6–3
West v. *C. & P. Tel. Co.* (1935)		x	x	x	x			x		x		—	—		—		6–3
Great Northern Ry. v. *Weeks* (1936)		x	x	x	x			x		x		—	—		—		6–3
Brimstone R.R. v. *U.S.* (1928)		x	x	x	x	x	x				—	x	—				7–2
Pac. Gas Co. v. *San Francisco* (1924)	x	x	x	x	x	x	x				—		—				7–2
McCardle v. *Indianapolis Co.* (1926)		x	x	x	x	x	x				x	—	—				7–2
McCart v. *Indianapolis Co.* (1938)		x	x		x			x		x		x	x		*	—	7–1
Lone Star Gas Co. v. *Texas* (1938)		x			x			x	x	x		x	x		*	—	7–1
Pub. Util. Comm. v. *Attleboro* (1927)		x	x	x	x	x	x				x	x	—				8–1
Davis v. *Portland Seed Co.* (1924)	x	x	x	x	x	x	x				x		—				8–1
So. Ry. Co. v. *Kentucky* (1927)		x	x	x	x	x	x				x	x	—				8–1
																	106–66
Totals	3–0	18–1	15–1	13–1	17–3	9–2	9–2	6–3	1–1	4–5	4–7	5–12	2–17	0–1	0–5	0–5 / 106–66	172
Scale positions	20	19	19	18	18	15	15	15	10	10	6	5	0	0	0	0	
Scale scores	1.00	.90	.90	.80	.80	.50	.50	.50	.00	.00	−.40	−.50	−1.00	−1.00	−1.00	−1.00	

$R = 1 - \frac{2}{120} = .983$ $S = 1 - \frac{4}{29} = .862$

Legend: x = vote for railroad or utility
— = vote against railroad or utility
* = not participating in decision but on the Court at time of decision

ically, it will ever be true, that the government is best which governs least."[24]

Those who expected Butler's religion to have some bearing on his judicial behavior were probably correct. The cases, however, from which that inference can be made are few. Two were unanimous decisions—*Pierce* v. *Society of Sisters,*[25] which struck down an Oregon law that required all persons between the ages of eight and sixteen to attend public schools, and *Cochran* v. *Louisiana Board of Education,*[26] which upheld the constitutionality of a statute that provided free textbooks for school children in private as well as public schools. Since the cases were unanimous, one might well conclude that Butler's religion was negligible in the Court's decisions.

The third case was *Buck* v. *Bell,*[27] which upheld the constitutionality of compulsory sterilization of the feeble-minded in Virginia. In that case, Butler dissented by himself without writing an opinion. One might presume that since Butler was a Roman Catholic, he believed that compulsory legal sterilization was immoral. In addition, Butler knew that if he had voted with the majority, members of the hierarchy like Archbishops Dowling and Glennon and Bishops Turner and Carroll might be disappointed, if not shocked, at his action. As it was, Monsignor John A. Ryan of Catholic University later asked Butler why he did not write a dissenting opinion in the *Buck* case.[28] It may be that certain members of the Catholic hierarchy were reference individuals for Butler in cases like *Buck* v. *Bell,* and his knowledge of their views on the immorality of compulsory legal sterilization may well have reinforced his decision to dissent in that case.[29]

The final case was *Hansen* v. *Haff,*[30] in which Butler again dissented by himself. In that case an unmarried alien woman left the United States in the company of a married man with whom she had been having sexual relations for some years. The intimate relationship continued abroad and the woman intended it to continue upon her return to the United States until she reached the city of her residence, where she was employed as a domestic. Upon these facts the immigration authorities refused to readmit her into the country on the ground that a federal statute excluded aliens who came to the United States "for the purpose of prostitution or for any other immoral purpose." Butler's colleagues held that the woman was entitled to readmission because her extra-marital relations fell short of concubinage, and, at any rate, she was not re-entering the country for the purpose of having such relations. Butler countered, citing Webster's definition, that the woman was indeed a concubine. Further, he said, she entered the country for an immoral purpose, and it made no difference whether that purpose was dominant or subordinate. Thus it appears that morality was Butler's primary value underlying his decision of the case.

Members of the Ku Klux Klan and like-minded persons, then, had exaggerated notions of the consequences of Butler's appointment for the Catholic Church. The most that can be said in that regard is that the hierarchy received some comfort in Butler's dissent in *Buck* v. *Bell.* Apparently Butler's religion had some bearing on his judicial behavior, but none, or practically none, on the Court's behavior.[31] LaFollette's expectations in regard to Butler's behavior in economic cases, on the other hand, proved to be extremely accurate, and that behavior, as LaFollette expected, was not only important in the Court but in the nation as well. Though Schaper's experience with Butler in 1917 was borne out in cases involving both the values of freedom and patriotism, his expectation concerning Butler's behavior in the area of due process was incorrect. In this one instance, Schaper, perhaps, was happy to have been proven wrong.

II

The Butler appointment also had consequences in the Senate, though they were less obvious than those in the Supreme Court. The controversy over Butler's confirmation marked the first significant attempt by liberals to oppose the appointment of conservatives to the Supreme Court.[32] Upon that experience, Senator Norris, particularly, would build. He was not discouraged by the Butler defeat; great numbers of citizens, he believed, had approved of his stand in regard to a man like Butler who was so obviously connected with the enemies of the common man. And there seemed to be no question that if the same situation rose in the future, Norris would act similarly.[33]

Two years later, as Norris saw it, the same situation had arisen in the nomination of Harlan F. Stone to the Supreme Court. As in Butler's case, the People's Legislative Service conducted an investigation of Stone, but it failed to come up with very much—only a memorandum showing his corporate connections through the law firms with which he was associated before and after he was dean of Columbia University Law School.[34] The day the debate occurred in the Senate on Stone's confirmation, Norris, with so little to go on, was not sure he was going to speak. As he listened to his colleagues, however, he felt that an important point—one LaFollette tried to make during the Butler controversy—was not being brought out, namely that in order to prevent the appointment of a Supreme Court Justice, it was necessary to show that he was dishonest, immoral, or lacked ability, when often the man against whom no such charges could be proven was the most dangerous to the welfare of the people because of his "viewpoint." [35] With LaFollette ill and not in the Chamber, Norris felt constrained to speak against Stone's confirmation.

> Why do we have 5 to 4 decisions, [asked Norris], and why is it that the five are usually the same and the four are usually the same? If you will examine, you will find that it is the viewpoint of the individual that they have carried with them, without charging any dishonesty, without charging any intention to do wrong to either side. After all, the close cases, the difficult cases in an appellate court, are often determined by human nature, by the viewpoint of the individual. That is a part of the man and remains a part of the judge.[36]

Norris convinced few, if any, of his colleagues; Stone was easily confirmed by a vote of 71 to 6. Even counting LaFollette's vote, the progressive's second attempt to stop a corporation lawyer from reaching the High Bench was no more successful than the first.

But again Norris was not disheartened. He circulated reprints of his Senate speech, which he entitled "The Viewpoint," feeling that it contained "food for thought" and that it would "appeal to most honest people." [37] That victory was possible in such cases was demonstrated a few months after Stone was confirmed, when the Senate rejected the nomination of Charles Beecher Warren as Attorney General to succeed Harry M. Daugherty. One of the major arguments made against Warren was his representation of the Sugar Trust.[38]

Five years went by without an appointment to the Supreme Court. Then Taft, broken in health and close to death, laid down the reins of the Chief Justiceship, and President Hoover nominated Charles Evans Hughes for the post. Norris knew that Hughes was perhaps the ablest lawyer in the country, but he also knew that Hughes was a Wall Street lawyer; hence he had to be opposed. At Norris' request the Legislative Reference Service of the Library of Congress prepared a list of Supreme Court cases in which Hughes had been counsel from 1916 to 1928. That list was the basis of Norris' statement in his minority report of the Judiciary Committee that Hughes had appeared before the Supreme Court fifty-four times "for corporations of untold wealth." Hughes's viewpoint was clouded, Norris charged. "He looks through glasses contaminated by the influence of monopoly as it seeks to get favors by means which are denied to the common, ordinary citizen." [39]

Norris' rhetoric was in the spirit of Fighting Bob LaFollette, who had gone to his grave five years before. And in the Senate, when Norris spoke against Hughes's confirmation, saying, "We are fearful of the encroachment of organized wealth upon our civilization," it was as though LaFollette himself were speaking. Norris attacked the Supreme Court's decisions in rate cases, suggesting that Hughes would join the majority that had decided them. The regulation of the utilities that the people want, Norris continued, they cannot have, and if they ask why not, the state commission tells them: "We cannot help you because the Supreme Court has settled the matter otherwise in the *Indianapolis Water Company* case" —a case in which Justice Butler wrote the majority opinion. Norris read at length from one of Justice Brandeis' dissenting opinions and argued that Brandeis' view, and not the view of the majority of the Court, was the correct one in rate cases. The Senator then made his point once more, now with eloquence: "The man who has never felt the pinch of hunger and who has never known what it was to be cold, who has never been associated with those who have earned their bread by the sweat of their faces, but who has lived in luxury, who has never wanted for anything that money could buy, is not fit to sit in judgment in a contest between organized wealth and those who toil." [40]

Although this time Norris had convinced a number of his colleagues, Hughes was confirmed by a vote of 52 to 26. Yet it represented three times the opposition to Butler's confirmation. It was not simply the force of Norris' argument, as he well knew, that made the difference. The economic conditions of the time had a lot to do with the vote confirming Hughes. "Butler had been chosen in the devil-may-care twenties, Hughes at the advent of the most terrible depression in American history. Arguments that the people would not heed when their wallets were full assumed grim significance as the vise of poverty tightened." [41]

Considering the magnitude of Hughes as a public figure in 1930, the fact that twenty-six senators voted against his confirmation was remarkable. "A lesser man of his views," the *Pittsburgh Press* stated editorially, "probably would have been defeated." [42] Two months later, President Hoover nominated such a man—Federal Circuit Judge John J. Parker —to fill the vacancy created by the death of Justice Sanford. Norris and Borah led the fight against Parker. Though Norris was told by one of his newspaper friends that nothing could be found in Parker's background that would justify Senate rejection, the A. F. of L. came out strongly against Parker because he upheld a "yellow-dog" contract in one of his court decisions, and the N.A.A.C.P. opposed him because it was alleged that he opposed Negro suffrage and political participation. In the Senate debate on confirmation, Norris made his point again: Parker, he charged, had but one idea—"big business" and "the virtue of large aggregations of wealth." The issue, Norris concluded, was not Parker, nor even the Supreme Court, but nothing less than "human liberty" and the "preservation of our government." Parker's nomination was rejected by a vote of 41 to 39. In 1922, when Butler's nomination was confirmed, Senator Nelson had remarked that the Lord was on the side of the strongest battalions. In 1930, when the Senate voted on Parker's nomination, it appeared that the Lord had changed sides.[43]

When Butler heard of the Senate's rejection of Parker, he probably had no idea that the controversy over his own confirmation was somehow related to it. Although the confirmation fights over Butler, Stone, Hughes, and Parker were distinct transactions separated in time, and hence cannot be explained except in terms of the activity comprising each of them, Norris' activity appears significant in all of them. His perception of Butler had something to do with his perception of Stone and later of Hughes and Parker; his commitment in the Butler controversy became a standing commitment; and the experience of each fight provided a foundation to build upon in the next fight. In terms of the discussion in Chapter 10, the Butler transaction was background activity for Norris in the transactions involving Stone, Hughes, and Parker.

III

For Nelson Phillips and Martin T. Manton the appointment of Butler meant that life would go on for them pretty much as before. Phillips passed from the national scene. An able and highly respected lawyer in Dallas, he continued to act as the Texas general counsel of the Southwestern Bell Telephone Company until 1935. He also continued in private practice with his own firm, Phillips, Townsend & Porter, and later with his son, Nelson, Jr., who had been a senior in law school the year Butler was appointed. Phillips died in 1939, the same year that death claimed Pierce Butler from the Supreme Court.[44]

Despite his setback in 1922, Manton would yet be famous —or rather infamous. The same year Butler and Phillips went honorably to their graves, Manton was convicted of selling justice and was on his way to the federal penitentiary at Lewisburg, Pennsylvania, to be remembered thereafter as "the Corrupt Judge."[45] It had taken the public seventeen years to learn what Taft believed was fact in 1922.

In his quest for judicial honor and power, Manton played the role of the manipulator up to the time he went to prison. In 1925, when the Catholic Justice McKenna retired, Manton was again a candidate for the Supreme Court and had enlisted the support of men like the New York banker Clarence H. Kelsey, an old Yale friend of Taft. Taft lectured Kelsey on how misguided his support was and added that he was unable to understand Manton's gall in using the Catholic hierarchy to work a promotion.[46] Manton's 1925 campaign made little headway, primarily because Stone was named to the Court immediately upon McKenna's retirement. The same thing occurred when Hughes succeeded Taft in 1930. But Manton seldom missed a trick in the game he was playing; he gave a dinner in honor of Hughes's appointment to which he invited all the leading members of New York's bench and bar.[47] When Franklin D. Roosevelt was elected to the Presidency in 1932, it was rumored that Manton was scheduled to succeed Butler. The rumor had plausibility, for Butler would reach retirement age in 1936, and at that time Manton would be only fifty-six years old—the same age that Butler had been when he was appointed. The month Butler was seventy, Manton made a radio address in which he castigated the conservative wing of the Supreme Court for thrusting its pet social and economic theories into the Constitution. It was dangerous, he said, for men like Butler, Van Devanter, Sutherland, and McReynolds to refuse "to see that the world moves on." During the court-packing dispute in 1937, Manton spoke in defense of Roosevelt's plan and sent copies of his speech to the President and various New Deal officials. Robert H. Jackson, who was an Assistant Attorney General at the time, later said he regarded the speech "as a part of Manton's plan eventually to become a candidate for the first Supreme Court vacancy." [48]

Manton's aspirations went even beyond the Supreme Court of the United States. Regarding himself as an expert in international law, he also sought appointment to the Permanent Court of International Justice. In 1935 a lawyer called on the international jurist and scholar, John Bassett Moore, in London, supposedly to discuss some international matter with which Manton was connected. The whole thing seemed mysterious to Moore, for all the lawyer did was give him some pamphlets by Manton on international law and ask him to read them. The following year Moore was able to make some sense out of the strange encounter when Joseph Buffington, senior circuit judge of the Third Circuit Court of Appeals, called on him and asked him to support Manton for the American vacancy on the World Court. Moore, long suspicious of Manton, refused to do so.[49]

Moore was not alone in his suspicions of Manton, yet it was hard to believe that this outstanding Catholic layman (a Knight of St. Gregory), highly respected citizen (holder of honorary degrees from four institutions of higher learning), and federal judge (senior circuit judge of the most important circuit in the nation) could be anything other than he held himself out to be. Moreover, he seemed rather strait-laced in moral matters. He dissented, for example, in the *Ulysses* case, maintaining that Joyce's masterpiece was obscene. In the course of his opinion, Judge Manton said:

> The people need and deserve a moral standard; it should be a point of honor with men of letters to maintain it. Masterpieces have never been produced by men given to obscenity or lustful thoughts—men who have no Master. Reverence for good work is the foundation of literary character. A refusal to imitate obscenity or to load a book with it is an author's professional chastity.[50] *

* Justice Butler never wrote anything as quotable as Manton's pas-

In 1939, the public learned about Judge Manton's lack of "professional chastity." The report was shocking: Manton was charged with accepting bribes and "loans" amounting to hundreds of thousands of dollars from litigants in cases entrusted to him for decision—and he was convicted.[51]

This, then, was the Martin T. Manton who had aspired to rise to the top of the judiciary in this country, and even the world. Perhaps things would have been different if he had been appointed to the Supreme Court in 1922 instead of Butler. Perhaps the shocking scandal that ruined him and embarrassed the federal judiciary would have never occurred. But then he still might have been "the Corrupt Judge," only on a grander scale.

IV

William A. Schaper had hoped that one of the consequences of the Butler controversy would be his vindication and return to university teaching, perhaps even with his old department at the University of Minnesota. There was some basis for his hope, for on December 12, 1922, the editors of the *Minnesota Alumni Weekly* confessed that they were "thoroughly ashamed" of the actions taken by the university during the war period, and they thought the administration probably felt the same way. Moreover, the articles and editorials in the *New Republic, Nation, Outlook,* and *Washington Times* at the time of Butler's appointment made Schaper's case a *cause célèbre*. And in early 1923 steps were already being taken in the Minnesota Legislature to investigate the actions of the Board of Regents of the university. Also at that time, Schaper began work on a manuscript dealing with his dismissal from the university. He felt that his cause had made progress during the Butler affair,* for at least the people of

---

sage above. In fact, one must look long and hard to find a single quotable line in Butler's opinions. His lack of quotability was no accident. Francis D. Butler said his father carefully went over each of his opinions and blue-penciled every line that he believed was quotable.

* The precise opposite, however, may have been the case, for it has been said that Schaper was being seriously considered for a teaching

Minnesota were now aware of what the Board of Regents of their university had done to him in 1917. A strong believer in democracy, Schaper felt that eventually his fellow citizens would do the right thing by him. "While the process of democracy may, on occasion, be blundering, lumbering and exasperatingly slow," he wrote in 1923, "ultimately a sense of justice and fair play will prevail." [52]

More than two years went by, and yet the demos continued to be "exasperatingly slow." But Schaper's friends and former colleagues at the University of Minnesota—men like William Anderson and Cephas Allin—did what they could to help him return to university teaching, and in 1925, largely through their efforts, he was appointed professor of finance at the University of Oklahoma. When he was told of this, Schaper wept. At Norman, Oklahoma he quietly completed his academic career.[53]

Back at Minnesota, however, consciences continued to rankle over Schaper's dismissal. Twenty years was not time enough to wash away the sense of injustice in the hearts of some of his colleagues. Members of his old department, political science, would not let the case die without changing the record. In 1938 Guy Stanton Ford, a historian who had been on the faculty when Schaper was dismissed, was Minnesota's acting president. Ford knew the case well and believed that Schaper was "fired incontinently to become a *cause célèbre* that is a blot on the University's otherwise excellent record in this century." [54] Ford corresponded with Charles Beard about the matter, and in January, 1938 Beard published an article in the *New Republic* discussing the Schaper dismissal. His point was that Minnesota owed it more to itself and the cause of academic freedom than to Schaper to confess that in a moment of passion it had falsely accused him of disloyalty and did him an injustice by dismissing him.[55]

The governor of Minnesota, Elmer Benson, who, ironically,

---

post by the University of Wisconsin at the time of Butler's nomination and that the publicity resulting from the confirmation controversy ended his chances for the position.

had been a law clerk in Pierce Butler's office when Schaper was dismissed, agreed that the Schaper dismissal deserved reconsideration by the Board of Regents even though more than twenty years had intervened. To compound irony, one of the regents of the university in 1938 was Albert Pfaender of New Ulm, whose loyalty had been called into question during the Schaper proceedings in 1917.[56] After discussing the matter, the board voted to make Schaper a professor emeritus and to pay him $5,000, his 1917–18 salary. Only Fred B. Snyder, who had been president of the board when Schaper was dismissed, dissented. In Norman, Oklahoma, Schaper, who had mellowed with the years, said that the board's action marked a step forward in the recognition of sound principles of academic freedom and tenure. The bitterness he had shown in 1922 was gone. "I look upon the University of Minnesota," he said, "as having given me the opportunity of my life."[57]

Mr. Justice Butler, now less than two years from his death, had also mellowed. Remembering the passions of the World War I period in Minnesota, he did not begrudge Professor Schaper's reinstatement or his salary for 1917–18. Apparently Butler meant what he had said soon after Schaper was dismissed: "I didn't want to fire that man, but he gave me no chance to save him."[58]

EPILOGUE

When the Supreme Court convened on November 16, 1939, the chair on the Chief Justice's left was empty. "It is my sad duty," said the Chief Justice, "to announce the passing early this morning, of our brother, Mr. Justice Pierce Butler." At eleven o'clock the next morning, six uniformed Supreme Court guards carried Pierce Butler's coffin into St. Matthew's Cathedral. The eight Justices and two of the retired Justices paid their final respects to the man Holmes characterized as a "monolith." For some of them, Chief Justice Hughes's comment on Butler the day before was still fresh in mind: "His fidelity, his courage and forthrightness, which were his outstanding characteristics, made him a doughty warrior for his convictions, and he served the Court with great ability and indefatigable industry and an unwavering loyalty to its traditions and to his lofty conception of its functions in preserving our constitutional heritage." [1]

In 1939, however, Butler's conception of the Constitution no longer represented the majority view in the Court or in the country. Patriotism, laissez faire, morality, and tradition were still valued by Americans, but not in the way Butler had valued them. In the end, LaFollette, Norris, Shipstead, and Schaper were the victors. And in the Court it was the dawn of a new era. Butler's death gave President Roosevelt his fifth appointment, which, when made, would bring the "Roosevelt Court" into being. Appropriately Charles Warren, the historian of the Court, was at St. Matthew's to witness the passing of the old era.

A number of persons who in some way were connected with his appointment to the Supreme Court in 1922 also attended the solemn requiem mass for Butler. Harding was dead, and Daugherty, in his eightieth year, was back in Ohio reminiscing about his political battles. But Justice Van Devanter, now retired, was at the Cathedral, and though his good friend and colleague William Howard Taft, who was so important in the Butler appointment, was dead, Taft's wife was present, representing, as it were, her late husband. Pierce, Jr., of course, was there; so were other members of the family. In the sanctuary were Archbishop John J. Glennon of St. Louis, who had told Harding in 1922 that Butler would "face the vexed problems of the day, seeking with American genius and courage, 'to mete the bounds of hate and love' and 'reach the law within the law,' " and also Bishop Hugh C. Boyle of Pittsburgh, who had written Harding about the same time that Butler would be "universally acceptable to Catholics throughout the country." And the successor of Archbishop Austin Dowling of St. Paul, John Gregory Murray, knelt beside the shepherds of St. Louis and Pittsburgh.[2]

Among the civil dignitaries at St. Matthew's were three Protestant judges, who perhaps felt a little out of place amid the incense and somber singing of the *Dies Irae*. Though they did not know it, each of them had had something in common with Butler—opposition to their nominations to the Supreme Court from Senator Norris and other progressives because of alleged sympathies with big business. Two of them—Charles Evans Hughes and Harlan F. Stone—were representing the Supreme Court at the service. The third judge—John J. Parker—was representing the inferior judiciary.

And the Irish were there in force—the Irish Minister, Robert Brennan, President Roosevelt's naval aide, Daniel J. Callaghan, Postmaster General James Farley, and Attorney General Frank Murphy. Murphy, resplendent in formal dress, was sought out after the service by reporters, for the day before the *New York Times* had referred to him as "a likely choice" to succeed Butler. There were some striking similarities between Murphy and Butler: like Butler, Murphy was

Irish, from the Middle West, a man of humble origin, a Roman Catholic, a member of a politically inactive family, a Democrat. Yet, it appears, he did not have Butler's eagerness for the High Bench. He loved the action of the Attorney General's office; moreover, he had his heart set on becoming Secretary of War. Nevertheless, the campaign to put Murphy on the Supreme Court was already well under way, and, oddly enough, even some of his enemies were supporting him. But that is another transaction.[3]

NOTES AND REFERENCES

Chapter 1: Pierce Butler

1. 67 L. Ed. 1226 (1923). There were only seven Justices on the bench on January 2, 1923, because Justice Pitney had retired the month before and his successor had not yet been chosen.

2. For a profile of the typical Supreme Court Justice through history, see John R. Schmidhauser, "The Justices of the Supreme Court: A Collective Portrait," *Midwest Journal of Political Science,* III (Feb., 1959), 1–57.

3. The biography of Pierce Butler is yet to be written. Useful short accounts of his life can be found in *Proceedings of the Bar and Officers of the Supreme Court of the United States in Memory of Pierce Butler* (Washington: privately printed, 1940); *In Memoriam, Hon. Pierce Butler, Proceedings Before the United States Court of Appeals for the Eighth Circuit* (Kansas City: privately printed, ca. 1941); Charles Fairman, "Pierce Butler," *Dictionary of American Biography* (New York: Chas. Scribner's Sons, 1958), XXII, 79–80; Richard J. Purcell, "Mr. Justice Pierce Butler," *Catholic Educational Review,* XLII (April, 1944), 193–215; Francis Joseph Brown, *The Social and Economic Philosophy of Pierce Butler* (Washington: Catholic University Press, 1945), pp. 1–6.

4. Evelyn Burke, "The Butler Family," *Northwest Life* (March, 1944), 18–20; "The Colorful Story of Five Bricklayers," *The Butler Miner,* III (May, 1944), 2–5; Frederick N. Dickson, *In Memoriam,* pp. 11–13; conversation with Francis D. Butler, December 18, 1962. Butler had five brothers and three sisters. All but his youngest sister, Effie, lived to maturity. His brothers went into the construction business in St. Paul and later turned to mining. Shrewd entrepreneurs with ingenious construction and mining methods, they became wealthy. Butler, who acted as their legal counsel, shared in the Butler Brothers enterprises and prospered with them.

5. Dickson, *In Memoriam,* p. 13; conversation with Francis D. Butler.

6. *Ibid.*

7. Pierce Butler, "Commencement Address," given at Carleton College on June 7, 1937, Pierce Butler Papers, Minnesota Historical Society.

8. Amasa Walker, *The Science of Wealth* (Philadelphia: J. B. Lippincott & Co., 1872), pp. 17, 31, 79, 101, 291, 409, 413, 417.

9. Thomas M. Cooley, *General Principles of Constitutional Law* (Boston: Little, Brown & Co., 1880); *Annual Catalogue of the Officers and Students of Carleton College,* 1886–87, pp. 24–25.

10. Clyde E. Jacobs, *Law Writers and the Courts* (Berkeley: University of California Press, 1954), p. 30.

11. Pierce Butler, " 'Valuation of Railway Property for Purposes of Rate Regulation'," *Journal of Political Economy,* XXIII (Jan., 1915), 24.

12. Dickson, *In Memoriam,* pp. 13–14; Butler, "Commencement Address."

13. Dickson, *In Memoriam,* p. 14; Official transcript of Pierce Butler, Carleton College, 1884–87; Delavan L. Leonard, *The History of Carleton College* (Chicago: Revell Co., 1904), p. 205

14. *Minnesota Law Journal,* II (Aug., 1894), 208; Burke, p. 19; Dickson, *In Memoriam,* p. 15; conversation with Francis D. Butler. The Butlers had eight children—Pierce, Jr., 1893; William and Mary (twins), 1894; Leo, 1896; Margaret, 1897; Francis, 1899; Kevin and Ann (twins), 1905.

15. Butler to Taft, Nov. 9, 1922, William Howard Taft Papers, Library of Congress; Dickson, *In Memoriam,* pp. 15–16.

16. George H. Hazzard to Knute Nelson, Nov. 28, 1922, Pierce Butler Confirmation Papers, University of Washington Library. This collection consists of copies of Senate Judiciary Committee papers relating to Butler's confirmation. They were found by John P. Frank in the basement of the Senate in 1939 and microfilmed by him. Mr. Frank kindly made copies of the papers available to the University of Washington Library in 1961.

17. *Minnesota Law Journal,* II, 208; Butler to Taft, Nov. 9, 15, 1922, Taft Papers; Butler to Knute Nelson, Nov. 24, 1922, Butler Confirmation Papers.

18. *Ibid.;* Butler to Taft, Nov. 9, 15, 1922, Taft Papers; Memorandum of Francis D. Butler, Dec. 18, 1962, p. 2.

19. *Ibid.,* pp. 2–3; Edwin Ames Jaggard, "William Mitchell," *Great American Lawyers,* ed. William Draper Lewis (Philadelphia: John C. Winston Co., 1909), VIII, 385–430; *Proceedings, Minnesota State Bar Association, 1908.*

20. Wilfrid E. Rumble, *Proceedings . . . in Memory of Pierce Butler,* p. 18; M. J. Doherty, Patrick J. Ryan, and Alexander Horn, "Memorial of Mr. Justice Butler," presented before the District Court of Ramsey County, Minnesota, 1940, unpublished manuscript, p. 5.

21. Francis L. Wellman, *The Art of Cross-Examination* (New York: Macmillan Co., 1903).

22. Conversation with Francis D. Butler.

23. Mitchell to Gertrude B. Mitchell, April 25, 1908, William DeWitt Mitchell Papers, Minnesota Historical Society.

24. Guy Stanton Ford to James L. Lee, Nov. 5, 1957, Schaper Case Papers, University of Minnesota Archives.

25. Abraham I. Harris, "A Reactionary for the Supreme Bench," *The New Republic,* XXXIII (Dec. 13, 1922), 66.

26. *In Memoriam,* p. 5.

27. William D. Mitchell, *Proceedings . . . in Memory of Pierce Butler,* p. 40.

28. James E. O'Brien, *In Memoriam,* p. 43.

29. *Ibid.*

30. *Lexington Mill & Elevator Co.* v. *United States,* 202 Fed. 615 (1913). The Supreme Court affirmed the Circuit Court's decision. 232 U. S. 399 (1914).

31. *United States* v. *Swift et al.,* 186 Fed. 1002 (1911); 188 Fed. 92 (1911); Memorandum of Francis D. Butler, p. 3.

32. 184 Fed. 765 (1911).

33. 169 U. S. 466 (1898).

34. 230 U. S. 352 (1913).

35. Butler to Taft, Nov. 9, 1922, Taft Papers; Memorandum of Francis D. Butler, p. 5. In 1915 the committee published the railroads' views on valuation, a project in which Butler had taken the lead. Pierce Butler, William G. Brantley, Herbert S. Hadley, and George S. Patterson, *In Re Certain Questions Arising under the Act of Congress of March 1, 1913, Providing for the Federal Valuation of All the Property Owned or Used by the Common Carriers Subject to the Act to Regulate Commerce* (Philadelphia: Presidents' Conference Committee, 1915).

36. Memorandum of Francis D. Butler, pp. 4–6; Butler to Taft, Nov. 9, 1922, Taft Papers.

37. Butler to Manahan, ca. Feb., 1904, James Manahan Papers, Minnesota Historical Society. Like Butler, Manahan was born on the Minnesota frontier in 1866. He taught school briefly, then went to law school at the University of Wisconsin. When the University of Minnesota opened its law school in 1888, Manahan transferred there, becoming Minnesota's first law graduate the following year. Though both men were Democrats, the value positions of Manahan and Butler were poles apart. Manahan was a staunch progressive, Butler a laissez-faire conservative. See James Manahan, *Trials of a Lawyer* (privately printed, 1933) and *Proceedings, Minnesota State Bar Association, 1911,* pp. 112–15.

38. Butler to Taft, Nov. 15, 1922, Taft Papers. As was the custom in the 1920's, Butler no longer voted after he came to the Court.

39. The only available speeches made by Butler within seven years of his appointment to the Court were to the Catholic Educational Association in 1915 and the Minnesota State Bar Association in 1916. In both cases, it appears, he chose his own subjects and parts of the 1915 speech are identical with the 1916 speech. Those speeches and another made by Butler to the American Bar Association in 1923, six months after his appointment, were analyzed to determine value content. For a description of the method used, see Ralph K. White,

Value-Analysis (Glen Gardner, N.J.: Society for the Psychological Study of Social Issues, 1953).

40. Pierce Butler, "Educating for Citizenship," *Catholic Educational Association Bulletin,* XII (Nov., 1915), 126.

41. Pierce Butler, "There Is Important Work for Lawyers as Citizens," *Proceedings, Minnesota State Bar Association, 1916,* p. 109.

42. *Ibid.;* cf. Butler, "Educating for Citizenship," 125.

43. Pierce Butler, "Some Opportunities and Duties of Lawyers," *American Bar Association Journal,* IX (Sept., 1923), 585.

44. John G. Williams to Harding, Nov. 7, 1922, File of Pierce Butler, Record Group 60, Department of Justice Records, National Archives.

45. The regents' views on Schaper's dismissal were quoted by the *Minneapolis Tribune,* Sept. 14, 1917.

46. Quoted in the *St. Paul Pioneer Press,* Sept. 14, 1917. The complete last sentence, as quoted in the newspaper, is: "We must see that sincere, loyal Americans are made the instructors of our youths, and not 'blatherskites,' such as this man." Butler denied he called Schaper a "blatherskite," and his son Francis who was present at the interview, said his father used the term but not in reference to Schaper.

47. Quoted in James Gray, *The University of Minnesota, 1851–1951* (Minneapolis: University of Minnesota Press, 1951), p. 248. Schaper's view of the proceedings was preserved in an unpublished manuscript by him. "Proceedings of the Board of Regents of the University of Minnesota in the Case of William A. Schaper," William A. Schaper Papers, University of Oklahoma Library.

48. Butler, "There Is Important Work for Lawyers as Citizens," p. 112.

49. Butler, "Educating for Citizenship," 131.

50. Pierce Butler, "Employees' Compensation for Injuries," *Proceedings, Minnesota State Bar Association, 1908,* pp. 32–45.

51. Pierce Butler, "Decisions of the Supreme Court in the Standard Oil and Tobacco Trust Cases," *Proceedings, Minnesota State Bar Association, 1911,* pp. 69–76.

52. *Ibid.,* pp. 81, 113, 125. See also Manahan, ch. 6.

53. Butler, "Educating for Citizenship," 127.

54. See, e.g., Butler, "Some Opportunities and Duties for Lawyers," 587.

55. Butler, "Educating for Citizenship," 128.

56. Patrick Butler was chosen as one of the delegates from the St. Paul diocese to the Catholic Lay Congress held in Baltimore in 1889. *Souvenir Volume of the Centennial Celebration and Catholic Congress* (Detroit: William H. Hughes, 1889), p. 91.

57. Conversation with Pierce Butler, III, Dec. 18, 1962; Butler, "Commencement Address"; Dickson, *In Memoriam,* p. 16.

58. See *Catholic Educational Association Bulletin,* XII (Nov., 1915), iii.

59. *Proceedings . . . in Memory of Pierce Butler,* p. 39.

60. Quoted in *Time,* XXXIV (Nov. 27, 1939), 14.

Chapter 2: Harding and Company

1. See Westley Marvin Bagby, *The Road to Normalcy* (Baltimore: Johns Hopkins University Press, 1962), pp. 98–99.
2. *Ibid.*, p. 88.
3. Mark Sullivan, *Our Times* (New York: Chas. Scribner's Sons, 1935), VI, 62.
4. See, e.g., Taft to Elihu Root, Sept. 17, 1926, Taft Papers; James E. Watson, *As I Knew Them* (Indianapolis: Bobbs-Merrill Co., 1936), pp. 226–28; Charles Evans Hughes, "Memorial Address," *In Memoriam, Warren G. Harding* (Washington: Government Printing Office, 1924), p. 14.
5. Samuel Hopkins Adams, *Incredible Era* (Boston: Houghton Mifflin Co., 1939), p. 195.
6. H. F. Alderfer, "The Personality and Politics of Warren G. Harding," unpublished doctoral dissertation, School of Citizenship and Public Affairs, Syracuse University, 1928, pp. 111–12.
7. Quoted in Clinton W. Gilbert, *The Mirrors of Washington* (New York: G. P. Putnam's Sons, 1921), p. 19. Cf. Alderfer, pp. 158–59, 170, 358.
8. Quoted in Sullivan, VI, 153.
9. Quoted in Adams, p. 8.
10. Sherman A. Cuneo, *From Printer to President* (Philadelphia: Dorrance, 1922), ch. 4; Alderfer, p. 159.
11. Harry M. Daugherty and Thomas Dixon, *The Inside Story of the Harding Tragedy* (New York: Churchill Co., 1932), pp. 9–10. Although this book is important to the understanding of Harding and Daugherty, it must be read, as William E. Leuchtenburg has pointed out, "*cum grano salis.*" *The Perils of Prosperity, 1914–32* (Chicago: University of Chicago Press, 1958), p. 284.
12. William Allen White, *Autobiography* (New York: Macmillan Co., 1946), p. 584.
13. Quoted in Adams, p. 151.
14. *Ibid.*, p. 154.
15. Harding to Malcolm Jennings, Jan. 20, 1920, Malcolm Jennings Papers, Ohio Historical Society; Daugherty, p. 18.
16. Quoted in Sullivan, VI, 108.
17. Quoted in White, p. 616.
18. John Q. Tilson to Ray Baker Harris, Sept 28, 1933; John B. Payne interview, Sept. 11, 1933, Ray Baker Harris Papers, Washington, D.C.
19. Quoted in Sullivan, VI, 95.
20. Daugherty to Harris, Nov. 28, 1932, Harris Papers.
21. Daugherty to Harris, June 7, 1932, *ibid.*
22. Sullivan, IV, 26.
23. Daugherty to Harris, May 24, 1934, Harris Papers.
24. Daugherty, pp. 9–10, 23–24.
25. Quoted in *ibid.*, p. 12.
26. Quoted in *ibid.*, p. 19. Contemporaries and historians corrob-

orate Daugherty's statements concerning his influence with Harding. See, e.g., Taft to Root, Sept. 17, 1926, Taft Papers; Irwin Hood (Ike) Hoover, *Forty-Two Years in the White House* (Boston: Houghton Mifflin Co., 1934), pp. 87, 249; Allan Nevins, "Warren Gamaliel Harding," *Dictionary of American Biography* (New York: Chas. Scribner's Sons, 1932), VIII, 252–57.

27. Daugherty to Harris, June 29, 1932, Harris Papers.

28. Daugherty, pp. 301–7.

29. Sutherland to Taft, Jan. 25, 1926, Taft Papers; Finley Peter Dunne, "A Look at Harding from the Side Lines," *Saturday Evening Post,* CCIX (Sept. 12, 1936), 76.

30. Joel Francis Paschal, *Mr. Justice Sutherland* (Princeton: Princeton University Press, 1951), pp. 105–8.

31. Quoted in Daugherty, p. 89.

32. *Ibid.,* p. 91.

33. Taft to Myron T. Herrick, Oct. 11, 1910, quoted in Henry F. Pringle, *The Life and Times of William Howard Taft* (New York: Farrar & Rinehart, Inc., 1939), II, 578–79.

34. Statement by Taft, Oct. 20, 1914; Taft to Harding, Nov. 10, 1914, quoted in *ibid.,* II, 888.

35. Daugherty to Hilles, Dec. 8, 1911, quoted in *ibid.,* II, 631.

36. See *ibid.,* II, 628–37; Sullivan, VI, 20–21.

37. Pringle, II, 827.

38. Quoted in *ibid.,* II, 828.

39. *Ibid.,* II, 636–37.

40. William Howard Taft, "Mr. Wilson and the Campaign," *Yale Review,* N.S., X (Oct., 1920), 19–20.

41. Taft to Helen H. Taft, Dec. 26, 1920, Taft Papers. See also Pringle, II, 954–55.

42. Harding to Taft, Jan. 4, 1921; Gus J. Karger to Taft, Jan. 14, 1921; Taft to Horace D. Taft, Jan. 18, 1921; Taft to Helen H. Taft, Feb. 1, 1921, Taft Papers.

43. Taft to Daugherty, Feb. 25, 1921, Harris Papers.

44. Taft to Helen H. Taft, March 1, 1921; Pam to Taft, March 21, 1921; Hilles to Taft, April 5, 1921, Taft Papers.

45. Dickinson to Taft, April 23, 1921; Taft to Helen H. Taft, March 1, 1921; Taft to Dickinson, April 25, 1921; Karger to Taft, April 1, 1921, *ibid.*

46. Karger to Taft, May 24, 25, 26, June 21, 1921; Luther A. Brewer to Taft, June 9, 1921; Wickersham to Taft, June 14, 1921, Taft Papers; Henry Fountain Ashurst, *A Many-Colored Toga* (Tucson: University of Arizona Press, 1962), p. 148.

47. Quoted in Karger to Taft, June 30, 1921, Taft Papers.

48. Daugherty to Taft, April 14, 1921; Taft to Daugherty, May 2, 1921; Daugherty to Taft, May 6, 1921, *ibid.*

49. Taft to Hilles, Jan. 20, 1923, *ibid.*

50. Taft to Horace D. Taft, Feb. 29, 1924; Taft to Root, Sept. 17, 1926, *ibid.*

51. Taft to Daugherty, June 5, 1922, *ibid.*

52. Taft to Helen H. Taft, Sept. 28, 1923, *ibid.*

53. Taft to Robert A. Taft, Jan. 27, 1924, *ibid.*

54. See, e.g., John D. Hicks, *Republican Ascendancy, 1921–1933* (New York: Harper & Bros., 1960), p. 26; Sullivan, VI, 153, n. 14.

55. See David J. Danelski, "The Influence of the Chief Justice in the Decisional Process," *Courts, Judges, and Politics,* Walter F. Murphy and C. Herman Pritchett, eds. (New York: Random House, 1961), pp. 499–502.

56. For an account of Van Devanter's appointment, see Daniel S. McHargue, "President Taft's Appointments to the Supreme Court," *Journal of Politics,* XII (Aug., 1952), 497–500. McHargue has done one of the most comprehensive studies of the Supreme Court appointment process. See his unpublished Ph.D. dissertation, "Appointments to the Supreme Court of the United States: The Factors That Have Affected Appointments, 1789–1932," Department of Political Science, University of California, Los Angeles, 1949.

57. Remarks of William D. Mitchell, 316 U. S. xvii (1941).

58. Taft to William Lyon Phelps, May 30, 1927, Taft Papers.

59. Felix Frankfurter, "Chief Justices I Have Known," *Of Law and Men,* ed. Phillip Elman (New York: Harcourt, Brace & Co., 1956), p. 129.

60. Taft to Daugherty, June 5, 1922, Taft Papers.

61. See Walter F. Murphy, "In His Own Image: Mr. Chief Justice Taft and Supreme Court Appointments," *The Supreme Court Review,* Phillip Kurland, ed. (Chicago: University of Chicago Press, 1961), pp. 159–93.

Chapter 3: Choosing a Candidate

1. Taft to Helen Taft Manning, Jan. 28, 1922; McKenna to Taft, Feb. 7, 1922; Taft to Horace D. Taft, April 17, Oct. 8, 1922; Taft to Harding, Aug. 27, 1922; Taft to Hilles, Sept. 9, 1922; Taft to Robert A. Taft, Oct. 6, 1922; Taft to Clarence H. Kelsey, Oct. 6, 1922, Taft Papers; Van Devanter to Clarke, Oct. 9, 1922, Willis Van Devanter Papers, Library of Congress; Van Devanter to Clarke, Oct. 4, 1922; Taft to Clarke, Nov. 15, 1922, John H. Clarke Papers, Western Reserve University Library.

2. Taft to Daugherty, Aug. 21, 1922; Taft to Charles P. Taft, II, Sept. 4, 1922; Taft to Horace D. Taft, Sept. 13, 17, 1922, Taft Papers; Taft to Sutherland, July 2, 1921; Hilles to Sutherland, Sept. 19, 1922, George Sutherland Papers, Library of Congress.

3. Taft to Miller, May 19, 1922, Taft Papers.

4. Miller to Taft, May 22, 1922; Taft to Van Devanter, Aug. 31, 1922; Taft to Horace D. Taft, Sept. 7, 17, 1922, *ibid.*

5. Taft to Harding, Aug. 19, 1922; Taft to Daugherty, Aug. 21, 1922; Harding to Taft, Aug. 24, 1922; Daugherty to Taft, Aug. 28, 1922; Harding to Taft, Aug. 30, 1922, *ibid;* Day to Van Devanter, Aug. 21, Sept. 2, 1922, Van Devanter Papers; Day to Harding, June 19, 1922, Warren G. Harding Papers, Ohio Historical Society; Harding to Day, June 23, 1920, William R. Day Papers, Library of Congress.

6. Clarke to Taft, Aug. 31, 1922; Taft to Van Devanter, Aug. 31, 1922; Taft to Harding, Sept. 5, 1922; Taft to Horace D. Taft, Sept. 7,

1922; Taft to Root, Sept. 13, 1922, Taft Papers; Clarke to Van Devanter, Aug. 23, 1922, Van Devanter Papers; Clarke to Day, Sept. 7, 1922, Day Papers.

7. Laski to Holmes, Sept. 6, 1922, Mark DeWolfe Howe, ed., *Holmes-Laski Letters: The Correspondence of Mr. Justice Holmes and Harold J. Laski, 1916–1935* (Cambridge: Harvard University Press, 1953), I, 446.

8. Harding to Taft, Sept. 8, 1922, Taft Papers.

9. *Ibid.*

10. Day to Van Devanter, Sept. 2, 1922, Van Devanter Papers; Taft to Van Devanter, Aug. 31, 1922; Taft to Hilles, Sept. 9, 1922; Van Devanter to Taft, Sept. 10, 1922, Taft Papers.

11. Hilles to Taft, ca. Sept. 15, 1922, *ibid.* Quoted with permission.

12. Taft to Hilles, Sept. 17, 1922, *ibid.*

13. Hilles to Taft, Sept. 22, 1922, *ibid.*

14. W. B. Woodbury to Daugherty, Sept. 25, 1922; Daugherty to Woodbury, Sept. 28, 1922, File of Martin T. Manton, Department of Justice.

15. Wickersham to Taft, Sept. 25, 1922; Taft to Wickersham, Sept. 28, 1922, Taft Papers.

16. Wickersham to Taft, Sept. 30, 1922, *ibid.*

17. Wickersham to Taft, Oct. 10, 1922, *ibid.*

18. Wickersham to Taft, Oct. 10, 11, 1922, *ibid.* Wickersham was referring to Manton's opinion in *F.T.C.* v. *P. Lorillard Co.,* 283 Fed. 999 (1922).

19. Henry W. Taft to Taft, Oct. 26, 1922, Taft Papers; Calder to Harding, Oct. 9, 1922; Munsey to Harding, Oct. 6, 1922; Edge to Harding, Oct. 27, 1922, Harding Papers.

20. Hilles to Butler, Oct. 20, 1922; Butler to Hilles, Oct. 23, 1922, Charles D. Hilles Papers, Yale University Library.

21. Van Devanter to Sanborn, Oct. 11, 1922, Van Devanter Papers.

22. Sanborn to Van Devanter, Oct. 14, 1922, *ibid;* copy in Taft Papers.

23. Taft to Butler, Nov. 2, 1922, Taft Papers.

24. Wickersham to Taft, Oct. 10, 1922, *ibid.*

25. Butler to Taft, Oct. 22, 1922, *ibid.* (Butler's emphasis)

26. Taft to Butler, Oct. 25, 1922, *ibid.* (Taft's emphasis)

27. Henry W. Taft to Taft, Oct. 26, 1922, *ibid.* Henry W. Taft was called Harry by members of his family and his friends.

28. *Ibid.;* Taft to Van Devanter, Oct. 27, 1922, *ibid.*

29. Pam to Harding, Oct. 11, 1922, Harding Papers; Pam to Taft, Oct. 26, 1922, Taft Papers; Pam to Daugherty, Oct. 26, 1922; Daugherty to Pam, Oct. 28, 1922; U. S. Supreme Court Personnel, Series 82, General Records of the Department of Justice, National Archives.

30. Taft to Van Devanter, Oct. 27, 1922, Taft Papers.

31. Taft to Pam, Oct. 28, 1922, *ibid.*

32. Van Devanter to Davis, Oct. 28, 1922, Van Devanter Papers.

33. Davis to Van Devanter, Oct. 31, 1922, *ibid.*

34. Taft to Harding, Oct. 30, 1922, Taft Papers.

35. Harding to Taft, Oct. 31, 1922, *ibid.*
36. Van Devanter to Taft, Nov. 1, 1922, *ibid.*

Chapter 4: Campaigning

1. Taft to Henry W. Taft, Oct. 27, 1922; Taft to Butler, Nov. 7, 1922, Taft Papers. See James H. Moynihan, *The Life of Archbishop John Ireland* (New York: Harper & Bros., 1953), pp. 258–59, 262–63.
2. Van Devanter to Sanborn, Oct. 31, 1922, Van Devanter Papers; File memorandum with résumé of Harding to O'Connell, Oct. 31, 1922, Harding Papers.
3. Taft to Butler, Nov. 2, 1922, Taft Papers.
4. Sanborn to Van Devanter, Nov. 6, 1922, Van Devanter Papers; Butler to Taft, Nov. 5, 1922, Taft Papers.
5. Taft to Butler, Nov. 7, 1922, *ibid.*
6. *Ibid.*
7. *Ibid.*
8. Butler to Taft, Nov. 9, 1922, *ibid.*
9. James F. Twohy to D. J. D., Jan. 11, 1964.
10. Dowling to Harding, Nov. 6, 1922, File of Pierce Butler, Record Group 60, Department of Justice Records.
11. Glennon to Harding, Nov. 7, 1922, *ibid.*
12. Alexander Christie to Harding, Nov. 15, 1922; James J. Keane to Harding, Nov. 21, 1922; Hugh Boyle to Harding, Nov. 22, 1922; Philip R. McDevitt to Harding, undated, received Nov. 18, 1922; John P. Carroll to Harding, Nov. 17, 1922, *ibid.;* Edward J. Hanna to Harding, undated, acknowledged Nov. 27, 1922, Harding Papers.
13. Maher to Harding, Nov. 20, 1922, File of Pierce Butler, Record Group 60, Department of Justice Records; Butler to Taft, Nov. 11, 1922, Taft Papers.
14. Carroll to Harding, Nov. 17, 1922, File of Pierce Butler, Record Group 60, Department of Justice Records.
15. Butler to Taft, Nov. 11, 1922, Taft Papers; James F. Twohy to D. J. D., Jan. 11, 1964.
16. Root to Taft, Nov. 21, 1922, Taft Papers.
17. Taft to Butler, Oct. 25, 1922, *ibid;* Van Devanter to Sanborn, Nov. 2, 1922, Van Devanter Papers. There was some basis for Taft's concern about Severance as a possible candidate, for a few months earlier Harding offered him a place on the Mixed Claims Commission. Severance to Kellogg, Aug. 25, 31, 1922. Frank B. Kellogg Papers, Minnesota Historical Society.
18. Taft to Helen H. Taft, June 12, 1921; Taft to Butler, Oct. 25, 1922, Taft Papers; Van Devanter to Sanborn, Oct. 31, 1922, Van Devanter Papers.
19. Kellogg to Harding, Oct. 25, 30, 1922; Harding to Kellogg, Oct. 31, Nov. 2, 1922, Harding Papers; Butler to Taft, Oct. 30, Nov. 5, 11, 1922, Taft Papers; Preus to Nelson, Oct. 30, 1922, Knute Nelson Papers, Minnesota Historical Society; Preus to Daugherty, Nov. 4, 1922, File of Pierce Butler, Record Group 60, Department of Justice Records.

20. Haupt to Harding, Nov. 16, 1922; Michael to Harding, Nov. 17, 1922; Howard Everett to Harding, Nov. 18, 1922; Paul Doty to Harding, Nov. 16, 1922; Richard D. O'Brien to Harding, Nov. 18, 1922; Thomas D. O'Brien to Harding, Nov. 15, 1922; L. L. Brown to Harding, Nov. 15, 1922; Frank A. Day to Harding, Nov. 16, 1922; John Burke to Harding, Nov. 15, 1922, *ibid.*

21. Ashurst to Harding, Nov. 14, 1922; Sinnott to Harding, Nov. 15, 1922; Webster to Harding, Nov. 12, 1922, *ibid.*

22. Butler to Taft, Nov. 11, 1922, Taft Papers: Thompson to Harding, Nov. 11, 1922, Harding Papers. Butler had correctly gauged the relationship between Thompson and Harding. On January 4, 1923, Harding wrote to Malcolm Jennings: "There has been no thought of bringing Carmi Thompson into the Cabinet. I am very fond of him and I am under very great obligations to him, but there isn't a place for him at the present time, or any prospect in the Cabinet." Jennings Papers.

23. Calvin L. Brown, Andrew Holt, Oscar Hallan, James H. Quin, Homer L. Dibble, Myron D. Taylor, and Edward Lees to Harding, Nov. 15, 1922, File of Pierce Butler, Record Group 60, Department of Justice Records.

24. Calvin L. Brown to Harding, Nov. 15, 1922, *ibid.*

25. Stone to Harding, Nov. 15, 1922; Thomas D. O'Brien, Nov. 15, 1922; James E. O'Brien, Nov. 16, 1922; Neil M. Cronin to Harding, Nov. 17, 1922; Richard D. O'Brien, Nov. 18, 1922, *ibid.*

26. Guernsey to Taft, Nov. 2, 1922, Taft Papers.

27. Taft to Dickinson, Nov. 2, 1922; Dickinson to Taft, Nov. 2, 1922, *ibid.*

28. Bowers to Taft, Nov. 3, 10, 1922, *ibid.*

29. File of Francis E. Baker, U. S. Supreme Court Personnel, Series 82, Department of Justice Records.

30. Bowers to Taft, Nov. 3, 10, 17, 1922; Taft to Bowers, Nov. 13, 18, 1922, Taft Papers.

31. E. D. Hulbert to Harding, Oct. 31, 1922, Harding Papers; Homer P. Clark to Harding, Nov. 18, 1922; Harry E. Randall to Harding, Nov. 18, 1922; Spencer to Daugherty, Nov. 3, 1922; Holden to Harding, Nov. 7, 1922, File of Pierce Butler, Record Group 60, Department of Justice Records.

32. George H. Prince to Harding, Nov. 15, 1922; Edward W. Decker to Harding, Nov. 14, 1922; Weyerhaeuser to Harding, Nov. 16, 1922; Mitchell to Mellon, Nov. 14, 1922; Mellon to Daugherty, Nov. 16, 1922, *ibid.*

33. John S. Drum to Harding, Nov. 18, 1922; T. S. Montgomery to Harding, Nov. 18, 1922; James D. Phelan to Harding, Nov. 18, 1922; D. W. Twohy to Harding, Nov. 6, 1922, *ibid.*

34. Coffman to Harding, Nov. 6, 1922; Fraser to Harding, Nov. 10, 1922; John G. Williams to Harding, Nov. 7, 1922; Cowling to Harding, Nov. 22, 1922, *ibid.;* Butler to Taft, Nov. 11, 1922, Taft Papers.

Chapter 5: Nomination

1. Gary to Harding, Nov. 1, 1922; Schwab to Harding, Oct. 27, 1922, File of Martin T. Manton, Department of Justice Records, St. Louis, Mo.; McKinley to Harding, Nov. 1, 1922; Cannon to Harding, Nov. 4, 1922, File of Francis E. Baker, U. S. Supreme Court Personnel, Series 82, Department of Justice Records, National Archives; Reed to Daugherty, Oct. 28, 1922, File of Robert von Moschzisker, *ibid.* Gary's and Schwab's support of Manton was significant, for, in their time, they were perceived as two of the most powerful men in the country. See Ida M. Tarbell, *The Life of Elbert H. Gary* (New York: Appleton-Century Co., 1933) and E. G. Grace, *Charles M. Schwab* (New York: privately printed, 1947). Later Gary also recommended Judge Francis E. Baker. Gary to Harding, Nov. 9, 1922, Harding Papers.

2. Henry W. Taft to Taft, Nov. 3, 6, 1922; Hilles to Taft, Nov. 3, 1922; Taft to Henry W. Taft, Nov. 4, 1922; Taft to Butler, Nov. 7, 1922, Taft Papers.

3. Wynne to Taft, Nov. 13, 1922; Taft to Wynne, Nov. 14, 1922, *ibid.*

4. Mary Deasy Hogan to Harding, Oct. 26, 1922; George B. Christian to Hogan, Oct. 28, 1922, Harding Papers.

5. Moeller to Harding, Oct. 13, 1922; Hartley to Harding, Oct. 17, 1922; Schrembs to Harding, Oct. 23, 1922; Harding to Jennings, Oct. 30, 1922, Jennings Papers.

6. Christian to Harrison R. Webber, Nov. 18, 1922, *ibid.*

7. File of Robert C. Alston, U. S. Supreme Court Personnel, Series 82, Department of Justice Records.

8. Files of the candidates named, *ibid.*

9. Simmons to Harding, Sept. 23, 1922; Robinson to Harding, Sept. 25, 1922; Underwood to Harding, Sept. 26, 1922; Overman to Harding, Nov. 1, 1922; Stanley to Harding, Nov. 11, 1922; Broussard to Harding, Nov. 14, 1922; Reed to Harding, Nov. 15, 1922, *ibid.;* Taylor to Harding, Nov. 13, 1922; Smith to Harding, Sept. 8, 1922, Harding Papers; Dickinson to Taft, Nov. 1, 1922; A. C. Denison to Taft, Nov. 2, 1922; Taft to Dickinson, Nov. 2, 1922; Taft to A. C. Denison, Nov. 7, 1922, Taft Papers.

10. Creager to Harding, Oct. 26, 1922; Harding to Daugherty, Oct. 30, 1922; Daugherty to Harding, Nov. 1, 1922; File of Nelson Phillips, U. S. Supreme Court Personnel, Series 82, Department of Justice Records.

11. File of Nelson Phillips, *ibid.;* Creager to Harding, Oct. 31, 1922, Harding Papers; Bascom N. Timmons, *Jesse H. Jones* (New York: Henry Holt and Co., 1956), pp. 104–5, 124.

12. Taft to Harding, Nov. 2, 1922, Taft Papers. Taft correctly identified Phillips as a Joe Bailey Democrat. See Sam Hanna Acheson, *Joe Bailey, The Last Democrat* (New York: Macmillan Co., 1932), pp. 233, 405. Bailey was aware of the importance of Taft's

endorsement of Phillips and on November 13, wired Taft recommending the former Texas judge. Taft answered Bailey the next day, saying he would keep Phillips in mind "should I be consulted."

13. Harding to Taft, Nov. 2, 1922, Taft Papers.

14. Taft to Meek, Nov. 4, 1922, *ibid.*

15. Henry W. Taft to Taft, Nov. 3, 1922; Taft to Harding, Nov. 4, 1922, *ibid.*

16. Taft to Harding, Nov. 5, 1922, *ibid.*

17. Harding to Taft, Nov. 6, 1922, *ibid.*

18. Taft to Harding, Nov. 7, 1922, Harding Papers.

19. Guernsey to Taft, Nov. 6, 1922; E. C. Lufkin to Guernsey, Nov. 6, 1922; Taft to Harding, Nov. 8, 1922; Harding to Taft, Nov. 8, 1922, *ibid.*

20. James A. Baker to R. Lovett, Nov. 6, 1922; Dickinson to Taft, Nov. 7, 15, 1922; A. T. Bledsoe to Lathrop, Nov. 11, 1922; P. W. Terry to Lathrop, Nov. 13, 1922; Samuel W. Hayes to Lathrop, Nov. 19, 1922; Lathrop to Taft, Nov. 20, 1922; Meek to Taft, Nov. 13, 15, 17, 1922; John J. Byrne to Taft, ca. Nov. 1–15, 1922, *ibid.*

21. Oscar W. Underwood Papers, Department of Archives and History, State of Alabama, Montgomery, Alabama.

22. *Birmingham Age-Herald,* Nov. 22, 1922; Dickinson to Taft, Nov. 1, 1922, Taft Papers.

23. Underwood to Harding, Nov. 10, 1922, Underwood Papers.

24. *New York Times,* Nov. 8, 9, 1922.

25. Quoted in Taft to Root, Nov. 19, 1922, Taft Papers.

26. Taft to Harding, Nov. 17, 1922; Taft to Butler, Nov. 17, 1922, *ibid.*

27. Smith to Daugherty, Nov. 18, 1922, File of Martin T. Manton, Department of Justice.

28. Daugherty to Harding, Nov. 21, 1922, File of Pierce Butler, Record Group 60, Department of Justice Records.

29. Daugherty to Smith, Nov. 21, 1922, File of Martin T. Manton, Department of Justice. On March 31, 1933 Daugherty wrote Ray Baker Harris: "I always considered [Governor Smith] . . . a good and unafraid friend of mine and Harding's friends and mine were generally the same." Harris Papers.

30. Van Devanter to Pollock, Nov. 22, 1922, Van Devanter Papers; U. S. *Congressional Record,* 67th Cong., 3d Sess., 1922, LXIII, 27, 68.

Chapter 6: Reaction

1. Taft to Butler, Nov. 17, 1922; Taft to Horace D. Taft, Nov. 24, 1922, Taft Papers.

2. Burlingham to Taft, Dec. 4, 1922; Wickersham to Taft, Nov. 23, 27, 1922; Taft to Wickersham, Nov. 25, 1922, *ibid.*

3. Van Devanter to Butler, Nov. 23, 1922, Van Devanter Papers.

4. *New York World,* Nov. 25, 1922.

5. *New York Times,* Nov. 25, 1922.

6. *New York World,* Nov. 25, 1922; *Milwaukee Journal,* Nov. 24, 1922; *Philadelphia Evening Bulletin,* Nov. 24, 1922; *Cleveland Plain Dealer,* Nov. 26, 1922.

7. *Boston Pilot,* Dec. 2, 1922.

8. *Michigan Catholic,* Dec. 14, 1922.

9. M. B. Grace to Harding, Dec. 9, 1922; W. O. Jones to Harding, Dec. 10, 1922; E. E. Cunningham to Harding, Nov. 15, 1922; C. S. Case to Harding, Nov. 25, 1922, File of Pierce Butler, Record Group 60, Department of Justice Records.

10. John Walso to Nelson, Nov. 28, 1922; Albert M. Lawton to Nelson, Dec. 8, 1922, Butler Confirmation Papers; R. L. Grubb to Norris, Dec. 8, 1922, George Norris Papers, Library of Congress; Levi Wright to Jones, Dec. 18, 1922, Wesley L. Jones Papers, University of Washington Library; *Belleville Messenger,* Dec. 29, 1922.

11. F. A. Pike to Harding, Nov. 16, 1922, Protest file of Pierce Butler, Record Group 60, Department of Justice Records; *The New Majority,* Dec. 16, 1922; John F. Sinclair to Norris, Nov. 26, 1922, Norris Papers.

12. *Ibid.*

13. "Why Pierce Butler?" *American Federationist,* XXX (Jan., 1923), 77. Excerpts from the article were quoted in the *Minneapolis Journal,* Dec. 18, 1922.

14. Eugene W. Reed to Norris, Dec. 8, 1922, Norris Papers; *Minneapolis Journal,* Dec. 9, 1922.

15. John F. McGee to Nelson, Nov. 26, 1922, Nelson Papers; *New York Times,* Nov. 25, 1922.

16. Willis to Harding, Dec. 12, 1922, Protest file of Pierce Butler, Record Group 60, Department of Justice Records.

17. D. J. Leary to Nelson, Nov. 25, Dec. 6, 1922, Butler Confirmation Papers.

18. Quoted in the *St. Paul Pioneer Press,* Nov. 26, 1922.

19. Gerhard Dietrichson to M. L. Burton, June 13, 1918; "Memorandum of the Appeal of Mr. G. Dietrichson," undated; "Findings upon the Charges Made by Gerhard Dietrichson against Dean Frankforter, with Explanations and Reference to Supporting Testimony," undated; President's Office Papers, University of Minnesota Archives; confidential source.

20. Berdahl to Sterling, Dec. 8, 1922, Schaper Papers, University of Oklahoma Library.

21. Sterling to Berdahl, Dec. 11, 1922, *ibid.*

22. Rypins to Shipstead, Dec. 7, 1922; Pierce Butler, Jr. to Nelson, Dec. 7, 1922; F. W. Murphy to Butler, June 16, 1920; Butler to M. L. Burton, May 4, 1920, Butler Confirmation Papers.

23. Quoted in Upton Sinclair, *The Goose-Step* (Pasadena: published by author, 1922), p. 221.

24. George E. Vincent to Gray, April 27, 1917; Gray to E. Dana Durand, April 30, 1917; E. Dana Durand to Gray, May 1, 1917; Gray to George E. Vincent, May 14, 1917, William Watts Folwell Papers, University of Minnesota Archives; confidential source.

25. William A. Schaper, "Proceedings of the Board of Regents of the University of Minnesota in the Case of Professor William A.

Schaper," March 5, 1923, pp. 2–3, Schaper Papers, University of Oklahoma Library.

26. *Ibid.,* p. 3.

27. J. A. A. Burnquist to William Anderson, July 11, 1958, Schaper Case Papers, 1919–58, University of Minnesota Archives.

28. Schaper, "Proceedings," pp. 4–6, Schaper Papers, University of Oklahoma Library.

29. *Ibid.,* p. 6.

30. *Ibid.,* pp. 6–7.

31. *Ibid.,* p. 2.

32. Schaper to Lowenthal, Dec. 21, 1922, *ibid.*

33. *Ibid.;* Schaper to John McCall, Dec. 22, 1922, *ibid.*

34. Lowenthal to Schaper, Dec. 21, 26, 1922, *ibid.*

35. "No Longer Supreme," *The Nation* CXV (Dec. 13, 1922), 653; "Pierce Butler and the Rule of Reason," *The New Republic,* XXXIII (Dec. 20, 1922), 82.

36. Clippings of Hard's articles are in the Schaper Papers, University of Oklahoma Library.

37. The editorial, somewhat revised, appeared in the *Washington Herald* on December 13, 1922. See p. 133.

38. Schaper to F. A. Pike, Dec. 18, 1922, Schaper Papers, University of Oklahoma Library; Nelson to Butler, Nov. 29, 1922, Nelson Papers; *St. Paul Dispatch,* Dec. 4, 1922.

39. Shipstead to Committee on the Judiciary, Dec. 7, 1922, Butler Confirmation Papers; Norris Papers; Taft Papers. The charges are paraphrased in the text.

Chapter 7: In Committee

1. Taft to Butler, Nov. 17, 1922, Taft Papers.

2. *Ibid.*

3. Taft to Butler, Dec. 5, 1922, *ibid.*

4. On Nelson generally, see Martin W. Odland, *The Life of Knute Nelson* (Minneapolis: The Lund Press, Inc., 1926).

5. Butler Confirmation Papers, *passim;* Taft to Max Pam, Dec. 12, 1922, Taft Papers.

6. U. S. Congress, Senate, Committee on the Judiciary, *Hearings on the Nomination of Pierce Butler, of Minnesota, to be Associate Justice of the Supreme Court of the United States* (unpublished transcript), pp. 1–3, Butler Confirmation Papers, hereafter cited as *Hearings.*

7. *Ibid.,* pp. 4–5.

8. *Ibid.,* pp. 5–7.

9. *Ibid.,* pp. 8–10.

10. *Ibid.,* pp. 10–11.

11. *Ibid.,* pp. 11–14.

12. *Ibid.,* pp. 19–21.

13. *Ibid.,* pp. 21–22.

14. *Ibid.,* pp. 26–31.

15. *Ibid.,* pp. 30–31, 34; Shipstead to Nelson, Dec. 9, 1922, Memo-

randum Concerning Professor John H. Gray, undated, Butler Confirmation Papers.

16. Resolution of Working People's Nonpartisan Political League, Nov. 29, 1922; Burghild Kuhlney to Nelson, Dec. 6, 1922; John Fitzpatrick to Nelson, Dec. 6, 1922; O. P. B. Jacobson to Nelson, Dec. 9, 1922; Albert M. Lawton to Nelson, Nov. 28, Dec. 8, 1922; H. E. Soule to Nelson, Dec. 9, 1922; John Walso to Nelson, Nov. 28, 1922; F. C. Wurdell to Nelson, Nov. 28, 1922; Samuel M. Adams to Harding, Nov. 24, 1922; L. Lund, Sr. to Nelson, Dec. 9, 1922; T. P. Schweiger to Nelson, Dec. 8, 1922; Herman O. Zuppke to Harding, Dec. 15, 1922, Butler Confirmation Papers.

17. McGee to Nelson, Nov. 26, 1922, Nelson Papers; J. J. Pettijohn to Nelson, Nov. 28, 1922; M. L. Burton to Nelson, Nov. 28, 1922; Snyder to Nelson, Nov. 28, 1922; Snyder, Williams and Partridge to Nelson, Dec. 12, 1922; Burnquist to Nelson, Nov. 28, 1922; Preus to Nelson, Dec. 5, 1922; William Louis Kelly *et al.* to Nelson, Dec. 6, 1922; George H. Hazzard to Nelson, Nov. 28, 1922; Charles E. Elmquist to Nelson, Dec. 5, 1922; A. V. Reike to Nelson, Dec. 18, 1922, *ibid.*

18. G. V. Barron to Nelson, Dec. 6, 1922; Samuel G. Overson to Nelson, Dec. 6, 1922; Pierce Butler, Jr. to Nelson, Dec. 9, 1922, *ibid.*

19. H. R. Leonard to Kellogg, Nov. 28, 1922, *ibid.*

20. Brantley to Nelson, Nov. 24, 1922; Halett to Nelson, Nov. 28, 1922, *ibid.*

21. Taft to Nelson, Dec. 7, 1922, Nelson Papers.

22. Nelson to Burton, Dec. 8, 1922; Nelson to McGee, Dec. 11, 1922; Affidavit of John F. McGee, Dec. 11, 1922, Butler Confirmation Papers; Nelson to J. J. Pettijohn, Dec. 8, 1922; J. J. Pettijohn to Nelson, Dec. 9, 1922; Pierce Butler, Jr. to J. J. Pettijohn, Dec. 9, 1922; Nelson to J. J. Pettijohn, Dec. 11, 1922; J. J. Pettijohn to Nelson, Dec. 11, 1922. President's Office Papers, University of Minnesota Archives.

23. Shipstead to Nelson, Dec. 9, 1922; Butler to Nelson, Dec. 12, 1922; Nelson to C. C. McChord, Dec. 13, 1922; B. H. Meyer to Nelson, Dec. 13, 1922; C. F. Staples to Nelson, Dec. 12, 1922, Butler Confirmation Papers.

24. Butler to Taft, Dec. 9, 1922, Taft Papers.

25. Butler to Taft, Dec. 14, 1922, *ibid.*

26. Butler to Taft, Dec. 9, 1922, *ibid.*

27. *Ibid.*

28. Taft to Butler, Dec. 12, 1922, *ibid.*

29. *Hearings,* pp. 18–19; Shipstead to Nelson, Dec. 9, 1922, Butler Confirmation Papers; Schaper to F. A. Pike, Dec. 18, 1922; Schaper to Max Lowenthal, Dec. 21, 1922, Schaper Papers, University of Oklahoma.

30. Schaper to Senate Judiciary Committee, Dec. 13, 1922, *Hearings,* pp. 54–55.

31. *Ibid.,* pp. 56–57.

32. *Ibid.,* pp. 39, 46–47.

33. Schaper to LaFollette, Dec. 21, 1922; Schaper to Senate Judiciary Committee, Dec. 21, 1922, Schaper Papers, University of Okla-

homa. The last letter, containing the statement Schaper wished to make to the subcommittee had it been receptive, apparently was never sent to the Judiciary Committee. Schaper, however, sent a copy to LaFollette.

34. *Hearings,* pp. 47–64.
35. *St. Paul Pioneer Press,* Dec. 14, 1922.
36. *Hearings,* pp. 67–70.
37. *Ibid.,* pp. 71–75.
38. *Ibid.,* pp. 75–79.
39. *Ibid.,* pp. 79–88.
40. *Ibid.,* pp. 91–93.
41. *Ibid.,* pp. 93–95.
42. *Ibid.,* pp. 95–96.
43. Butler Confirmation Papers, *passim.*
44. Sterling to Berdahl, Dec. 16, 1922, Schaper Papers, University of Oklahoma.
45. Taft to Butler, Dec. 17, 1922, Taft Papers; *New York Times,* Dec. 19, 1922.

Chapter 8: Confirmation

1. Robert M. LaFollette, *LaFollette's Autobiography* (Madison: published by author, 1913), p. 760 (emphasis LaFollette's); *Minneapolis Journal,* Dec. 4. 1922.
2. Belle C. and Fola LaFollette, *Robert M. LaFollette* (New York: Macmillan Co., 1953), II, 776–77, 1055–58, 1062–63; Edward N. Doan, *The LaFollettes and the Wisconsin Idea* (New York: Rinehart & Co., 1947), pp. 106–7.
3. Belle C. and Fola LaFollette, II, 1065–68; Doan, pp. 98–101; *Chicago Tribune,* Dec. 2, 1922.
4. Taft to Harding, Dec. 4, 1922, Taft Papers.
5. Schaper to LaFollette, Jan. 3, 1923, referring to LaFollette to Schaper, Dec. 27, 1922, Schaper Papers, University of Oklahoma Library.
6. Shipstead to LaFollette, Dec. 12, 1922; LaFollette to Nelson, Dec. 13, 1922, Butler Confirmation Papers.
7. U. S. *Congressional Record,* 67th Cong., 4th Sess., 1922, LXIV, Part I, 387.
8. Shipstead to Nelson, Dec. 16, 1922, Butler Confirmation Papers; Schaper to LaFollette, Dec. 20, 21, 1922; Schaper to Evjen, Dec. 20, 1922, Schaper Papers, University of Oklahoma Library; confidential source.
9. *Minneapolis Journal,* Dec. 20, 1922.
10. Taft to Henry W. Taft, Dec. 20, 1922; Taft to Horace D. Taft, Dec. 20, 1922, Taft Papers.
11. "Papers used by Senator Nelson in the Senate," Butler Confirmation Papers; *St. Paul Pioneer Press,* Dec. 22, 1922.
12. *Ibid.;* Belle C. and Fola LaFollette, II, 910–11, 929; Walsh to McAdoo, Nov. 28, 1922, William Gibbs McAdoo Papers, Library of Congress. See also Josephine O'Keane, *Thomas J. Walsh* (Frances-

town, N. H.: Marshal Jones Co., 1955). Professor J. Leonard Bates of the Department of History at the University of Illinois, who is writing a biography of Thomas J. Walsh, was consulted, and his research thus far sheds no further light on Walsh's role in the confirmation of Pierce Butler.

13. *St. Paul Pioneer Press,* Dec. 22, 1922; U. S. *Congressional Record,* 67th Cong., 2d Sess., 1922, LXII, Part 9, 9077.

14. Robert M. LaFollette, "Pierce Butler on the Supreme Court," *LaFollette's Magazine,* XV (Jan., 1923), 2, 5. It was usual for LaFollette to publish the substance of his Senate speeches as editorials in his magazine. Since there is independent evidence indicating he spoke in the Senate on the same points covered by his editorial, presumably the editorial substantially reflects his views on the Butler appointment as he expressed them in the Senate.

15. Sterling to Berdahl, Dec. 23, 1923, Schaper Papers, University of Oklahoma Library.

16. U. S. *Congressional Record,* 1922, LXIV, 813.

17. Quoted in the *St. Paul Pioneer Press,* Dec. 22, 1922.

18. *New York Times,* Dec. 23, 1922.

19. *St. Paul Dispatch,* Dec. 22, 1922.

20. *Philadelphia Evening Bulletin,* Dec. 22, 1922.

21. *St. Louis Post-Dispatch,* Dec. 22, 1922.

22. Schaper to Max Lowenthal, Jan. 15, 1923, Schaper Papers, University of Oklahoma Library.

23. Taft to Severance, Dec. 24, 1922, Taft Papers.

Chapter 9: Transactions

1. John Dewey and Arthur F. Bentley, *Knowing and the Known* (Boston: Beacon Press, 1949), p. 108.

2. *Ibid.,* p. 110.

3. Henry J. Abraham, *The Judicial Process* (New York: Oxford University Press, 1962), pp. 62, 64–65. Abraham was singled out for illustrative purposes because he has staunchly defended the use of motive as a means of explaining Supreme Court appointments. See *ibid.,* pp. 58–59.

4. Dewey and Bentley, p. 108.

5. "Autobiographical Notes," quoted in Eugene C. Gerhart, *America's Advocate: Robert H. Jackson* (Indianapolis: Bobbs-Merrill Co., 1958), p. 171.

6. Although the concept of *transaction* goes back to Polybius, the epistemological foundations for its use in scientific inquiry were not firmly laid until John Dewey and Arthur F. Bentley wrote a series of articles in the 1940's that were brought together in 1949 in *Knowing and the Known.* The following year, Bentley further elucidated his notion of transaction in "Kennetic Inquiry," *Science,* CXII (Dec. 29, 1950), 775–83. Some social psychologists have seen the relevance of the concept to their work. See, e.g., Hadley Cantril, *The "Why" of Man's Experience* (New York: Macmillan Co., 1950); William H. Ittelson and Hadley Cantril, *Perception: A Transactional Approach*

(Garden City, N. Y.: Doubleday & Co., 1954); F. P. Kilpatrick, ed., *Transactional Explorations in Psychology* (New York: New York University Press, 1962). William A. Caudill, an anthropologist, used the concept in his study, *The Psychiatric Hospital as a Small Society* (Cambridge: Harvard University Press, 1958). Thus far, the concept of transaction has had little impact on the study of politics. Charles B. Hagan, however, pointed out its analytical utility in "The Group in Political Science," *Life, Language, Law,* ed. Richard W. Taylor (Yellow Springs, Ohio: Antioch Press, 1957), pp. 109–24; and Arnold Brecht dealt critically with it in *Political Theory* (Princeton: Princeton University Press, 1959), pp. 512–13.

7. Occasionally one comes across discussions in the literature of political science that go beyond the traditional notion of interaction and suggest something like transaction. The following passage by Harold D. Lasswell and Abraham Kaplan in the preface of *Power and Society* is an example: "In particular, full emphasis is given to the multiplicity of factors involved in any political event—an emphasis that may be designated as a *principle of interdetermination.* This standpoint is sometimes formulated as a principle of 'multiple causation.' But more is involved than multiple causes; there are multiple effects as well, and more important, there are patterns of interaction in which it is impossible to distinguish between cause and effect. Hence we speak of the interdetermination of a set of variables—each correlated with the others." (New Haven: Yale University Press, 1950), p. xvii. And in *The President's Cabinet,* Richard F. Fenno wrote: "A discussion of the component variables in the appointment process reveals a diverse and complicated interaction of forces, no one of which can be said to dictate the result." (New York: Random House, 1959), p. 81.

8. Ittelson and Cantril, p. 2. The ideas attributed to Ittelson and Cantril are not exact quotations.

9. Ranyard West, *Conscience and Society* (New York: Emerson Books, 1945), p. 158.

10. Pierre Teilhard de Chardin, *The Phenomenon of Man* (New York: Harper, 1959), p. 30.

Chapter 10: Influence

1. Harold D. Lasswell, *Politics: Who Gets What, When, How* (New York: McGraw-Hill, 1936), p. 3.

2. Harold D. Lasswell and Abraham Kaplan, *Power and Society* (New Haven: Yale University Press, 1950), ch. v; Herbert Simon, "Notes on the Observation and Measurement of Power," *Journal of Politics,* XV (Nov., 1953), 500–16; James G. March, "An Introduction to the Theory and Measurement of Influence." *American Political Science Review,* XLIX (June, 1955), 431–51; "Measurement Concepts in the Theory of Influence," *Journal of Politics,* XIX (May, 1957), 202–26; Robert A. Dahl, "The Concept of Power," *Behavioral Science,* II (July, 1957), 201–15; Denis Sullivan, "The Concept of Power in International Relations," unpublished paper presented at the

Midwest Conference of Political Scientists, Bloomington, Indiana, April 29, 1960; Felix E. Oppenheim, *Dimensions of Freedom* (New York: St. Martin's Press, 1961), ch. ii; William H. Riker, "Some Ambiguities in the Notion of Power," *American Political Science Review,* LVII (June, 1964), 341–49; C. W. Cassinelli, *Freedom, Control, and Influence: An Analysis* (forthcoming), ch. iii.

3. Or, in other words, *x* was a sufficient condition or a necessary and sufficient condition for the occurrence of *y*.

4. Dahl's article and Sullivan's paper were helpful in clarifying the problems dealt with in this paragraph.

5. Taft to Horace D. Taft, Nov. 24, 1922, Taft Papers.

6. C. Wright Mills, *The Power Elite* (New York: Oxford University Press, 1956), p. 9. See also Suzanne Keller, *Beyond the Ruling Class* (New York: Random House, 1963).

7. George W. Norris, *Fighting Liberal* (New York: Macmillan Co., 1946), ch. xxxi.

8. John P. Frank, "The Appointments of Supreme Court Justices, III," *University of Wisconsin Law Review,* 1941 (July, 1941), 487.

9. Walsh to McAdoo, Nov. 28, 1922, McAdoo Papers; *Baltimore Catholic,* Dec. 15, 1922.

10. U. S. *Congressional Record,* 68th Cong., 2d Sess., 1925, LXVI, Part 3, 3057.

11. Frank, 487.

12. U. S. *Congressional Record,* LXVI, 3057. The Stone appointment transaction involved much more than Norris' activity. No attempt is made here to explain it. See Alpheus Thomas Mason, *Harlan Fiske Stone* (New York: Viking Press, 1956), ch. xii.

13. Gilbert C. Fite, *Peter Norbeck: Prairie Statesman* (Columbia: University of Missouri Press, 1948), pp. 39–40, 99–100, 111–12.

14. See pp. 191–94.

Chapter 11: Personality

1. The leading works by political scientists utilizing the concept of personality are Harold D. Lasswell, *Psychopathology and Politics* (Chicago: University of Chicago Press, 1930) and *Power and Personality* (New York: W. W. Norton & Co., 1948); Alexander L. and Juliette L. George, *Woodrow Wilson and Colonel House* (New York: John Day, 1956); Alex Gottfried, *Boss Cermak of Chicago* (Seattle: University of Washington Press, 1962); Arnold A. Rogow, *James Forrestal* (New York: Macmillan Co., 1963).

2. Perceptions of regularities in activity, whether of one's own or another's activity, are, of course, to some extent the creation of the perceiver; and past perceptions of personality, which tend to remain static, enter into present perceptions. That is one of the many difficulties in using personality theory to explain human phenomena. See F. P. Kilpatrick, "Personality in Transactional Psychology," *Journal of Individual Psychology,* XVII (May, 1961), 12–19.

3. Horney's theory of personality is contained in several of her works: *The Neurotic Personality of Our Time* (New York: W. W.

Norton & Co., 1937); *Self-Analysis* (New York: W. W. Norton & Co., 1942); *Our Inner Conflicts* (New York: W. W. Norton & Co., 1945); *Neurosis and Human Growth* (New York: W. W. Norton & Co., 1950).

4. Horney, *Our Inner Conflicts,* p. 48.

5. Horney, *Neurosis and Human Growth,* pp. 190–91.

6. See Horney, *Our Inner Conflicts,* ch. iii; *Neurosis and Human Growth,* chs. ix–x. Cf. *The Neurotic Personality of Our Time,* chs. vi–ix; *Self-Analysis,* ch. viii.

7. "Moving Toward People" is the title of ch. iii of *Our Inner Conflicts.*

8. *Ibid.,* p. 52.

9. Horney, *The Neurotic Personality of Our Time,* p. 97.

10. Horney, *Self-Analysis,* p. 55; *Our Inner Conflicts,* p. 50; *Neurosis and Human Growth,* pp. 242–45.

11. Horney, *Our Inner Conflicts,* pp. 53–54.

12. Alderfer, p. 158.

13. *Ibid.,* p. 358.

14. Vol. XIII, 252.

15. John Hays Hammond, *Autobiography* (New York: Farrar & Rinehart, 1935), II, 676.

16. Memoir fragment, p. 41, Newton H. Fairbanks Papers, Ohio Historical Society.

17. The content analysis of *The Inside Story of the Harding Tragedy* was done at the request of the author by two persons who had no knowledge of Horney's personality theory. A list of traits was supplied, but each coder was free to add additional traits.

18. See pp. 21–23, above.

19. Harding to Daugherty, Nov. 29, 1918, copy in Fairbanks Papers; Harding to Jennings, Jan. 20, 1920, Jennings Papers.

20. See pp. 25–27, above.

21. Quoted on p. 23, above.

22. See Horney, *Our Inner Conflicts,* ch. iv; *Neurosis and Human Growth,* pp. 198–215; cf. *The Neurotic Personality of Our Time,* chs. x–xi.

23. "Moving Against People" is the title of ch. iv of *Our Inner Conflicts.*

24. *Ibid.,* p. 64.

25. Horney, *Neurosis and Human Growth,* p. 204.

26. Horney, *Our Inner Conflicts,* p. 63; *Neurosis and Human Growth,* p. 203.

27. Taft to Horace D. Taft, Feb. 29, 1924, Taft Papers.

28. Taft to Root, Sept. 17, 1926, *ibid.*

29. Alderfer, p. 323.

30. *New York Times,* March 2, 1924.

31. Sullivan, VI, 22.

32. Daugherty, pp. 5, 8.

33. See pp. 24–27, above.

34. Quoted in the *Columbus Citizen,* Jan. 29, 1939.

35. Harding to Daugherty, Nov. 29, 1918; Daugherty to Harding, Dec. 17, 1918, copies in Fairbanks Papers.

36. Daugherty, p. 5; Daugherty to Harris, June 7, 1938, Harris Papers.

37. Members of Harding's "Poker Cabinet" are listed in Ike Hoover's memoir, pp. 249–50.

38. Quoted in the *Columbus Citizen,* Jan. 29, 1939.

39. See pp. 78–79.

40. Taft to Root, Sept. 17, 1926, Taft Papers.

41. Quoted in Daugherty, p. 149. Daugherty, however, vehemently denied that Fall made the statement. *Ibid.*

42. U. S. *Congressional Record,* 67th Cong., 2d Sess., 1922, LXII, 12346; Gompers to W. D. Mahon, Dec. 14, 1922, Samuel Gompers Papers, A.F. of L.–C.I.O.

Chapter 12: Consequences

1. One of the objects of the present chapter is to demonstrate the relation between Butler's pre-Court values and his behavior on the Court. If the values articulated by Butler in his speeches were related to his judicial behavior, it was assumed that at the minimum they could be inferred from his activity in cases in which he dissented alone or in cases in which he wrote a dissenting opinion in which no other justice joined. The results of an examination of those cases revealed: *Samuels* v. *McCurdy,* 267 U. S. 188 (1925) (laissez faire/freedom); *Buck* v. *Bell,* 274 U. S. 200 (1927) (morality/freedom); *Stromberg* v. *California,* 283 U. S. 359 (1931) (patriotism); *Dunn* v. *United States,* 284 U. S. 390 (1932) (due process/freedom); *Adams* v. *Mills,* 286 U. S. 397 (1932) (insufficient data to make any value inference); *Stephenson* v. *Binford,* 287 U. S. 251 (1932) (laissez faire); *Burnet* v. *Brooks,* 288 U. S. 378 (1933) (laissez faire); *Hansen* v. *Haff,* 291 U. S. 559 (1934) (morality/tradition); *United States* v. *American Sheet & Tin Plate Co.,* 301 U. S. 402 (1937) (laissez faire); *Palko* v. *Connecticut,* 302 U. S. 319 (1937) (due process/freedom); *O'Malley* v. *Woodrough,* 307 U. S. 277 (1939) (tradition). Francis J. Brown's dissertation, *The Social and Economic Philosophy of Pierce Butler* (Washington: Catholic University Press, 1945), which is a traditional study of Butler's work on the Court, complements the analysis presented in this chapter.

2. *Moore* v. *Dempsey,* 261 U. S. 86 (1923); *Carroll* v. *United States,* 267 U. S. 132 (1925); *United States ex rel. Hughes* v. *Gault,* 271 U. S. 142 (1926); *Casey* v. *United States,* 276 U. S. 413 (1928); *Olmstead* v. *United States,* 277 U. S. 438 (1928); *Aldridge* v. *United States,* 283 U. S. 308 (1931); *Dunn* v. *United States,* 284 U. S. 390 (1932); *Powell* v. *Alabama,* 287 U. S. 45 (1932); *Grau* v. *United States,* 287 U. S. 124 (1932); *Sgro* v. *United States,* 287 U. S. 206 (1932); *Snyder* v. *Massachusetts,* 291 U. S. 97 (1934); *United States* v. *Wood,* 299 U. S. 123 (1936); *District of Columbia* v. *Clawans,* 300 U. S. 617 (1937); *Palko* v. *Connecticut,* 302 U. S. 319 (1937); *Nardone* v. *United States,* 302 U. S. 379 (1937); *Johnson* v. *Zerbst,* 304 U. S. 458 (1938).

3. Nonunanimous cases were chosen for this analysis for the

reasons given in C. Herman Pritchett's pioneering work, *The Roosevelt Court: A Study in Judicial Politics and Values, 1937–1947* (New York: Macmillan Co., 1948), p. xii. Since a dissent by a single Justice on a due-process ground makes a case a due-process case for purposes of analysis, the percentages reported are obviously only rough measures. Just because one Justice perceives a due-process issue in a case does not mean necessarily that his Associates see the case the same way. The fact that the sixteen cases do not form an acceptable Guttman scale would seem to indicate that Justices were perceiving some of the same cases differently. Yet, on the assumption that values are related to perception, one could infer that the Justice who readily perceives a due-process issue highly values due process. Also, since he ordinarily communicates his perception of the case in the decisional process of the Court—usually in conference or opinion circulation—his colleagues must decide whether his perception is a plausible one, and it is assumed that the Justices who highly value due process would be inclined to see the case as he sees it. Hence Butler's high percentage of votes for the individual in due-process cases indicates, at least in a rough way, that he highly valued due process. Certainly it shows that Schaper's expectation was incorrect.

4. 302 U. S. 319 (1937).

5. 277 U. S. 438 (1928).

6. Taft to Horace D. Taft, June 8, 1928, Taft Papers.

7. *United States* v. *Motlow,* 10 F. 2d 657, 662 (1926).

8. *United States* v. *Olmstead,* 277 U. S. 438, 485, 488 (1928).

9. *Meyer* v. *Nebraska,* 262 U. S. 390 (1923); *Bartels* v. *Iowa,* 262 U. S. 404 (1923); *Gitlow* v. *New York,* 268 U. S. 652 (1925); *Buck* v. *Bell,* 274 U. S. 200 (1927); *Burns* v. *United States,* 274 U. S. 328 (1927); *United States* v. *Schwimmer,* 279 U. S. 644 (1929); *Stromberg* v. *California,* 283 U. S. 359 (1931); *United States* v. *Macintosh,* 283 U. S. 605 (1931); *United States* v. *Bland,* 283 U. S. 636 (1931); *Near* v. *Minnesota,* 283 U. S. 697 (1931); *Associated Press* v. *N.L.R.B.,* 301 U. S. 103 (1937); *Herndon v. Lowry,* 301 U. S. 242 (1937); *Kessler* v. *Strecker,* 307 U. S. 22 (1939); *Hague* v. *C.I.O.,* 307 U. S. 496 (1939).

10. 279 U. S. 644 (1929).

11. *Gitlow* v. *New York; Burns* v. *United States; Stromberg* v. *California; United States* v. *Macintosh; United States* v. *Bland; Herndon* v. *Lowry;* and *Kessler* v. *Strecker*. An important unanimous case that must also be mentioned is *De Jonge* v. *Oregon,* 299 U. S. 353 (1937), apparently the sole Communist case in which Butler voted for the individual.

12. *Near* v. *Minnesota* and *Hague* v. *C.I.O.*

13. For additional evidence of Butler's strong commitment to *stare decisis,* see John R. Schmidhauser, "*Stare Decisis,* Dissent, and the Background of the Justices of the Supreme Court of the United States," *University of Toronto Law Journal,* XIV (May, 1962), 196–212. Schmidhauser found that in the entire history of the Court up to 1957 only three Justices showed stronger resistance to overruling precedents than Butler. At the memorial proceedings before the Court of Appeals for the Eighth Circuit in honor of Butler, James E.

O'Brien said that Butler's "respect for precedent and his strict adherence to the principle of *stare decisis* caused him to be classed as one of the most conservative members of the Court." *In Memoriam,* p. 44. Protesting the Supreme Court's departure from precedent in the late 1930's, Butler wrote: "Our decisions ought to be sufficiently definite and permanent to enable counsel usefully to advise clients. Generally speaking, at least, our decisions of yesterday ought to be the law of today." *R. R. Comm.* v. *Pacific Gas & Elec. Co.,* 302 U. S. 388, 418 (1938).

14. Scaling is a precise way of describing voting behavior in the Supreme Court. If the theory underlying Guttman scaling is applicable to Supreme Court decision-making and the Justices perceive a set of cases in terms of essentially the same values, then a scalogram of those cases should indicate the presence of those values and the intensity with which they are held. See Glendon A. Schubert, *Quantitative Analysis of Judicial Behavior* (Glencoe, Ill.: The Free Press, 1959), ch. v; S. Sidney Ulmer, "Scaling Judicial Cases: A Methodological Note," *American Behavioral Scientist,* IV (April, 1961), 31–34; and Warren S. Torgerson, *Theory and Method of Scaling* (New York: John Wiley & Sons, Inc., 1958). If a scale has a coefficient of reproducibility of .90 or better and a coefficient of scalability of .65 or better, the scale pattern is regarded as significant.

15. 298 U. S. 587 (1936).

16. 298 U. S. 513 (1936).

17. 279 U. S. 461 (1929).

18. *Smyth* v. *Ames,* 169 U. S. 466 (1898); *Willcox* v. *Consolidated Gas Co.,* 212 U. S. 19 (1909); *Minnesota Rate Cases,* 230 U. S. 352 (1913).

19. *Bluefield Water Works Co.* v. *Public Service Comm.,* 262 U. S. 679 (1923); *McCardle* v. *Indianapolis Water Co.,* 272 U. S. 400 (1926).

20. *Southwestern Bell Telephone Co.* v. *Public Service Comm.,* 262 U. S. 276 (1923), in which Justice McReynolds wrote the opinion of the Court.

21. The nonunanimous cases involving contract rights during Butler's period on the Court scale with high coefficients of reproducibility and scalability. That is not surprising, for those cases are probably a portion of the same universe partially shown in Tables I and II.

22. In *B. and W. Taxi Co.* v. *B. and Y. Taxi Co.,* 276 U. S. 518 (1928), Butler quoted Sir George Jessel, M.R., as saying that persons "shall have the utmost liberty of contracting, and that their contracts, when entered into fairly and voluntarily, shall be held sacred, and shall be enforced by Courts of justice."

23. Walker, p. 291. The cases are *Adkins* v. *Childrens Hospital,* 261 U. S. 525 (1923); *Morehead* v. *New York ex rel. Tipaldo,* 298 U. S. 587 (1936); *West Coast Hotel Co.* v. *Parrish,* 300 U. S. 379 (1937).

24. Walker, p. 101.

25. 268 U. S. 510 (1925).

26. 281 U. S. 370 (1930).

27. 274 U. S. 200 (1927). Butler's vote in this case probably re-

flects both the values of freedom and morality. Though morality appears primary, the case was also counted earlier with cases raising substantive issues of freedom.

28. Conversation with Francis D. Butler, Dec. 18, 1962. In 1927 the morality of compulsory legal sterilization was still argued by a few moral theologians in the Church, but the prevailing view was strongly otherwise. In 1930 Pope Pius XI condemned such sterilization as immoral in his encyclical on Christian marriage. The same year Monsignor John A. Ryan wrote that "it is clear that no Catholic is morally justified in promoting either the enactment or execution of sterilization laws. This applies to private citizens as well as to public officials and public employees, but especially to legislators, physicians and surgeons." *Moral Aspects of Sterilization* (Washington: National Catholic Welfare Conference, 1930), p. 22. The views of Ryan and Butler on economic matters, however, were poles apart. See Francis L. Broderick, *Right Reverend New Dealer John A. Ryan* (New York: Macmillan Co., 1963).

29. For a discussion of the importance of the concept of reference individual, see Herbert H. Hyman, "Reflections on Reference Groups," *Public Opinion Quarterly,* XXIV (Fall, 1960), 390–92.

30. 291 U. S. 559 (1934).

31. For a similar view, see Harold W. Chase, Margaret Jane Green, and Robert Mollan, "Catholics on the Court," *New Republic,* CXXXIII (Sept. 26, 1960), 13–15.

32. Joseph P. Harris, in *The Advice and Consent of the Senate* (Berkeley and Los Angeles: University of California Press, 1953), did not take into account the controversy in the Senate over Butler's confirmation and marks the fight over Stone's confirmation as the liberals' first attempt to block the confirmation of a conservative appointee. See pp. 115–17.

33. Norris to H. M. Crumbliss, Jan. 4, 1923, Norris Papers.

34. "Corporate Connections of Harlan F. Stone Through the Law Firms With Which He Is Connected," *ibid.*

35. Norris to C. A. Sorensen, April 7, 1925, *ibid.*

36. U. S. *Congressional Record,* 68th Cong., 2d Sess., 1925, Part 3, LXVI, 3053.

37. Norris to C. A. Sorensen, April 7, 1925, Norris Papers.

38. Felix A. Nigro, "The Warren Case," *Western Political Quarterly,* XI (Dec., 1958), 835–56.

39. Quoted in Richard L. Neuberger and Stephen B. Kahn, *Integrity: The Life of George W. Norris* (New York: Vanguard Press, 1937), pp. 343–44.

40. U. S. *Congressional Record,* 71st Cong., 2d Sess., 1930, Part 4, LXXII, 3564–81.

41. Neuberger and Kahn, p. 345.

42. *Pittsburgh Press,* Feb. 15, 1930.

43. Ray Tucker to Norris, undated, Norris Papers; U. S. *Congressional Record,* 71st Cong., 2d Sess., 1930, Part 8, LXXII, 8182, 8192; William J. Burris, *The Senate Rejects a Judge: A Study of the John J. Parker Case* (Chapel Hill: Dept. of Political Science, University of North Carolina, 1962); Richard L. Wetson, Jr., "The Defeat of Judge

Parker: A Study in Pressure Groups and Politics," *Mississippi Valley Historical Review,* L (Sept., 1963), 213–34. See also Kenneth C. Cole, "The Role of the Senate in the Confirmation of Judicial Nominations," *American Political Science Review,* XXVIII (Oct., 1934), 875–94.

44. Nelson Phillips, Jr. to D. J. D., Sept. 23, 1963.

45. See Joseph Borkin, *The Corrupt Judge* (New York: Clarkson N. Potter, Inc., 1962), pp. 23–93.

46. Taft to Kelsey, Jan. 2, 1925, Taft Papers.

47. Moore to Stone, Dec. 5, 1939, Stone Papers, Library of Congress.

48. *New York Times,* March 9, 1936; Robert H. Jackson, "Autobiographical Notes," quoted in Gerhart, p. 171.

49. Moore to Stone, Dec. 5, 1939, Stone Papers.

50. *United States* v. *One Book Entitled Ulysses,* 72 F. 2d 705, 711 (1934).

51. For the details of the Manton scandal, see Borkin.

52. Schaper, "Proceedings of the Board of Regents of the University of Minnesota in the Case of William A. Schaper," p. 36. Schaper Papers, University of Oklahoma Library.

53. Gray, *The University of Minnesota, 1851–1951,* p. 249; *Nebraska City Press,* Feb. 12, 1938.

54. Guy Stanton Ford to James L. Lee, Nov. 5, 1957, Schaper Case Papers, University of Minnesota Archives.

55. Charles Beard, "Mine Eyes May Behold," *New Republic,* LXXXXIII (Jan. 19, 1938), 306.

56. See above, p. 101*n*.

57. Gray, pp. 386–90; *Nebraska City Press,* Feb. 12, 1938.

58. Quoted in Gray, p. 248.

Epilogue

1. 84 L. Ed. 1425 (1939); *New York Times,* Nov. 17, 1939.

2. *St. Paul Catholic Bulletin,* Nov. 25, 1939; Glennon to Harding, Nov. 7, 1922; Boyle to Harding, Nov. 22, 1922, Record Group 60, Justice Department Records.

3. *New York Times,* Nov. 17, 18, 1939; Francis Biddle, *In Brief Authority* (New York: Doubleday & Co., 1962), pp. 80, 86–87, 91–95.

BIBLIOGRAPHY

Manuscripts

Pierce Butler Papers. Minnesota Historical Society, St. Paul, Minn.

Pierce Butler Confirmation Papers. University of Washington Library, Seattle, Wash.

John H. Clarke Papers. Western Reserve University Library, Cleveland, Ohio.

William R. Day Papers. Library of Congress, Washington, D.C.
Ohio.

Newton H. Fairbanks Papers. Ohio Historical Society, Columbus,

William Watts Folwell Papers. University of Minnesota Archives, Minneapolis, Minn.

Samuel Gompers Papers. A.F. of L.—C.I.O., Washington, D.C.

Warren G. Harding Papers. Ohio Historical Society, Columbus, Ohio.

Ray Baker Harris Papers. Washington, D.C.

Charles D. Hilles Papers. Yale University Library, New Haven, Conn.

Malcolm Jennings Papers. Ohio Historical Society, Columbus, Ohio.

Wesley L. Jones Papers. University of Washington Library, Seattle, Wash.

Frank B. Kellogg Papers. Minnesota Historical Society, St. Paul, Minn.

William Gibbs McAdoo Papers. Library of Congress, Washington, D.C.

James Manahan Papers. Minnesota Historical Society, St. Paul, Minn.

William DeWitt Mitchell Papers. Minnesota Historical Society, St. Paul, Minn.

Knute Nelson Papers. Minnesota Historical Society, St. Paul, Minn.

George Norris Papers. Library of Congress, Washington, D.C.

William A. Schaper Papers. University of Oklahoma Library, Norman, Okla.

Schaper Case Papers. University of Minnesota Archives, Minneapolis, Minn.

Harlan Fiske Stone Papers. Library of Congress, Washington, D.C.

George Sutherland Papers. Library of Congress, Washington, D.C.

William Howard Taft Papers. Library of Congress, Washington, D.C.

Oscar W. Underwood Papers. Department of Archives and History, State of Alabama, Montgomery, Ala.

U. S. Department of Justice Records. File of Martin T. Manton. St. Louis, Mo.

U. S. Department of Justice Records. Record Group 60. National Archives, Washington, D.C.

U. S. Department of Justice Records. U. S. Supreme Court Personnel, Series 82. National Archives, Washington, D.C.

University of Minnesota. President's Office Papers. University of Minnesota Archives, Minneapolis, Minn.

Willis Van Devanter Papers. Library of Congress, Washington, D.C.

Personal Interviews

Francis D. Butler
Pierce Butler III
Fola LaFollette
Rev. Richard Twohy, S.J.

Public Documents

U. S. *Congressional Record,* Vols. LXII, LXIV, LXVI, LXXII.

Books

Abraham, Henry J. *The Judicial Process.* New York: Oxford University Press, 1962.

Acheson, Sam Hanna. *Joe Bailey, The Last Democrat.* New York: Macmillan Co., 1932.

Adams, Samuel Hopkins. *Incredible Era.* Boston: Houghton Mifflin Co., 1939.

Annual Catalogue of the Officers and Students of Carleton College, 1886–87.

Ashurst, Henry Fountain. *A Many-Colored Toga.* Tucson: University of Arizona Press, 1962.

Bagby, Westley Marvin. *The Road to Normalcy.* Baltimore: Johns Hopkins University Press, 1962.

Biddle, Francis. *In Brief Authority.* New York: Doubleday & Co., 1962.

Borkin, Joseph. *The Corrupt Judge.* New York: Clarkson N. Potter, Inc., 1962.

Brecht, Arnold. *Political Theory.* Princeton: Princeton University Press, 1959.

Broderick, Francis L. *Right Reverend New Dealer John A. Ryan.* New York: Macmillan Co., 1963.

Brown, Francis Joseph. *The Social and Economic Philosophy of Pierce Butler.* Washington: Catholic University Press, 1945.

Burris, William J. *The Senate Rejects a Judge: A Study of the John J.*

Parker Case. Chapel Hill: Dept. of Political Science, University of North Carolina, 1962.

Butler, Pierce, Brantley, William G., Hadley, Herbert S., and Patterson, George S. *In Re Certain Questions Arising, under the Act of Congress of March 1, 1913, Providing for the Federal Valuation of All the Property Owned or Used by the Common Carriers Subject to the Act to Regulate Commerce*. Philadelphia: Presidents' Conference Committee, 1915.

Cantril, Hadley. *The "Why" of Man's Experience*. New York: Macmillan Co., 1950.

Cassinelli, C. W. *Freedom, Control, and Influence: An Analysis*. Forthcoming.

Caudill, William A. *The Psychiatric Hospital as a Small Society*. Cambridge: Harvard University Press, 1958.

Cooley, Thomas M. *Constitutional Limitations*. 5th ed. Boston: Little, Brown & Co., 1883.

———, *General Principles of Constitutional Law*. Boston: Little, Brown & Co., 1880.

Croly, Herbert. *Marcus Alonzo Hanna*. New York: Macmillan Co., 1912.

Cuneo, Sherman S. *From Printer to President*. Philadelphia: Dorrance, 1922.

Daugherty, Harry M., and Dixon, Thomas. *The Inside Story of the Harding Tragedy*. New York: Churchill Co., 1932.

Dewey, John, and Bentley, Arthur F. *Knowing and the Known*. Boston: Beacon Press, 1949.

Doan, Edward N. *The LaFollettes and the Wisconsin Idea*. New York: Rhinehart & Co., 1947.

Fenno, Richard F. *The President's Cabinet*. New York: Random House, 1959.

Fite, Gilbert C. *Peter Norbeck: Prairie Statesman*. Columbia: University of Missouri Press, 1948.

George, Alexander L. and Juliette L. *Woodrow Wilson and Colonel House*. New York: John Day, 1956.

Gerhart, Eugene C. *America's Advocate: Robert H. Jackson*. Indianapolis: Bobbs-Merrill Co., 1958.

Gilbert, Clinton W. *The Mirrors of Washington*. New York: G. P. Putnam's Sons, 1921.

Gottfried, Alex. *Boss Cermak of Chicago*. Seattle: University of Washington Press, 1962.

Grace, E. G. *Charles M. Schwab*. New York: privately printed, 1947.

Gray, James. *The University of Minnesota, 1851–1951*. Minneapolis: University of Minnesota Press, 1951.

Hammond, John Hays. *Autobiography*. 2 vols. New York: Farrar & Rhinehart, 1935.

Harris, Joseph P. *The Advice and Consent of the Senate*. Berkeley and Los Angeles: University of California Press, 1953.

Hicks, John D. *Republican Ascendency, 1921–1933*. New York: Harper & Bros., 1960.

Hoover, Irwin Hood (Ike). *Forty-Two Years in the White House*. Boston: Houghton Mifflin Co., 1934.

Horney, Karen. *Neurosis and Human Growth*. New York: W. W. Norton & Co., 1950.

———, *The Neurotic Personality of Our Time*. New York: W. W. Norton & Co., 1937.

———, *Our Inner Conflicts*. New York: W. W. Norton & Co., 1945.

———, *Self-Analysis*. New York: W. W. Norton & Co., 1942.

Howe, Mark DeWolfe ed. *Holmes-Laski Letters*. 2 vols. Cambridge: Harvard University Press, 1953.

In Memoriam, Hon. Pierce Butler, Proceedings Before the United States Court of Appeals for the Eighth Circuit. Kansas City: privately printed, ca. 1941.

Ittelson, William H., and Cantril, Hadley. *Perception: A Transactional Approach*. Garden City, N.Y.: Doubleday & Co., 1953.

Jacobs, Clyde E. *Law Writers and the Courts*. Berkeley: University of California Press, 1954.

Keller, Suzanne. *Beyond the Ruling Class*. New York: Random House, 1963.

Kilpatrick, F. P. ed. *Explorations in Transactional Psychology*. New York: New York University Press, 1962.

LaFollette, Belle C., and LaFollette, Fola. *Robert M. LaFollette*. New York: Macmillan Co., 1953.

LaFollette, Robert M. *LaFollette's Autobiography*. Madison: published by author, 1913.

Lasswell, Harold D. *Politics: Who Gets What, When, How*. New York: McGraw-Hill, 1936.

———, *Power and Personality*. New York: W. W. Norton & Co., 1948

———, *Psychopathology and Politics*. Chicago: University of Chicago Press, 1930.

———, and Kaplan, Abraham. *Power and Society*. New Haven: Yale University Press, 1950.

Leonard, Delavan L. *The History of Carleton College*. Chicago: Revell Co., 1904.

Manahan, James. *Trials of a Lawyer*. Privately printed, 1933.

Mason, Alpheus Thomas. *Harlan Fiske Stone*. New York: Viking Press, 1956.

Mills, C. Wright. *The Power Elite*. New York: Oxford University Press, 1956.

Moynihan, James H. *The Life of Archbishop John Ireland*. New York: Harper & Bros., 1953.

Neuberger, Richard L., and Kahn, Stephen B. *Integrity: The Life of George W. Norris*. New York: Vanguard Press, 1937.

Norris, George W. *Fighting Liberal*. New York: Macmillan Co., 1946.

Odland, Martin W. *The Life of Knute Nelson*. Minneapolis: The Lund Press, Inc., 1926.

O'Keane, Josephine. *Thomas J. Walsh*. Francestown, N. H.: Marshall Jones Co., 1955.

Oppenheim, Felix E. *Dimensions of Freedom*. New York: St. Martin's Press, 1961.

Paschal, Joel Francis. *Mr. Justice Sutherland.* Princeton: Princeton University Press, 1951.

Pringle, Henry F. *The Life and Times of William Howard Taft.* 2 vols. New York: Farrar & Rinehart, Inc., 1939.

Pritchett, C. Herman. *The Roosevelt Court: A Study in Judicial Politics and Values, 1937–1947.* New York: Macmillan Co., 1948.

Proceedings in the Supreme Court of Texas Touching the Death of Nelson Phillips. Austin: privately printed, 1939.

Proceedings of the Bar and Officers of the Supreme Court of the United States in Memory of Pierce Butler. Washington: privately printed, 1940.

Rogow, Arnold A. *James Forrestal.* New York: Macmillan Co., 1963.

Ryan, John A. *Moral Aspects of Sterilization.* Washington: National Catholic Welfare Conference, 1930.

Schubert, Glendon A. *Quantitative Analysis of Judicial Behavior.* Glencoe, Ill.: The Free Press, 1959.

Sinclair, Upton. *The Goose-Step.* Pasadena: published by author, 1922.

Souvenir Volume of the Centennial Celebration and Catholic Congress. Detroit: William H. Hughes, 1889.

Swaine, Robert T. *The Cravath Firm and Its Predecessors, 1819–1948.* 2 vols. New York: privately printed, 1946, 1948.

Tarbell, Ida M. *The Life of Elbert H. Gary.* New York: Appleton-Century Co., 1933.

Teilhard de Chardin, Pierre. *The Phenomenon of Man.* New York: Harper, 1959.

Timmons, Bascom N. *Jesse H. Jones.* New York: Henry Holt and Co., 1956.

Torgerson, Warren S. *Theory and Method of Scaling.* New York: John Wiley & Sons, Inc., 1958.

Walker, Amasa. *The Science of Wealth.* Philadelphia: J. B. Lippincott & Co., 1872.

Watson, James E. *As I Knew Them.* Indianapolis: Bobbs-Merrill Co., 1936.

Wellman, Francis L. *The Art of Cross-Examination.* New York: Macmillan Co., 1903.

West, Ranyard. *Conscience and Society.* New York: Emerson Books, 1945.

White, Ralph K. *Value-Analysis.* Glen Gardner, N.J.: Society for the Psychological Study of Social Issues, 1953.

White, William Allen. *Autobiography.* New York: Macmillan Co., 1946.

Articles and Periodicals

Beard, Charles. "Mine Eyes May Behold," *New Republic,* LXXXXIII (Jan. 19, 1938), 306.

Bentley, Arthur F. "Kennetic Inquiry," *Science,* CXII (Dec. 29, 1950), 775–83.

Burke, Evelyn. "The Butler Family," *Northwest Life* (March, 1944), 18–20.

Butler, Pierce. "Decisions of the Supreme Court in the Standard Oil and Tobacco Trust Cases," *Proceedings, Minnesota State Bar Association, 1911,* pp. 69–76.

———, "Educating for Citizenship," *Catholic Educational Association Bulletin,* XII (Nov., 1915), 123–32.

———, "Employees' Compensation for Injuries," *Proceedings, Minnesota State Bar Association,* 1908, pp. 32–45.

———, "Some Opportunities and Duties of Lawyers," *American Bar Association Journal,* IX (Sept., 1923), 583–87.

———, "There Is Important Work for Lawyers as Citizens," *Proceedings, Minnesota State Bar Association,* 1916, pp. 106–19.

———, " 'Valuation of Railway Property for Purposes of Rate Regulation,' " *Journal of Political Economy,* XXII (Jan., 1915), 17–33.

Chase, Harold W., Green, Margaret Jane, and Mollan, Robert. "Catholics on the Court," *New Republic,* CXXXIII (Sept. 26, 1960), 13–15.

Cole, Kenneth C. "The Role of the Senate in the Confirmation of Judicial Nominations," *American Political Science Review,* XXVIII (Oct., 1934), 875–94.

"The Colorful Story of Five Bricklayers," *The Butler Miner,* III (May, 1944), 2–5.

Dahl, Robert A. "The Concept of Power," *Behavioral Science,* II (July, 1957), 201–15.

Danelski, David J. "The Influence of the Chief Justice in the Decisional Process," in *Courts, Judges and Politics.* Eds. Walter F. Murphy and C. Herman Pritchett. New York: Random House, 1961.

Dunne, Finley Peter. "A Look at Harding from the Side Lines," *Saturday Evening Post,* CCIX (Sept. 12, 1936), 24–25, 74, 76, 79.

Fairman, Charles. "Pierce Butler," in *Dictionary of American Biography.* Vol. XXII. New York: Chas. Scribner's Sons, 1958.

Frank, John P. "The Appointment of Supreme Court Justices, III," *University of Wisconsin Law Review* (July, 1941), 461–512.

Frankfurter, Felix. "Chief Justices I Have Known," in *Of Law and Men.* ed. Philip Elman. New York: Harcourt Brace and Co., 1956.

Gompers, Samuel. "Why Pierce Butler?" *American Federationist,* XXX (Jan., 1923), 76–77.

Hagan, Charles B. "The Group in Political Science," in *Life, Language, Law.* ed. Richard W. Taylor. Yellow Springs, Ohio: Antioch Press, 1957.

Harris, Abraham I. "A Reactionary for the Supreme Bench," *The New Republic,* XXXIII (Dec. 13, 1922), 65–67.

Hughes, Charles Evans. "Memorial Address," in *In Memoriam, Warren G. Harding.* Washington: Government Printing Office, 1924.

Hyman, Herbert H. "Reflections on Reference Groups," *Public Opinion Quarterly,* XXIV (Fall, 1960), 390–92.

Jaggard, Edwin Ames. "William Mitchell," in *Great American Lawyers,* Vol. VIII. ed. William Draper Lewis. Philadelphia: John C. Winston Co., 1909.

Kilpatrick, F. P. "Personality in Transactional Psychology," *Journal of Individual Psychology,* XVII (May, 1961), 12–19.

LaFollette, Robert M. "Pierce Butler on the Supreme Court," *LaFollette's Magazine,* XV (Jan., 1923), 2, 5.

March, James G. "An Introduction to the Theory and Measurement of Influence," *Journal of Politics,* XIX (May, 1957), 202–26.

McHargue, Daniel S. "President Taft's Appointments to the Supreme Court," *Journal of Politics,* XII (Aug., 1952), 497–500.

Minnesota Law Journal, II (Aug., 1894), 208.

Murphy, Walter F. "In His Own Image: Mr. Chief Justice Taft and Supreme Court Appointments," *The Supreme Court Review.* ed. Phillip Kurland. Chicago: University of Chicago, 1961.

Nevins, Allan. "Warren Gamaliel Harding," in *Dictionary of American Biography.* Vol. VIII. New York: Chas. Scribner's Sons, 1958.

Nigro, Felix A. "The Warren Case," *Western Political Quarterly,* XI (Dec., 1958), 835–56.

"No Longer Supreme," *The Nation,* CXV (Dec. 13, 1922), 653.

"Pierce Butler and the Rule of Reason," *The New Republic,* XXXIII (Dec. 20, 1922), 81–82.

Proceedings, Minnesota State Bar Association, 1908, 1911, 1916.

Purcell, Richard J. "Mr. Justice Pierce Butler," *Catholic Educational Review,* XLII (April, 1944), 193–215.

Riker, William H. "Some Ambiguities in the Notion of Power," *American Political Science Review,* LVII (June 1964), 341–49.

Schmidhauser, John R. "The Justices of the Supreme Court: A Collective Portrait," *Midwest Journal of Political Science,* III (Feb., 1959), 1–57.

———, "*Stare Decisis,* Dissent, and the Background of the Justices of the Supreme Court of the United States," *University of Toronto Law Journal,* XIV (May, 1962), 196–212.

Simon, Herbert. "Notes on the Observation and Measurement of Power," *Journal of Politics,* XV (Nov., 1953), 500–16.

Taft, William Howard. "Mr. Wilson and the Campaign," *Yale Review,* N. S., X (Oct., 1920), 1–25.

Time, XXXIV (Nov. 27, 1939).

Ulmer, S. Sidney, "Scaling Judicial Cases: A Methodological Note," *American Behavioral Scientist,* IV (April, 1961), 31–34.

Newspapers

Atlanta Constitution
Baltimore Catholic
Belleville Messenger
Boston Pilot
Chicago Daily News
Chicago Tribune
Cleveland Plain Dealer
Columbus Citizen
Michigan Catholic
Milwaukee Journal
Minneapolis Journal
Minneapolis Tribune

Nebraska City Press	St. Louis Post-Dispatch
New Majority	St. Paul Catholic Bulletin
New York Call	St. Paul Dispatch
New York Times	St. Paul Pioneer Press
New York World	Washington Herald
Philadelphia Evening Bulletin	Washington Times

Unpublished Material

Alderfer, H. F. "The Personality and Politics of Warren G. Harding." Unpublished Ph.D. dissertation, School of Citizenship and Public Affairs, Syracuse University, 1928.

Butler, Francis D. Memorandum for the author, Dec. 18, 1962.

Doherty, M. J., Ryan, Patrick J., and Horn, Alexander. "Memorial of Mr. Justice Butler." Presented before the District Court of Ramsey County, Minnesota, 1940.

McHargue, Daniel S. "Appointments to the Supreme Court of the United States: The Factors That Have Affected Appointments. 1789–1932." Unpublished Ph.D. dissertation, Department of Political Science, University of California, Los Angeles, 1949.

Sullivan, Denis. "The Concept of Power in International Relations." Paper presented at the Midwest Conference of Political Scientists, Bloomington, Indiana, April 29, 1960.

INDEX